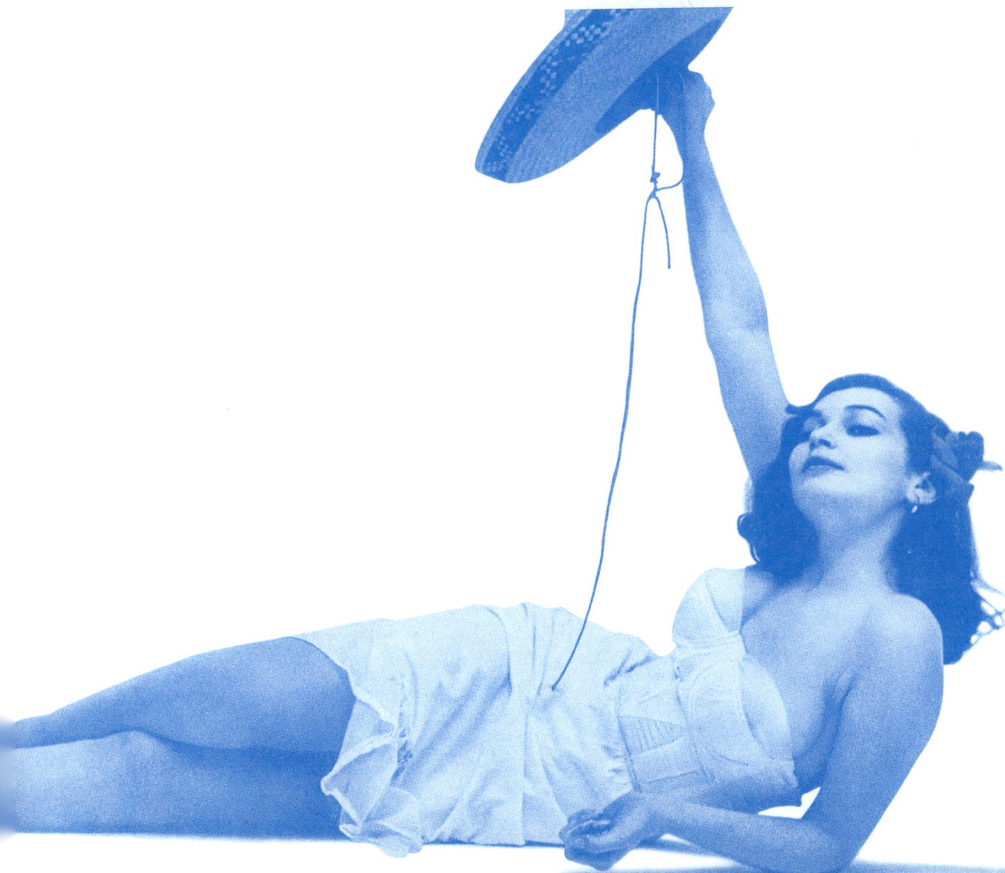

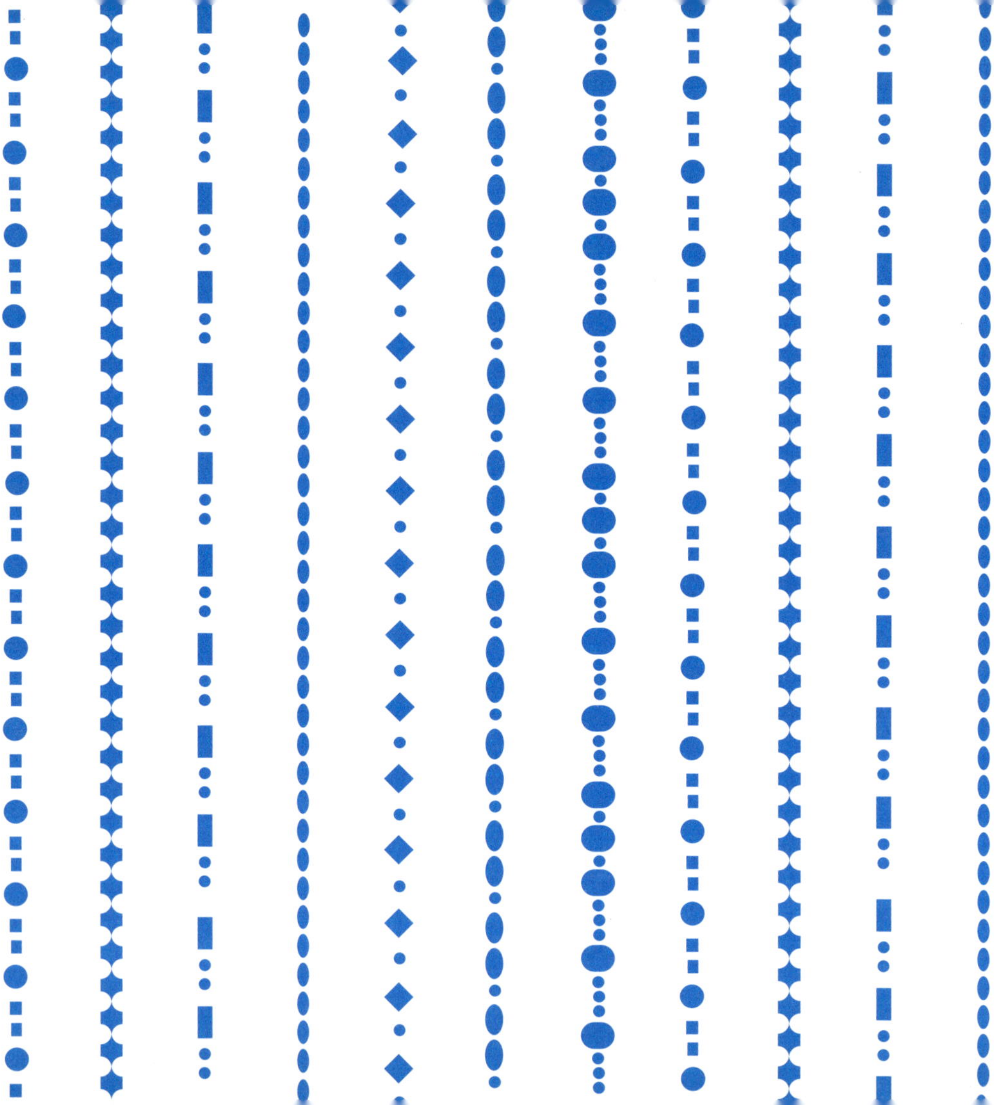

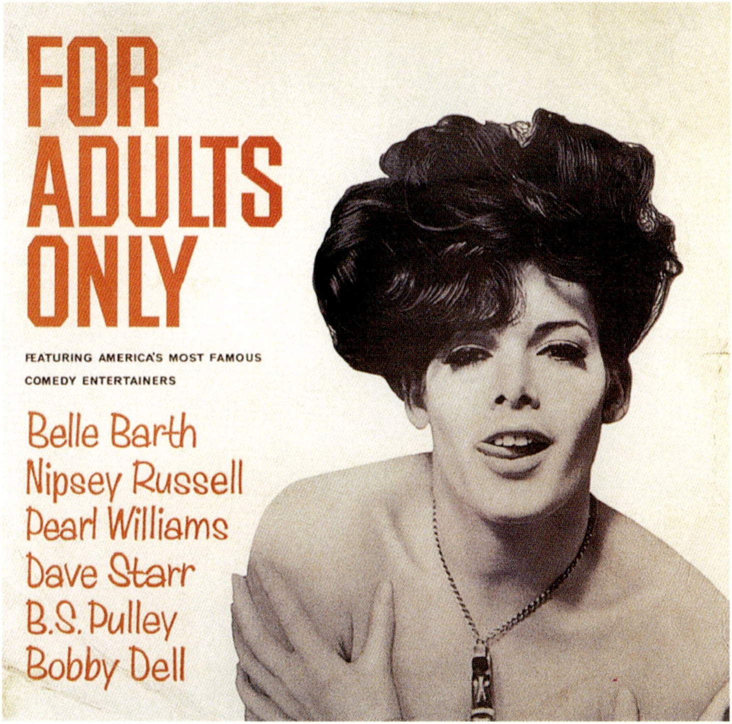
FOR ADULTS ONLY
FEATURING AMERICA'S MOST FAMOUS COMEDY ENTERTAINERS
Belle Barth
Nipsey Russell
Pearl Williams
Dave Starr
B.S. Pulley
Bobby Dell

Vixens

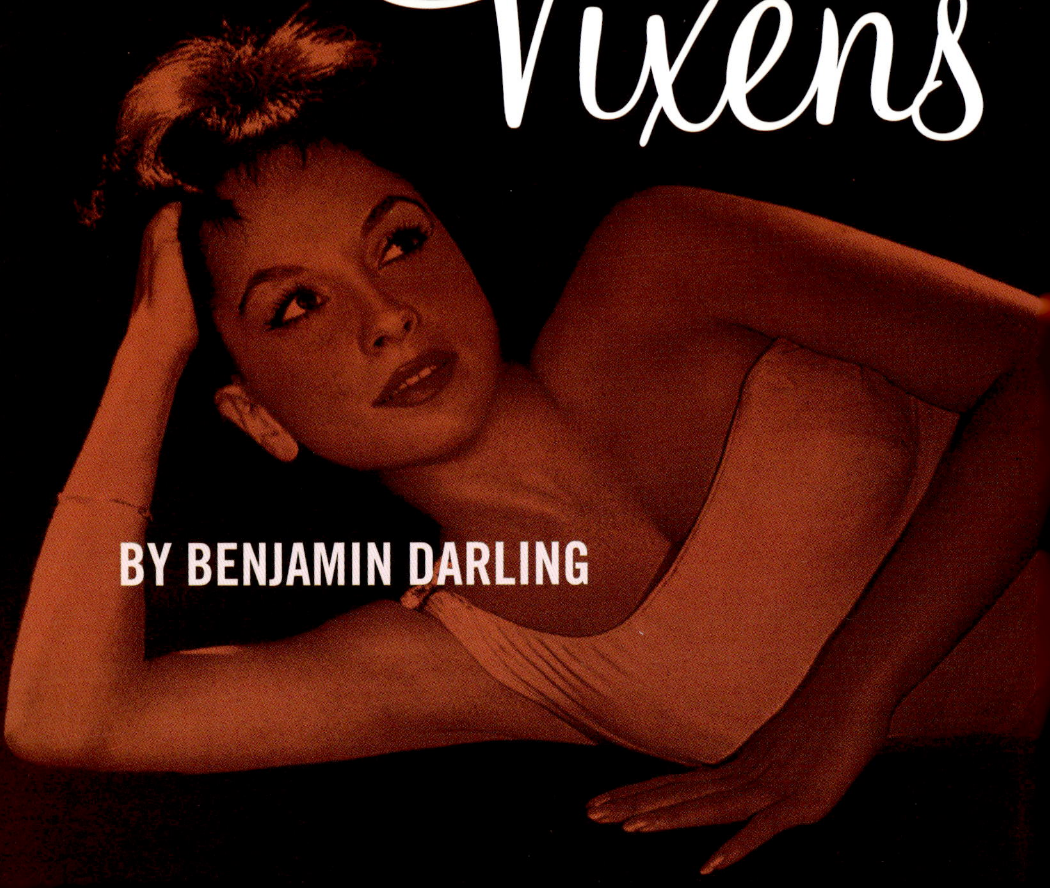

BY BENJAMIN DARLING

of Vinyl

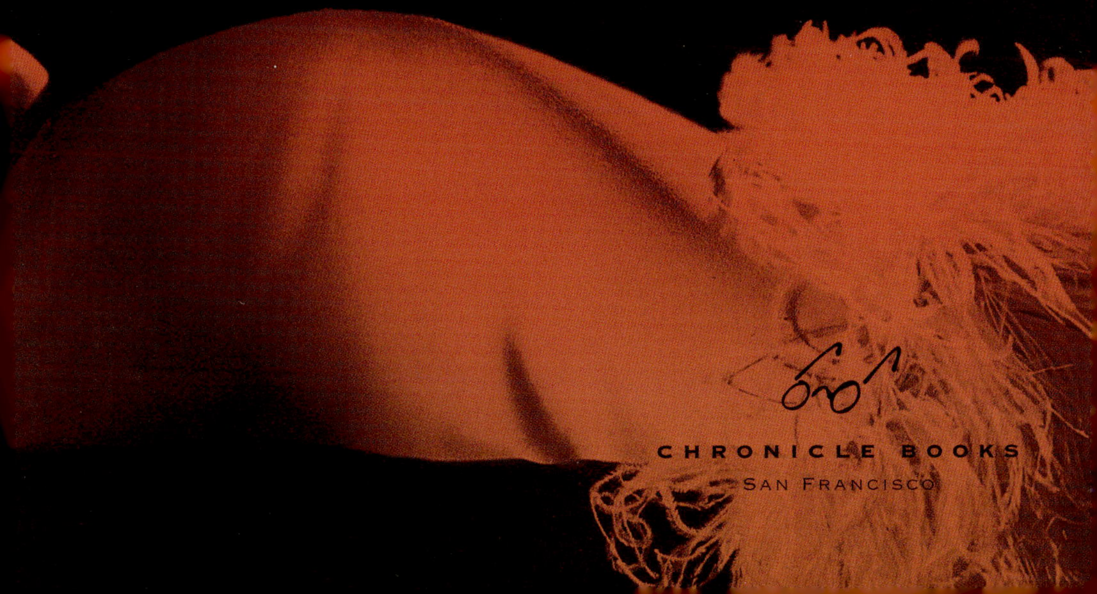

CHRONICLE BOOKS
SAN FRANCISCO

The author would like to thank Lia Friedman for her invaluable contributions, and Elisabeth Darling for her general invaluableness.

Library of Congress Cataloging-in-Publication Data available.
ISBN 0-8118-3134-5

Printed in Hong Kong.

Distributed in Canada by Raincoast Books
9050 Shaughnessy Street
Vancouver, BC V6P 6E5

10 9 8 7 6 5 4 3 2 1

Chronicle Books LLC
85 Second Street
San Francisco, California 94105

www.chroniclebooks.com

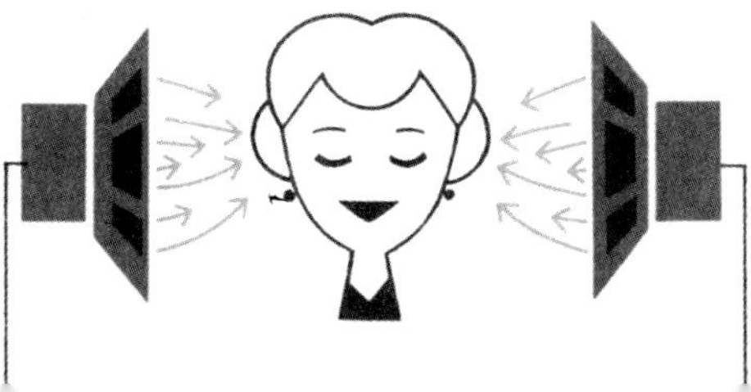

Contents

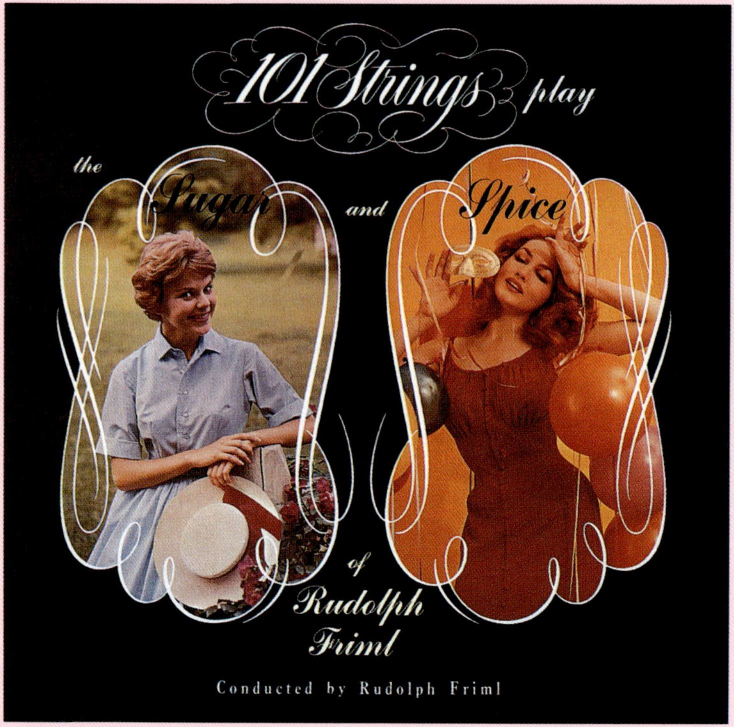
101 Strings play
the Sugar and Spice
of Rudolph Friml
Conducted by Rudolph Friml

The Vixen: What She Is and Is Not

8:30 P.M. When I tossed the idea of this book to my editor, Ed, his first verbal response was "Oh yes, Daddy!"

We were sitting in the Persian Zam Zam Room at the time, sipping vodka martinis (just try ordering something other than a martini at the Persian Zam Zam: oh baby, you'll see). I ordered two more to celebrate and leaned back in my barstool to bask in the glow. Vixens of vinyl . . . cool, I thought to myself.

"Are vixens different from vamps, or are they synonymous?" Ed asked in that annoying way editors have of asking you to organize your thoughts.

"Vixens do and vamps don't," the bartender growled at us. I had never heard him stray from subjects related to ordering and paying for drinks; this must be an important distinction! I was grateful for the help.

"There—that settles that," I said triumphantly, reaching for my fresh martini.

"Are there other types as well?" Ed asked no one in particular, meaning me (the bartender had exceeded his conversational quota for the decade). It was clear Ed wasn't going to let me off easy.

Why fight it? I put the proverbial yoke on without complaint. I grabbed a stack of cocktail napkins (my preferred medium), and took out my pen. "Okay, Daddy-o, let's go."

10:45 P.M. "To know what she is, we have to identify what she isn't, see?" I said to Ed as I spread a collage of napkins across the bar in the Tonga Room.

"So show me," he said, a little testily, I thought. Perhaps the Tonga's Pu Pu Platter wasn't the right choice after all.

I began laying it out for him, slowly and clearly for a cat that might be fighting his own inner demons, if you know what I mean. "It's like the periodic table. At one end you've got nice college girls—they're the lightest—and at the other end you've got vixens—they're the heaviest. In between you've got all kinds of elements—some you may have never heard of, and some that haven't even been discovered yet, dig it?"

"Yeah, I'm just not seein' it, man." Ed signaled for another seltzer. Poor guy; I knew he should have gone for the duck.

I ordered another cognac to show solidarity to my fallen comrade. "Well, how 'bout we slide on over to my pad after this, and I'll show you the real goods, dig?"

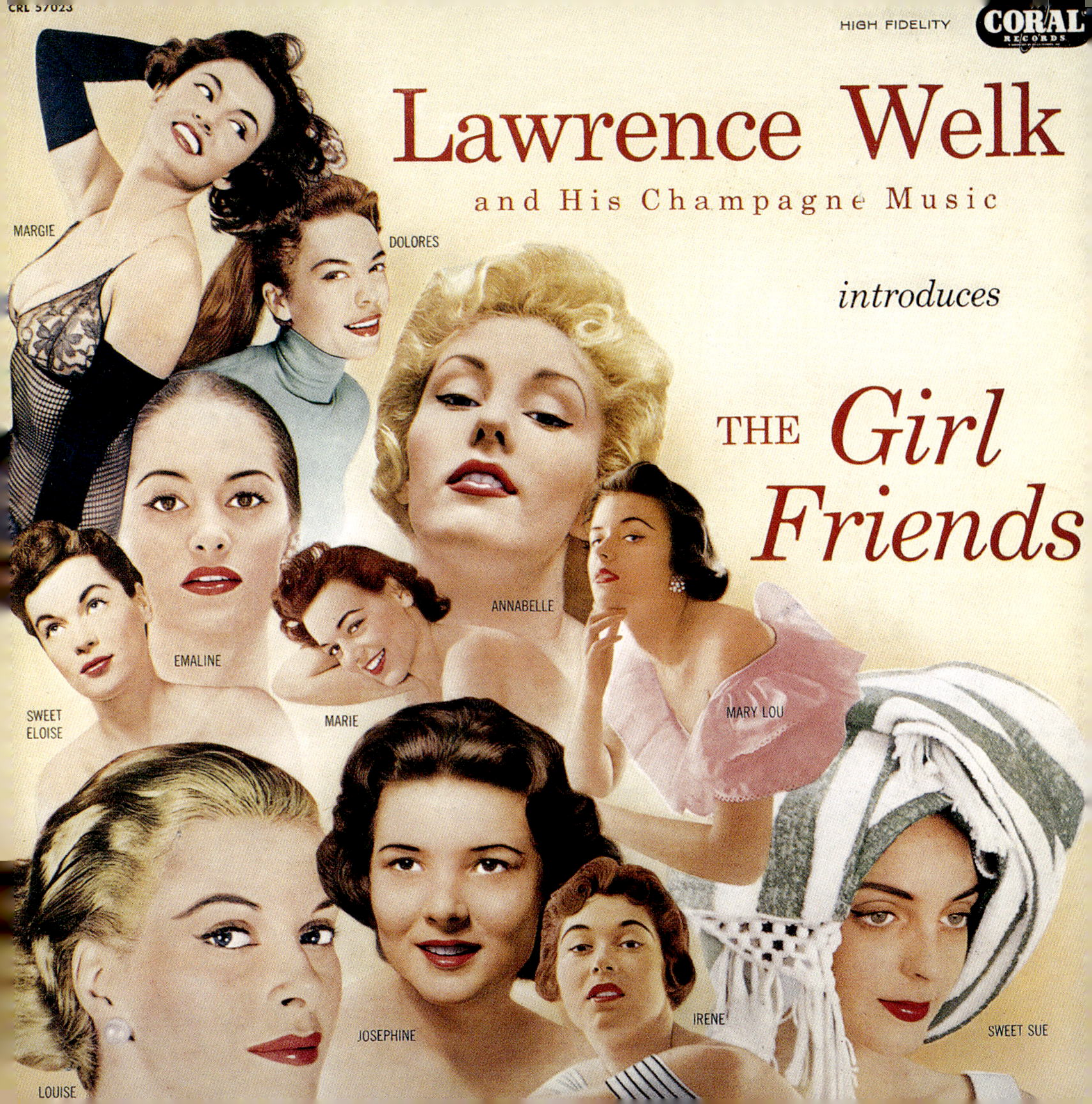
CRL 57023
HIGH FIDELITY
CORAL RECORDS
Lawrence Welk
and His Champagne Music
introduces
THE Girl Friends
MARGIE
DOLORES
ANNABELLE
EMALINE
SWEET ELOISE
MARIE
MARY LOU
LOUISE
JOSEPHINE
IRENE
SWEET SUE

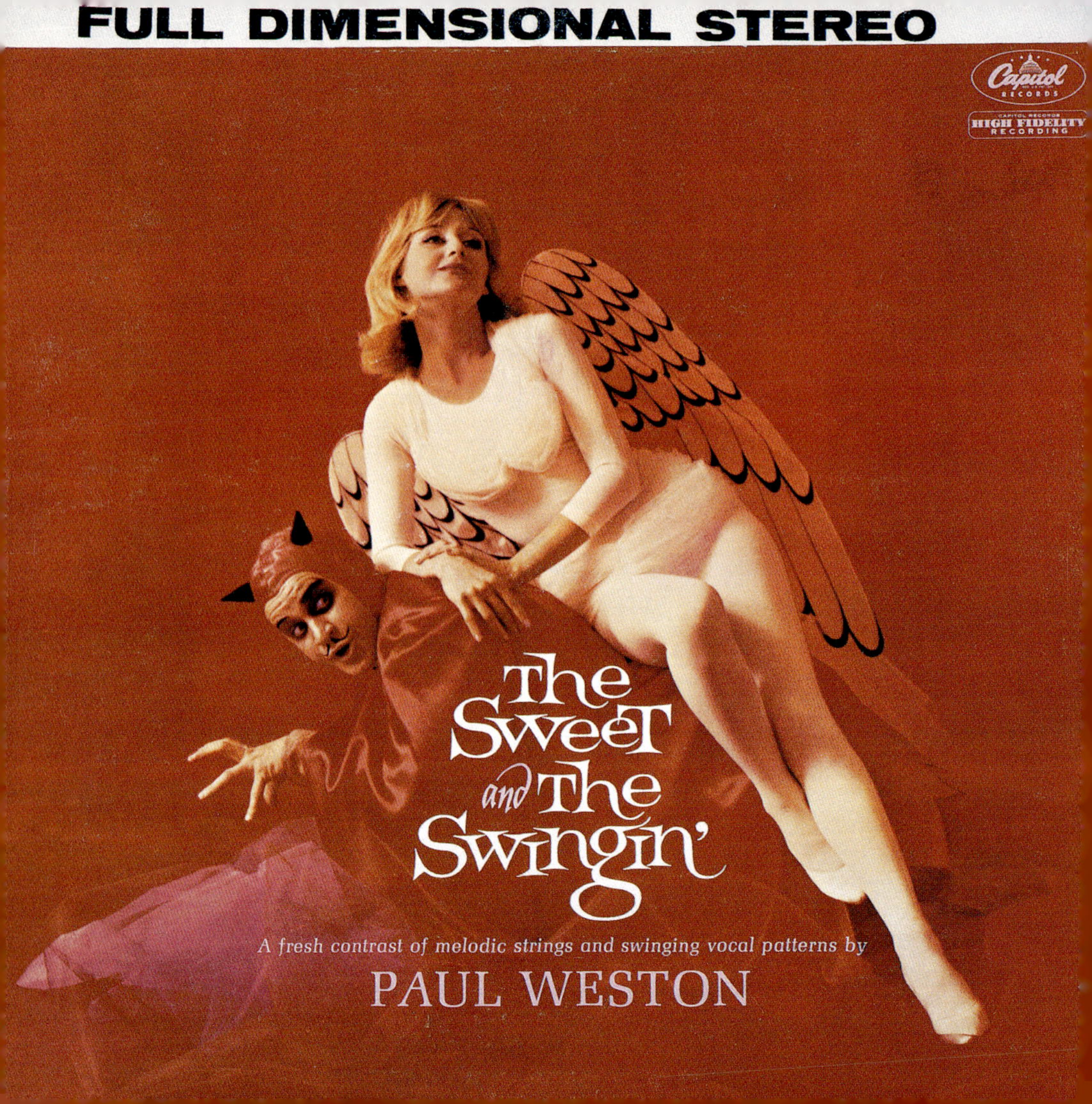
FULL DIMENSIONAL STEREO
Capitol
RECORDS
HIGH FIDELITY
RECORDING
The Sweet and The Swingin'
A fresh contrast of melodic strings and swinging vocal patterns by
PAUL WESTON

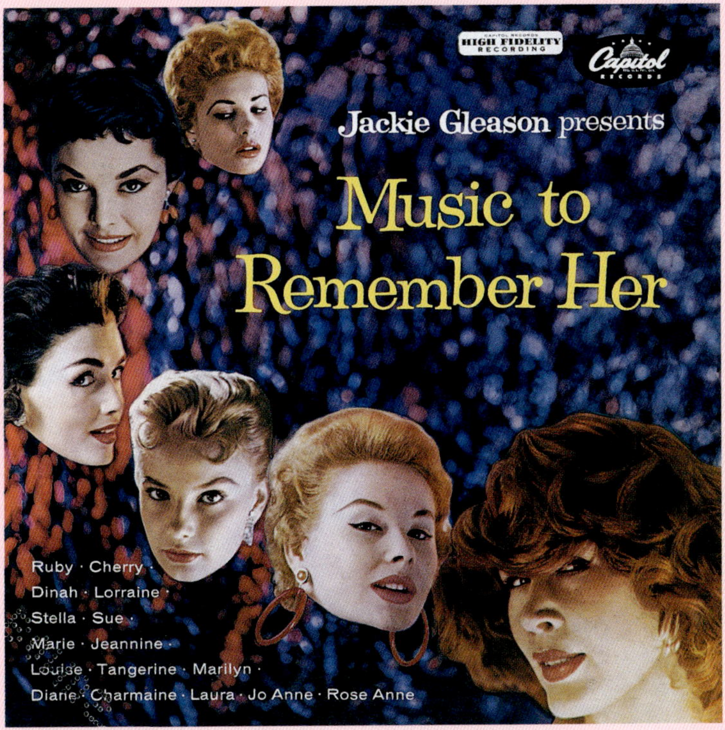

Liner Note: Of the innumerable things that may evoke memories of a girl—from perfume to laughter to a clear bright shade of lipstick—there is nothing so thoroughly, so absorbingly evocative as music.

11:30 P.M. To put Ed in the mood for vixens, I spun a little Herb Alpert and spread out a batch of albums on the coffee table in front of us. I began my speech: "College girls—well, at least the ones on album covers, not the kind you and I encounter —they're innocent, I mean *real* innocent. Later on—the amount of time depends on whether she grew up in Manhattan or Midvale—she becomes either a good girl, all soft sweaters and fresh, healthy skin . . . " I handed Ed the angora-clad sweetheart on the cover of *Music for the Girl You Love.*

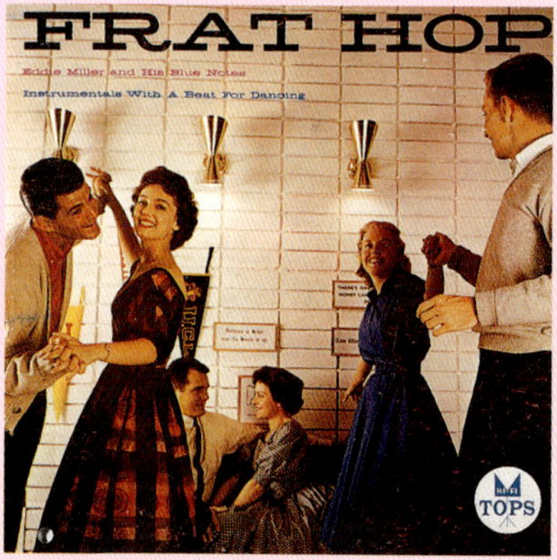

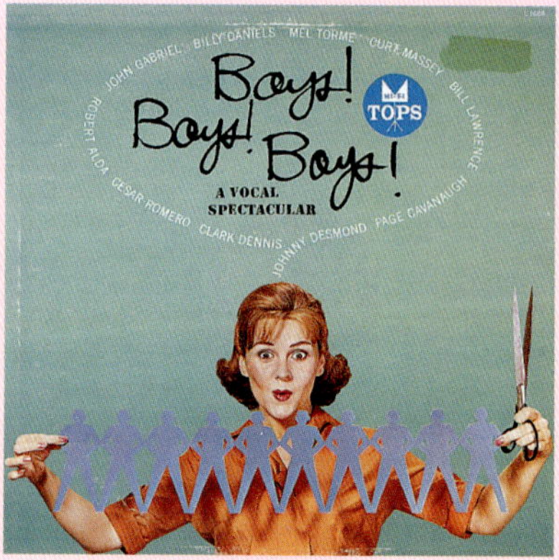

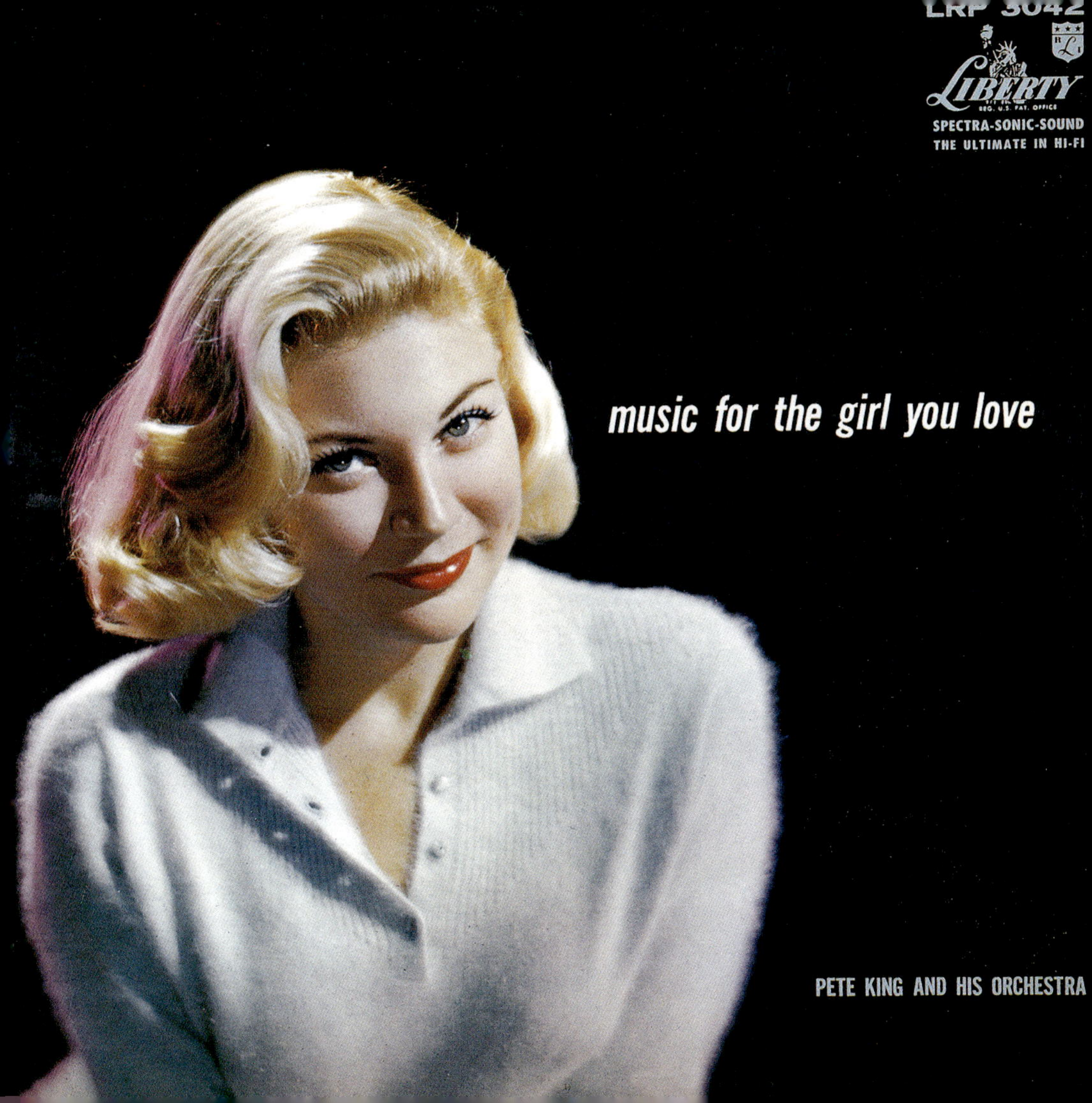
LRP 3042
LIBERTY
REG. U.S. PAT. OFFICE
SPECTRA-SONIC-SOUND
THE ULTIMATE IN HI-FI
music for the girl you love
PETE KING AND HIS ORCHESTRA

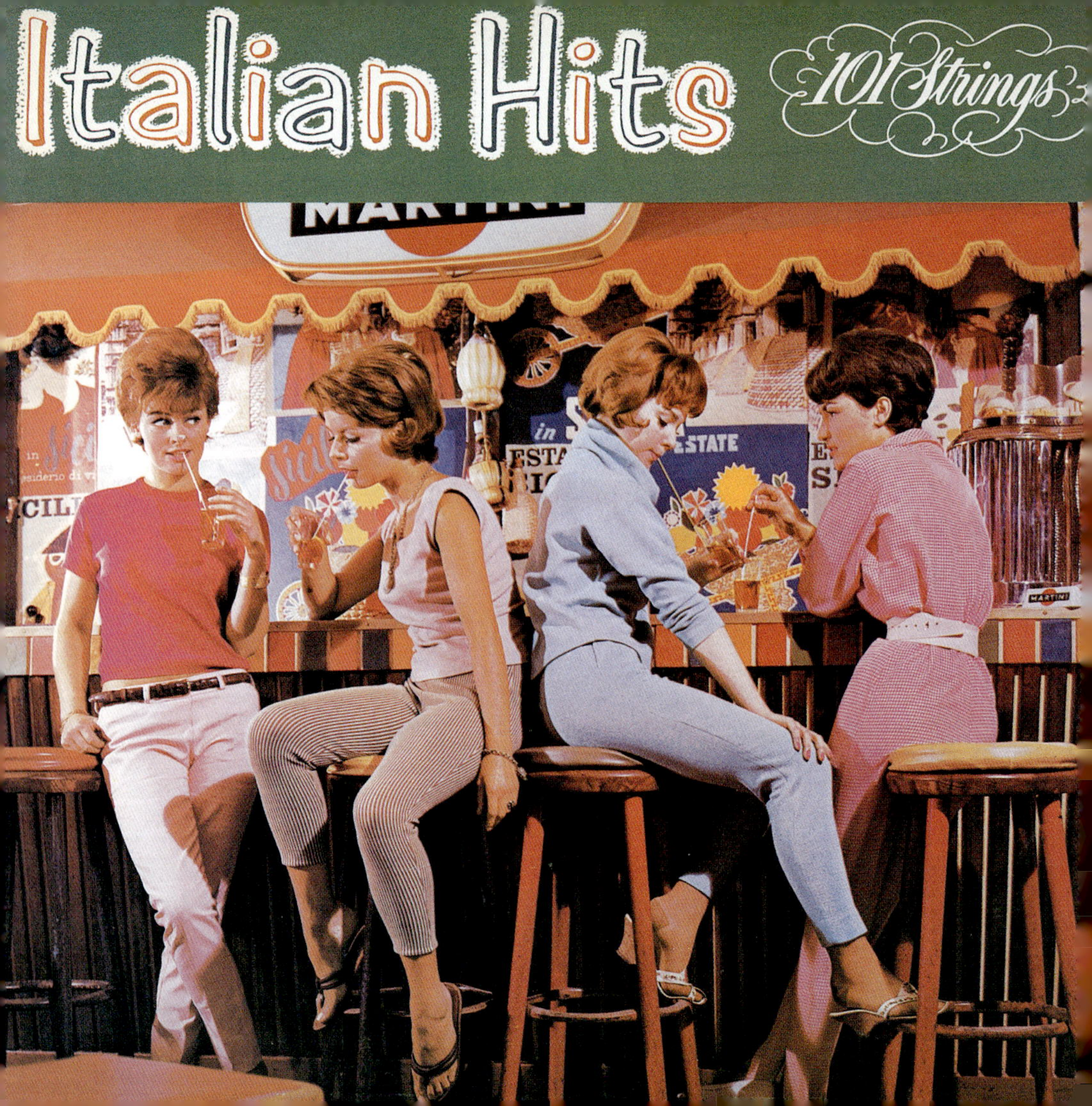
Italian Hits
101 Strings
MARTINI
ESTATE
MARTINI

"Or she's a good girl going bad: capri pants and wicked shades of lipstick. Look at the looks on these girls' faces," I said as I handed Ed a copy of *Italian Hits.*

"I know what I like," Ed said. The wolf, no matter how dyspeptic, is always on the prowl.

"Back in your cage, Tiger. You're throwing me off my groove." I continued: "Such a girl can turn out one of two ways. A lonely girl, she should have stayed a good girl, and now that it's too late, she knows it. A bad girl, on the other hand, she has no regrets." I lined up two Jackie Gleason albums for Ed's delectation. "Jackie knew how to make an album cover. He knew it was just as much about the doll on the cover as it was about the music. His covers are some of the best. Sometimes a bad girl becomes a vixen, sort of a bad girl with attitude—an *über* bad girl, if you will."

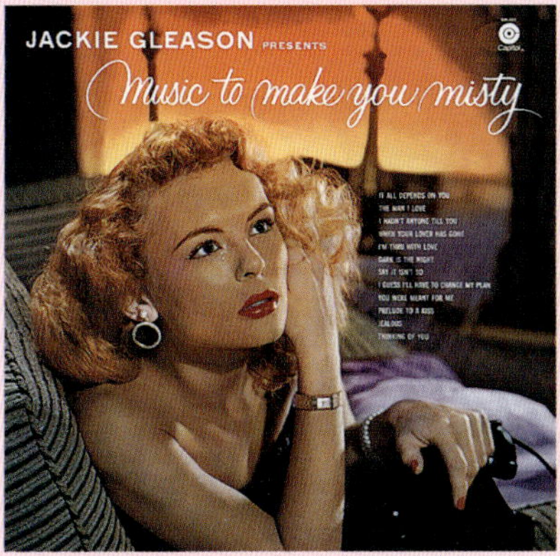

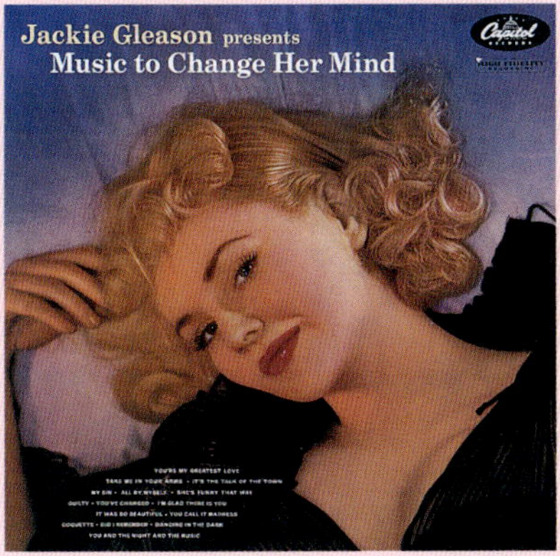

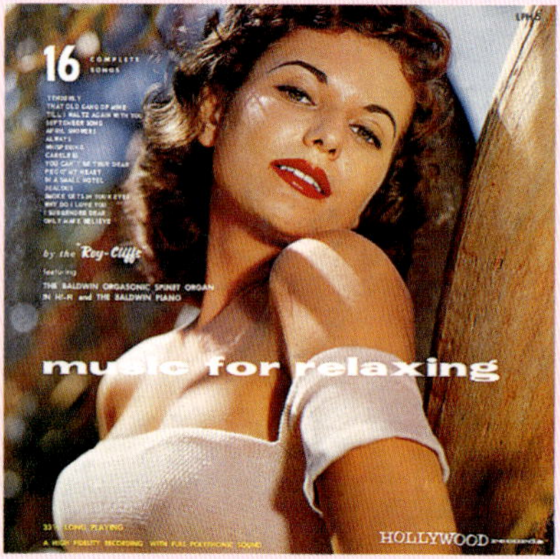
16
COMPLETE SONGS
music for relaxing
HOLLYWOOD

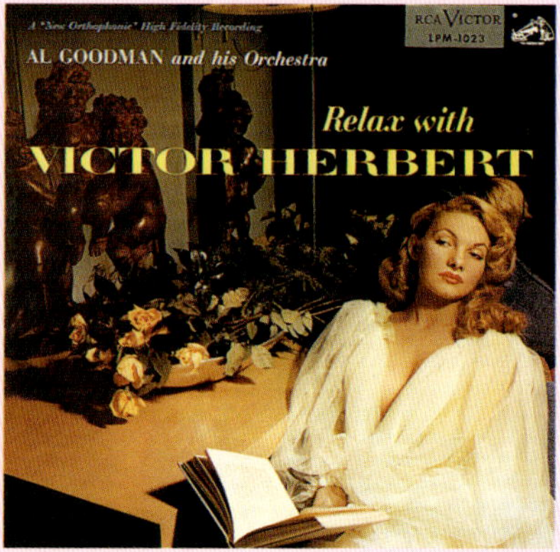
A "New Orthophonic" High Fidelity Recording
RCA VICTOR
LPM-1023
AL GOODMAN and his Orchestra
Relax with
VICTOR HERBERT

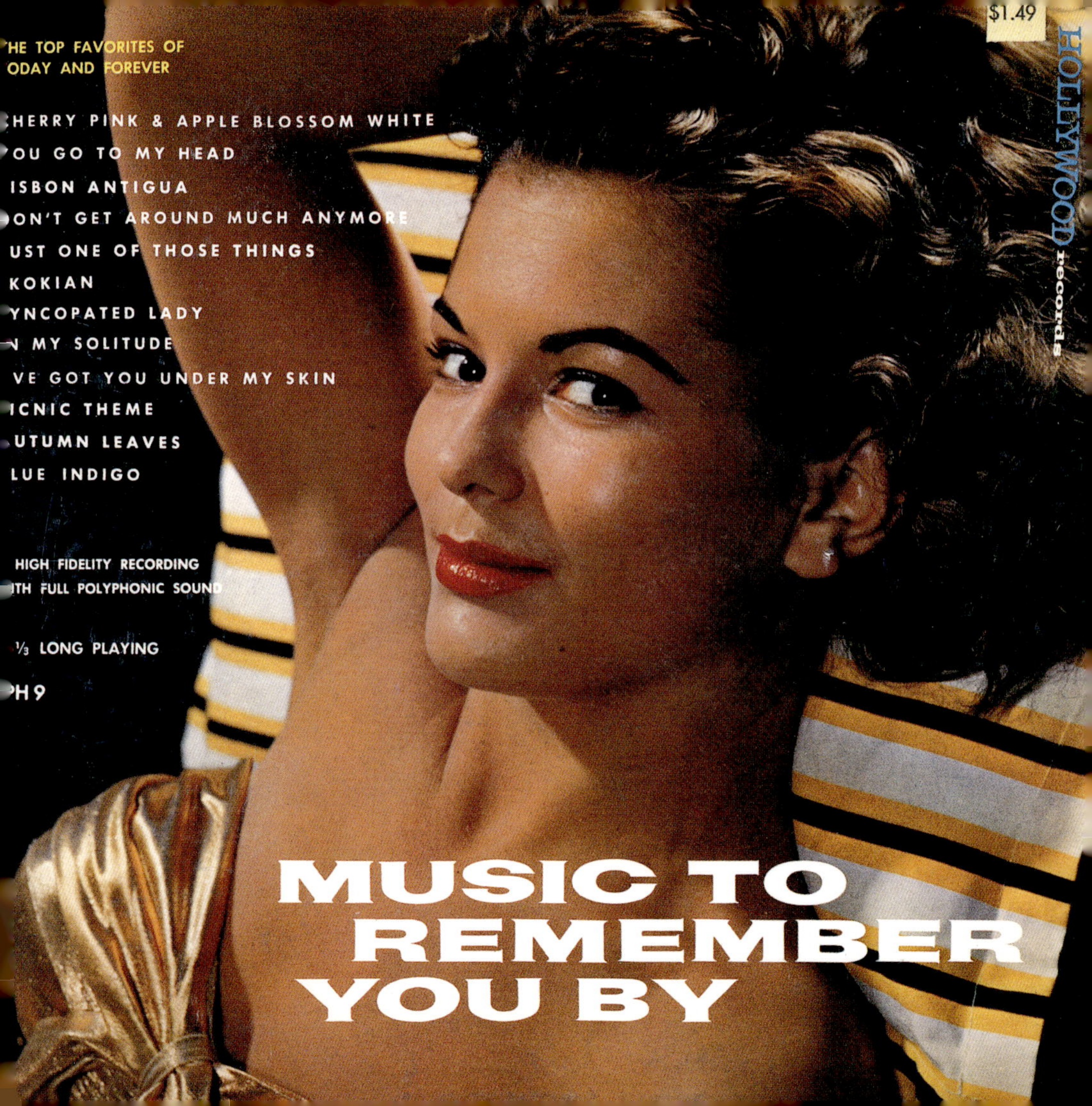

$1.49
HOLLYWOOD records
HE TOP FAVORITES OF
ODAY AND FOREVER
HERRY PINK & APPLE BLOSSOM WHITE
OU GO TO MY HEAD
ISBON ANTIGUA
ON'T GET AROUND MUCH ANYMORE
UST ONE OF THOSE THINGS
KOKIAN
YNCOPATED LADY
N MY SOLITUDE
VE GOT YOU UNDER MY SKIN
ICNIC THEME
UTUMN LEAVES
LUE INDIGO
HIGH FIDELITY RECORDING
ITH FULL POLYPHONIC SOUND
⅓ LONG PLAYING
H9
MUSIC TO
REMEMBER
YOU BY

I was getting a little thirsty, but Ed looked either concerned or impressed with how much I actually knew about the subject. I too wondered about this heretofore untapped font of knowledge—is this what my subconscious had been working on all these years? I forged on. "After the present or former good girls, you have the married set; they've got their own gig going on. There is the good housewife and the bad housewife, and I don't mean their cooking and cleaning. I know you're a confirmed bachelor, Ed, but check out *How to Strip for Your Husband.* Kinda makes you wonder if you're missing something. Marriage doesn't agree with some bad housewives, and they end up as elegant hostesses, or gay divorcées—take your pick. I like 'em both."

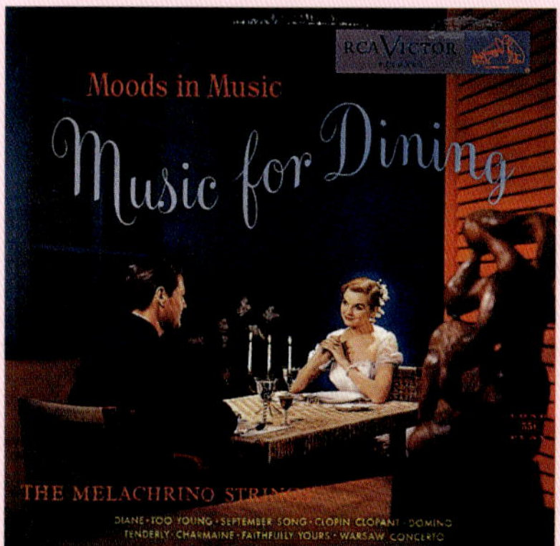

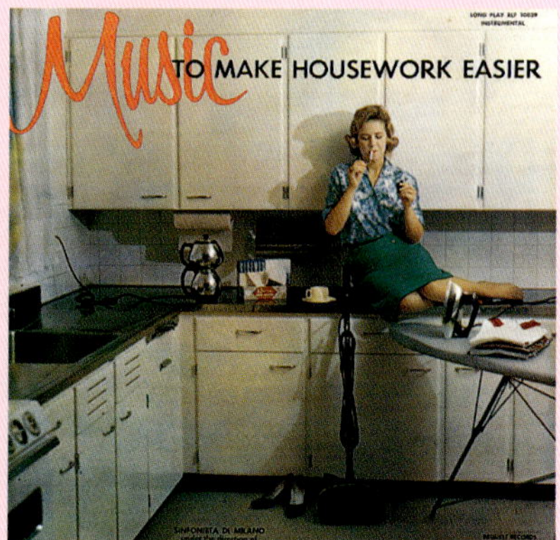

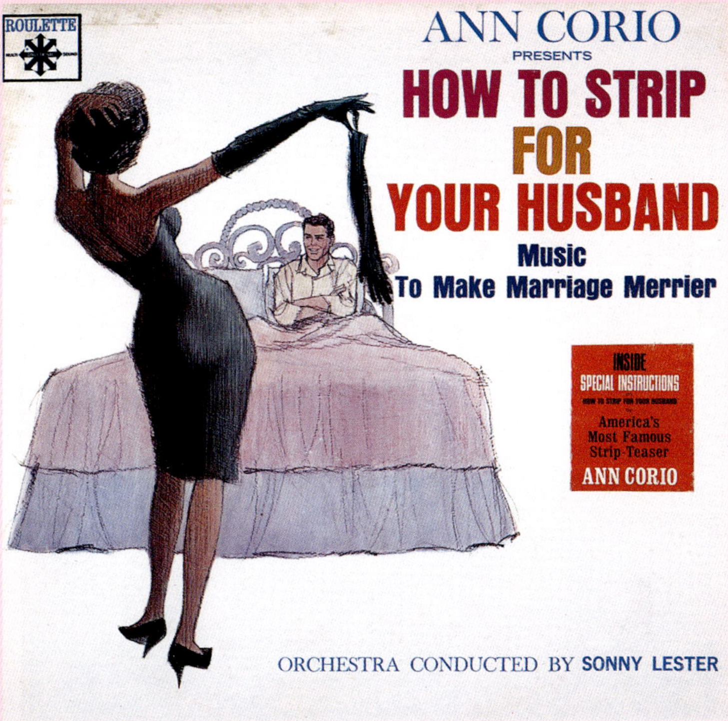

Liner Note: For the girls—here's your big moment, the chance for you to become, in the privacy of your own fancy, and perhaps the enjoyment of your spouse, an ecdysiast—(stripteaser to you!)

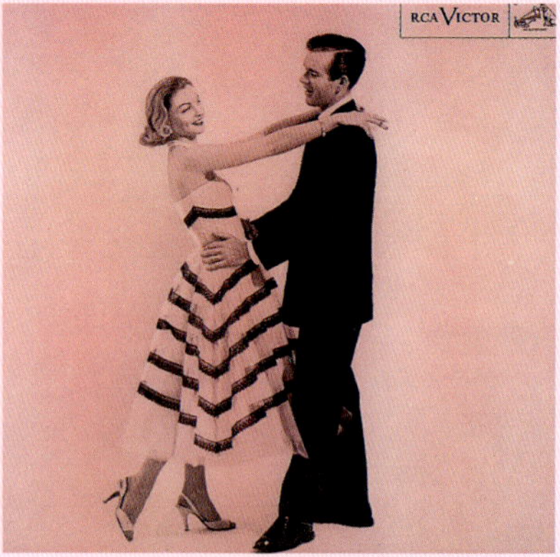

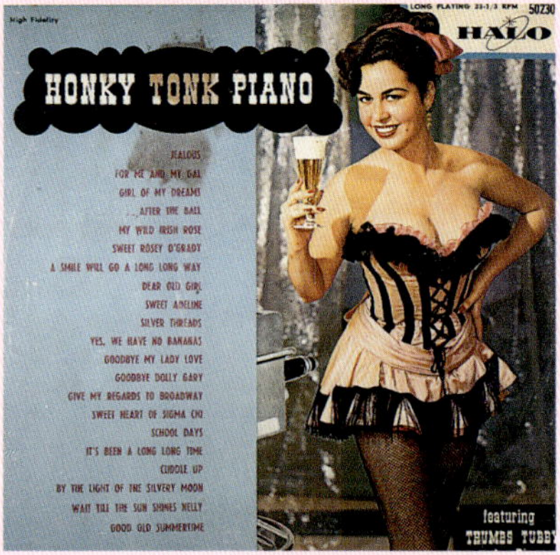

"Coo-coo ca-choo, Mrs. Robinson!" Either the Pu Pu was settling down, or Ed was digging my rap.

"Cool it; I'm almost finished. There are lots of other types mixed in there, like smiling buxom barmaids." Copies of *Honky Tonk Piano* and *Barbershop Ballads* made their way into Ed's eager hands. "They're too jolly to be vixens. Of course, there are types we haven't even discussed: sophisticated ladies and wholesome beach babes. There's even a whole subgenus of exercise mavens."

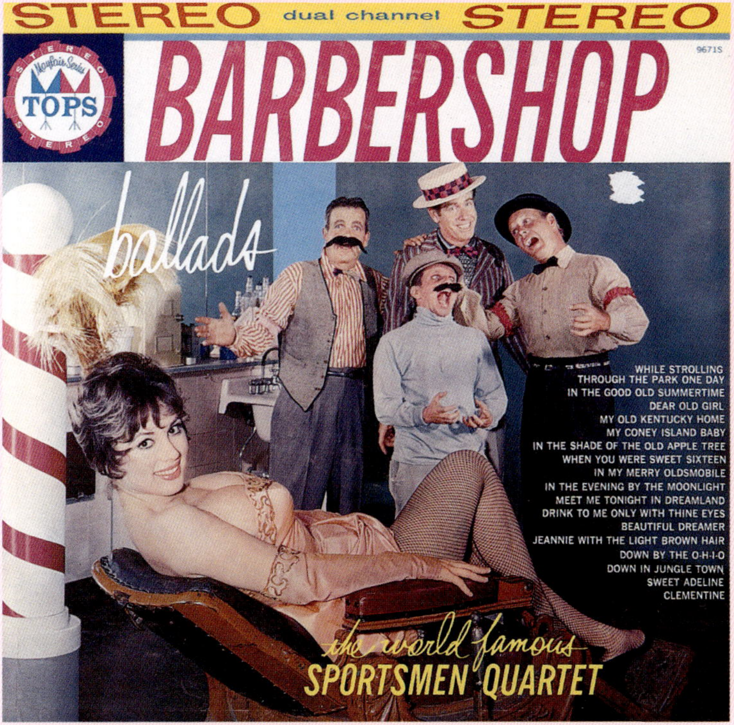
STEREO dual channel STEREO
STEREO Mayfair Series TOPS STEREO
9671S
BARBERSHOP
ballads
WHILE STROLLING THROUGH THE PARK ONE DAY
IN THE GOOD OLD SUMMERTIME
DEAR OLD GIRL
MY OLD KENTUCKY HOME
MY CONEY ISLAND BABY
IN THE SHADE OF THE OLD APPLE TREE
WHEN YOU WERE SWEET SIXTEEN
IN MY MERRY OLDSMOBILE
IN THE EVENING BY THE MOONLIGHT
MEET ME TONIGHT IN DREAMLAND
DRINK TO ME ONLY WITH THINE EYES
BEAUTIFUL DREAMER
JEANNIE WITH THE LIGHT BROWN HAIR
DOWN BY THE O-H-I-O
DOWN IN JUNGLE TOWN
SWEET ADELINE
CLEMENTINE
the world famous
SPORTSMEN QUARTET

I could see that I was losing Ed's interest, so I cut right to the chase. "Finally, at the other end of our periodic table of album covers, there are true vixens." I poured Ed and me a couple of fresh whiskies, allowing suspense to build, and got a new pile of records from off the hi-fi. "Many cool albums—and perhaps more interestingly, many square ones—were sold because of the picture on the cover. And what type of picture was most common? A vixen's, of course! To confirm the supremacy of this approach, one need only think of Herb Alpert's *Whipped Cream & Other Delights.*

"What particularly makes them vixens, you ask?" (Actually, he hadn't.) "This baddest of the bad girls looks out at us in the eye, straight out at us. Invitingly, engagingly, she looks out from the album cover, commanding us with her come-hither stare." I handed Ed *Shangri-La* and *Warm and Willing:* more than ample evidence. "Music appeals to our passions; vixens do as well. When they were big on marketing that crazy new stereophonic sound, you could always rely on the vixen to attract a Square Sam.

"It's what the college crowd might call symbiotic. Hip chicks dig the vixen because she doesn't fall for any wolf's line and knows how to give him what-for if he asks for it. Hep cats like vixens because if she digs you, she's liable to set a trap of her own."

"Oh yes, Daddy!" Ed had come full circle from unbridled enthusiasm to unbridled enthusiasm. I handed him a stack of vixen album covers to peruse and leaned back, drink in hand. Man, am I good.

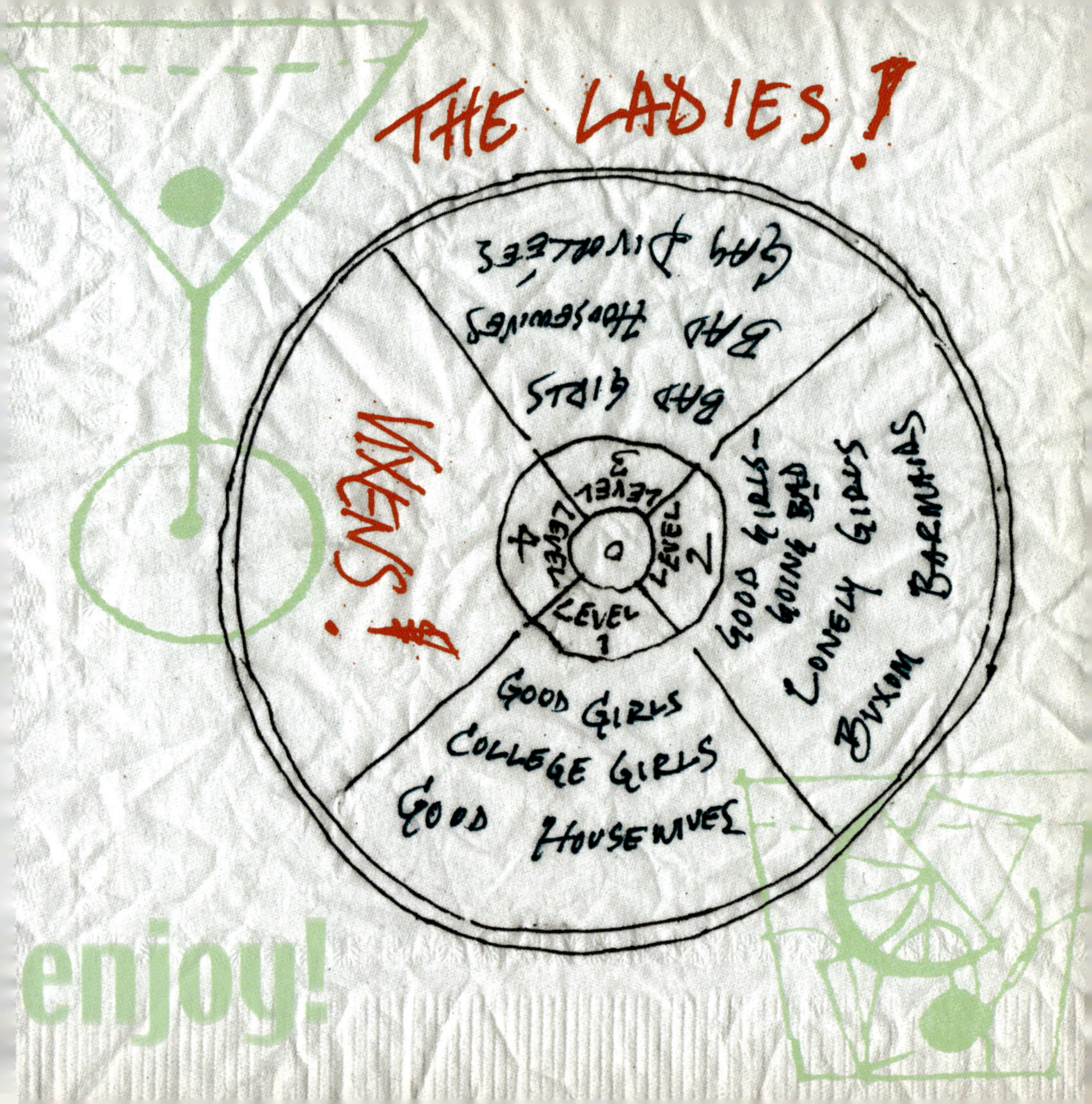
THE LADIES!
VIXENS!
GOOD GIRLS
COLLEGE GIRLS
GOOD HOUSEWIVES
GOOD GIRLS–GOING BAD
LONELY GIRLS
BUXOM BARMAIDS
BAD GIRLS
BAD HOUSEWIVES
GAY DIVORCÉES
LEVEL 1
LEVEL 2
LEVEL 3
LEVEL 4
0
enjoy!

VIXENS, GLORIOUS VIXENS!

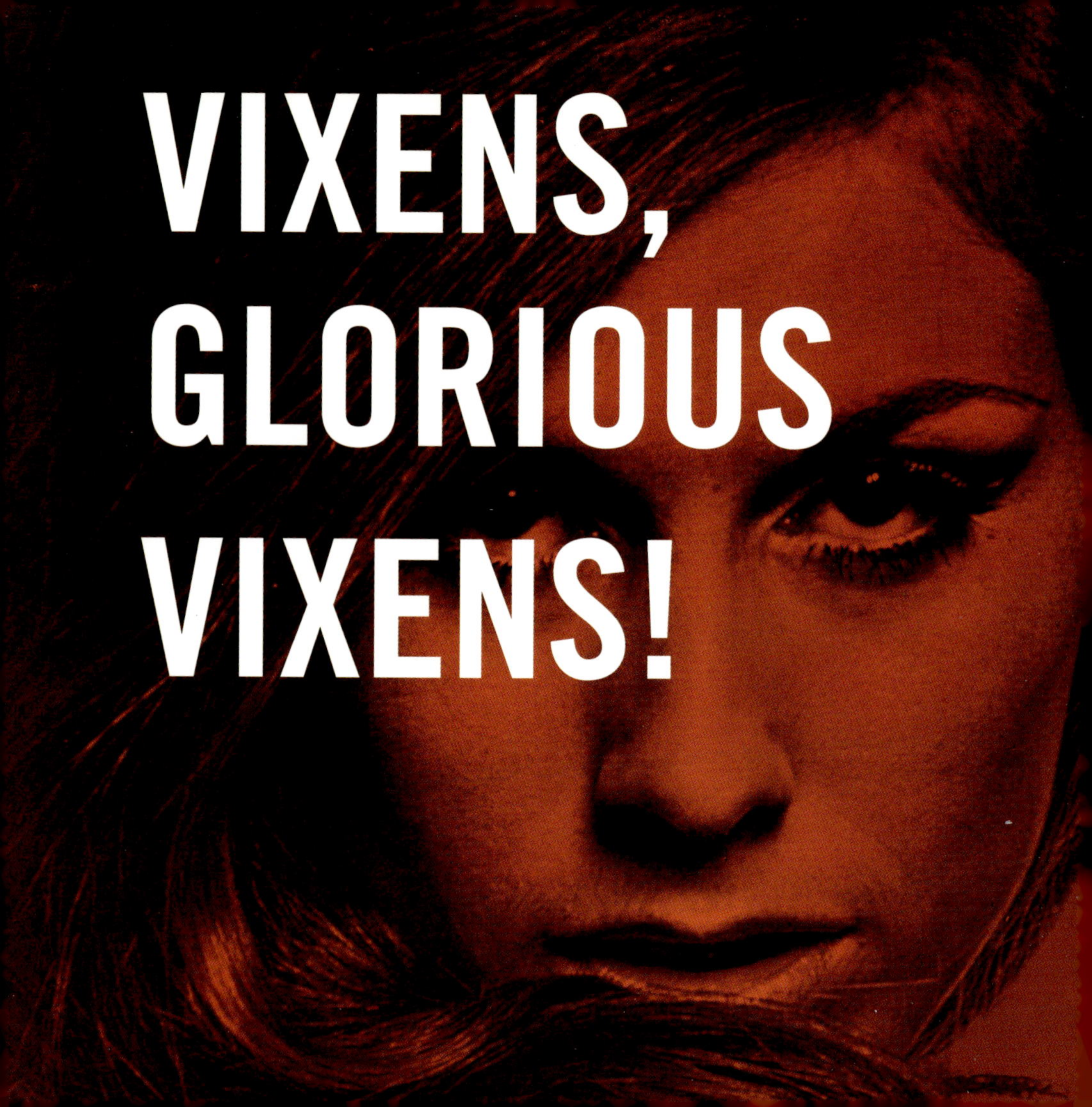

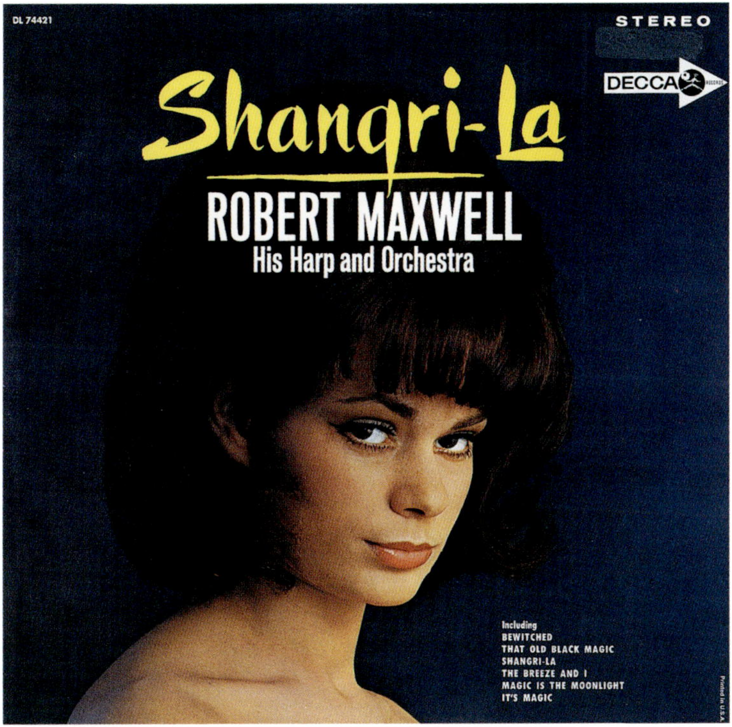
DL 74421
STEREO
DECCA
Shangri-La
ROBERT MAXWELL
His Harp and Orchestra
Including
BEWITCHED
THAT OLD BLACK MAGIC
SHANGRI-LA
THE BREEZE AND I
MAGIC IS THE MOONLIGHT
IT'S MAGIC
Printed in U.S.A.

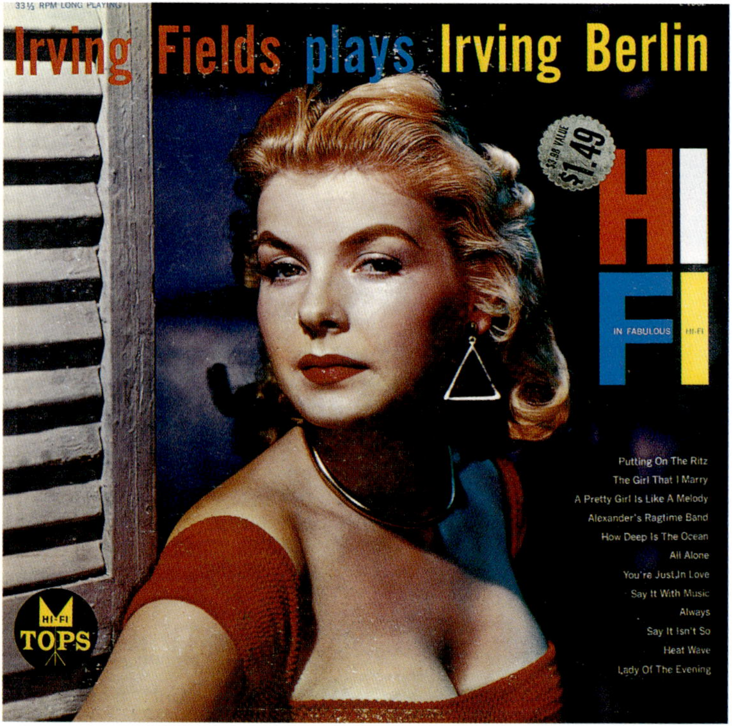

Do you really think you could handle a vixen? You're pretty ambitious, Loverboy.

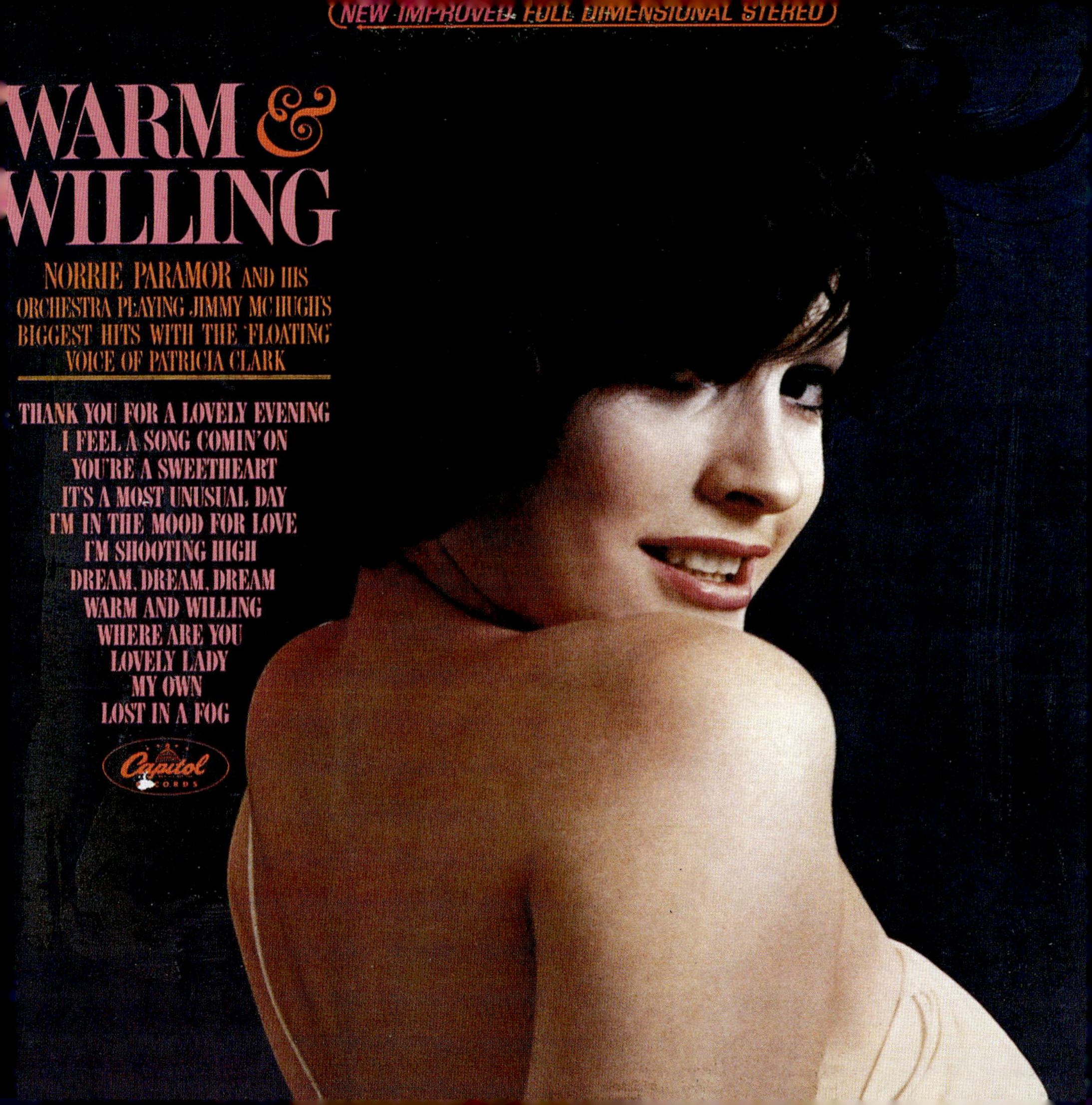
NEW IMPROVED FULL DIMENSIONAL STEREO
WARM & WILLING
NORRIE PARAMOR AND HIS ORCHESTRA PLAYING JIMMY MCHUGH'S BIGGEST HITS WITH THE 'FLOATING' VOICE OF PATRICIA CLARK
THANK YOU FOR A LOVELY EVENING
I FEEL A SONG COMIN' ON
YOU'RE A SWEETHEART
IT'S A MOST UNUSUAL DAY
I'M IN THE MOOD FOR LOVE
I'M SHOOTING HIGH
DREAM, DREAM, DREAM
WARM AND WILLING
WHERE ARE YOU
LOVELY LADY
MY OWN
LOST IN A FOG
Capitol RECORDS

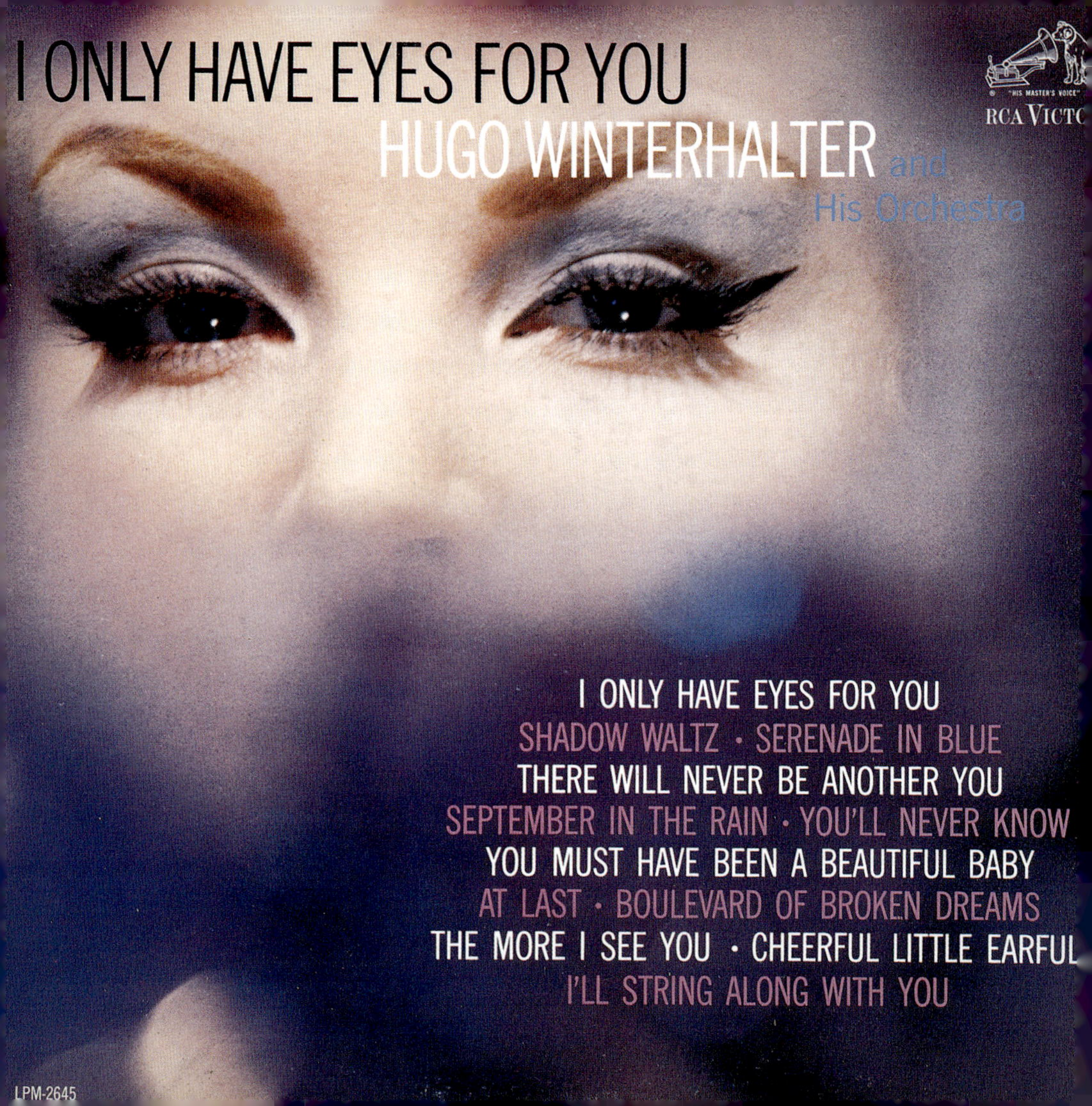
I ONLY HAVE EYES FOR YOU
HUGO WINTERHALTER and His Orchestra
I ONLY HAVE EYES FOR YOU
SHADOW WALTZ · SERENADE IN BLUE
THERE WILL NEVER BE ANOTHER YOU
SEPTEMBER IN THE RAIN · YOU'LL NEVER KNOW
YOU MUST HAVE BEEN A BEAUTIFUL BABY
AT LAST · BOULEVARD OF BROKEN DREAMS
THE MORE I SEE YOU · CHEERFUL LITTLE EARFUL
I'LL STRING ALONG WITH YOU
LPM-2645

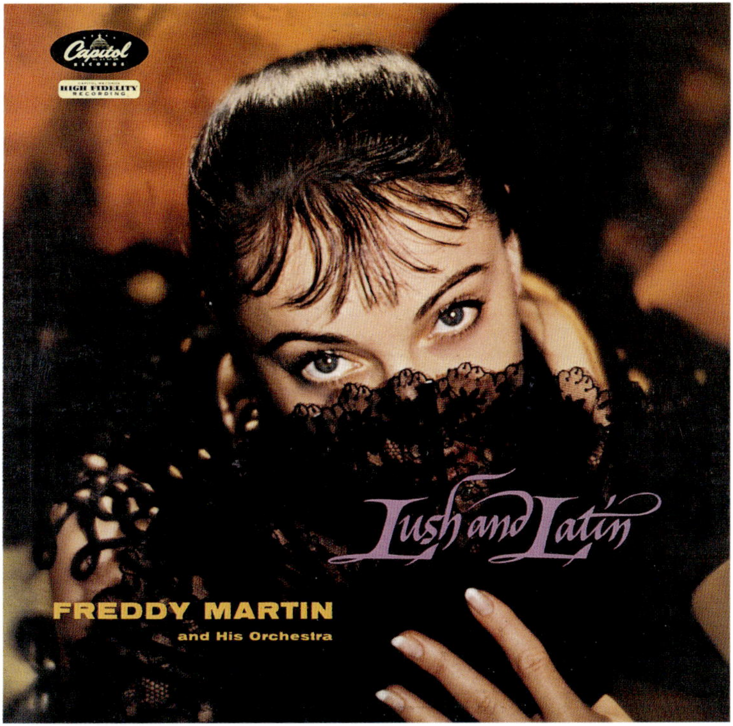

The transfixing gaze of the vixen. She's not afraid to look you in the eye.

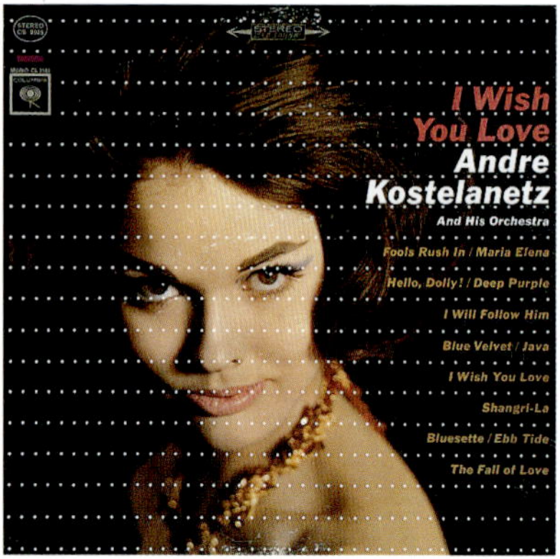
I Wish
You Love
Andre
Kostelanetz
And His Orchestra
Fools Rush In / Maria Elena
Hello, Dolly! / Deep Purple
I Will Follow Him
Blue Velvet / Java
I Wish You Love
Shangri-La
Bluesette / Ebb Tide
The Fall of Love

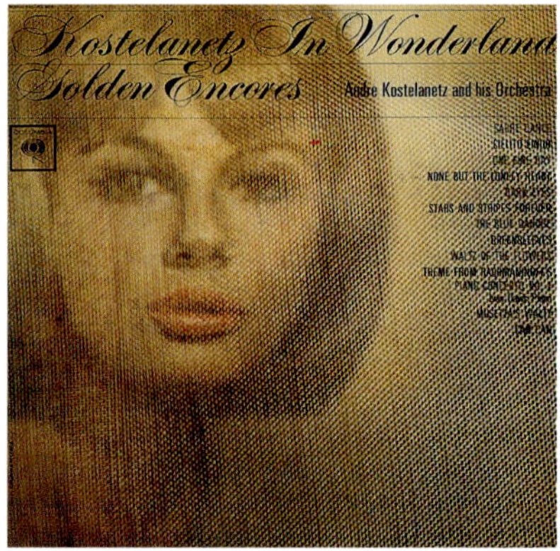
Kostelanetz In Wonderland
Golden Encores
Andre Kostelanetz and his Orchestra
NONE BUT THE LONELY HEART
STARS AND STRIPES FOREVER

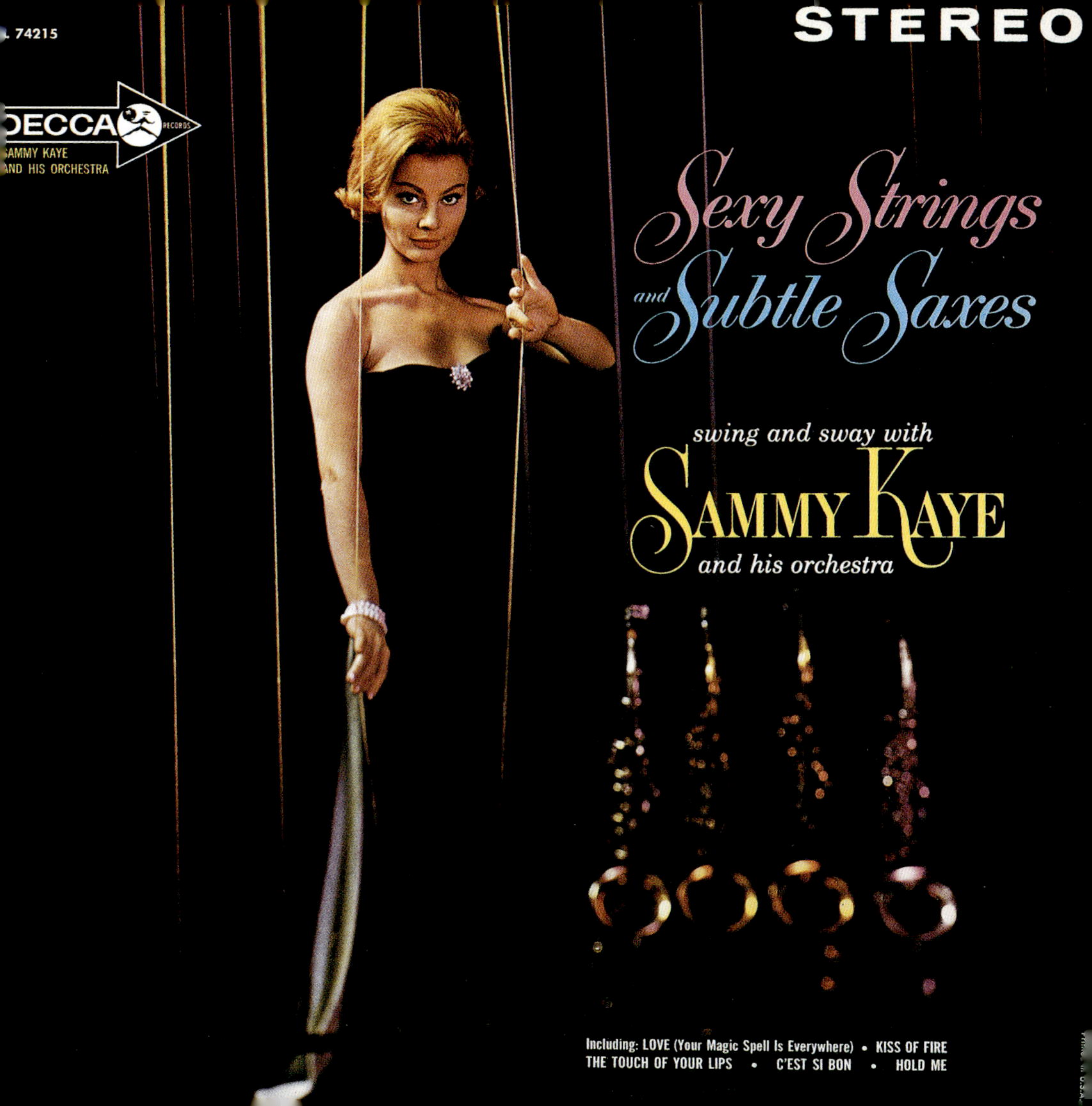
74215
STEREO
DECCA
RECORDS
SAMMY KAYE
AND HIS ORCHESTRA
Sexy Strings
and Subtle Saxes
swing and sway with
SAMMY KAYE
and his orchestra
Including: LOVE (Your Magic Spell Is Everywhere) • KISS OF FIRE
THE TOUCH OF YOUR LIPS • C'EST SI BON • HOLD ME

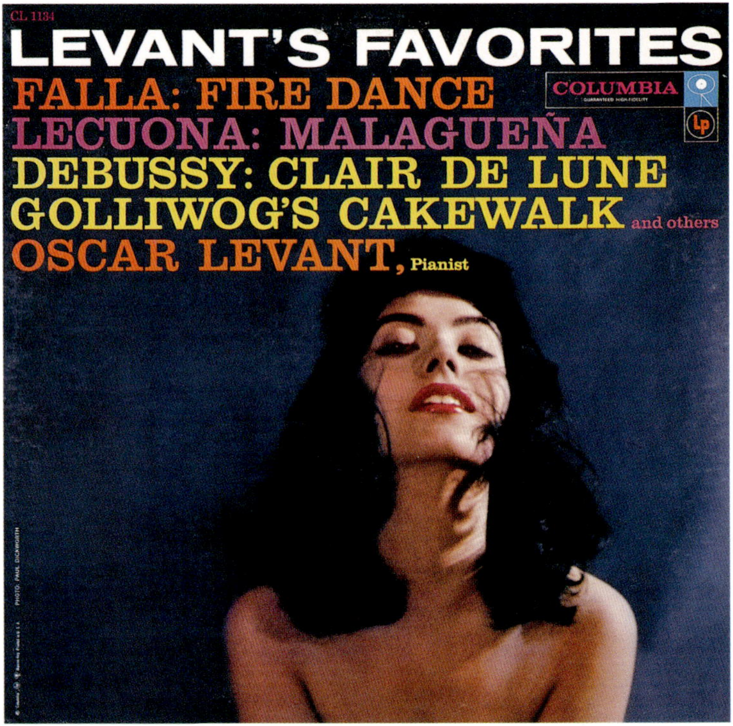
CL 1134
LEVANT'S FAVORITES
FALLA: FIRE DANCE
LECUONA: MALAGUEÑA
DEBUSSY: CLAIR DE LUNE
GOLLIWOG'S CAKEWALK and others
OSCAR LEVANT, Pianist
COLUMBIA
GUARANTEED HIGH-FIDELITY
PHOTO: PAUL DICKWORTH

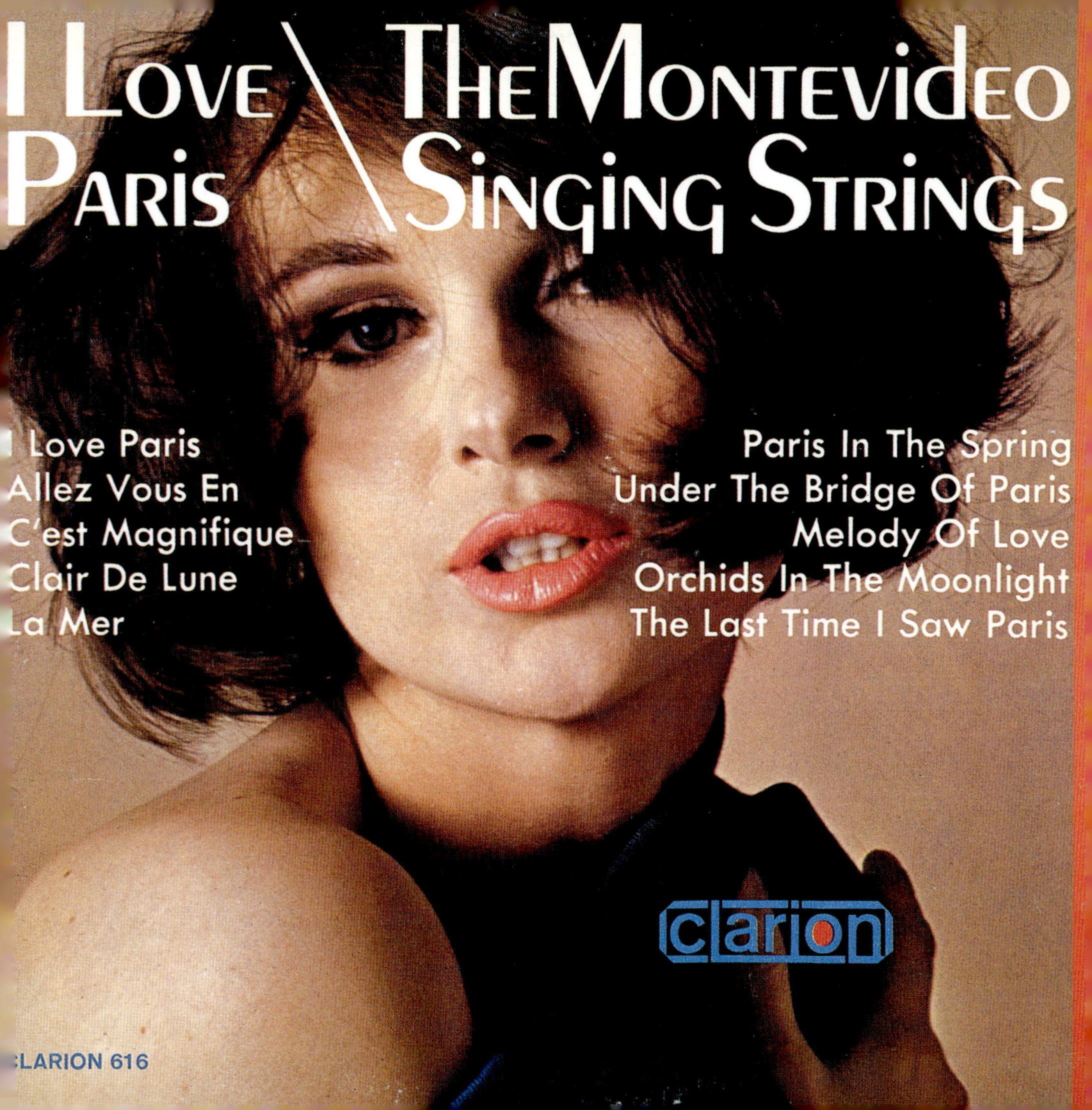
I Love Paris
The Montevideo Singing Strings
I Love Paris
Allez Vous En
C'est Magnifique
Clair De Lune
La Mer
Paris In The Spring
Under The Bridge Of Paris
Melody Of Love
Orchids In The Moonlight
The Last Time I Saw Paris
clarion
CLARION 616

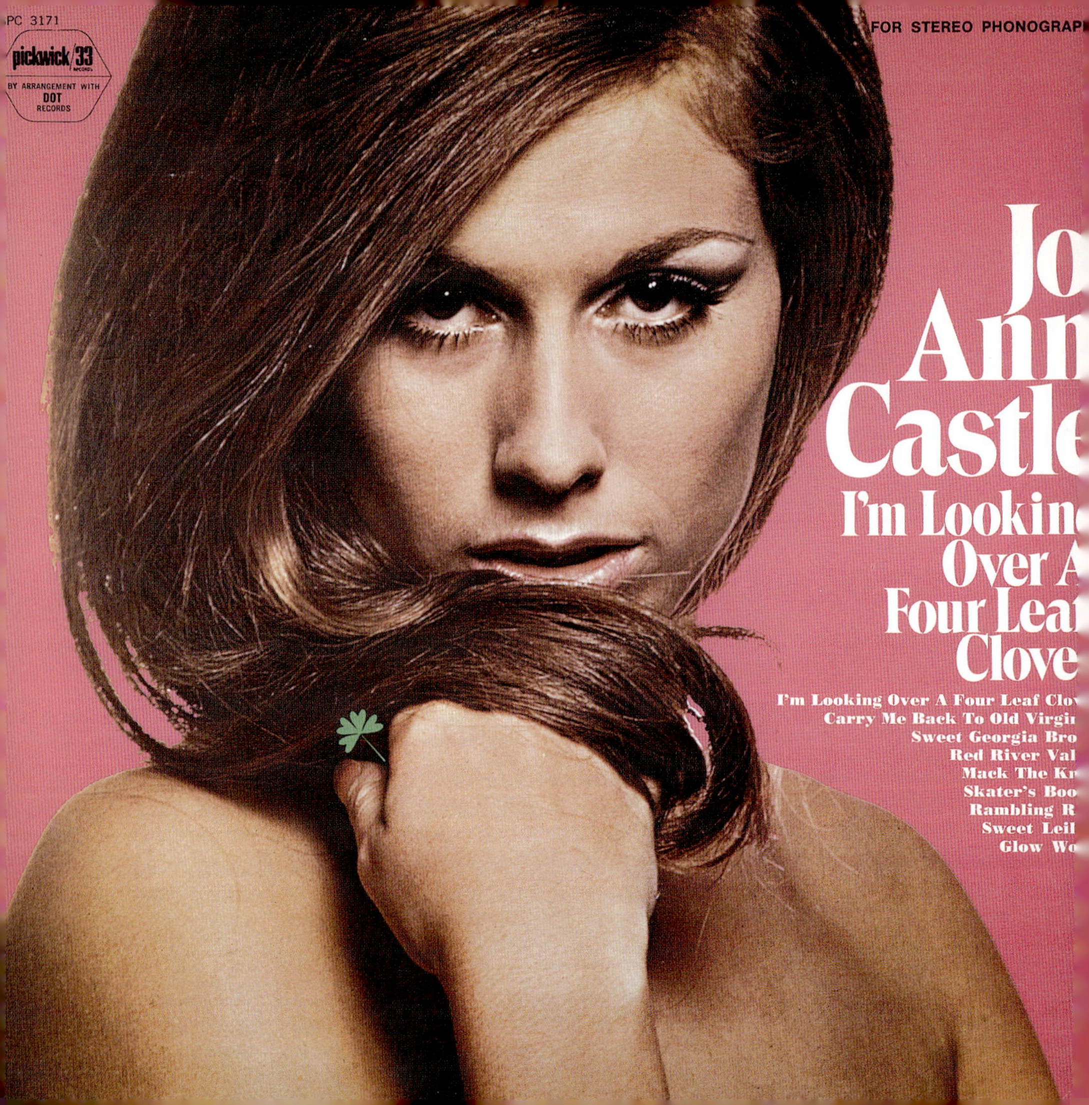
PC 3171
pickwick/33 RECORDS
BY ARRANGEMENT WITH DOT RECORDS
FOR STEREO PHONOGRAP
Jo
Ann
Castle
I'm Lookin
Over A
Four Lea
Clove
I'm Looking Over A Four Leaf Clo
Carry Me Back To Old Virgi
Sweet Georgia Bro
Red River Val
Mack The K
Skater's Boo
Rambling R
Sweet Leil
Glow W

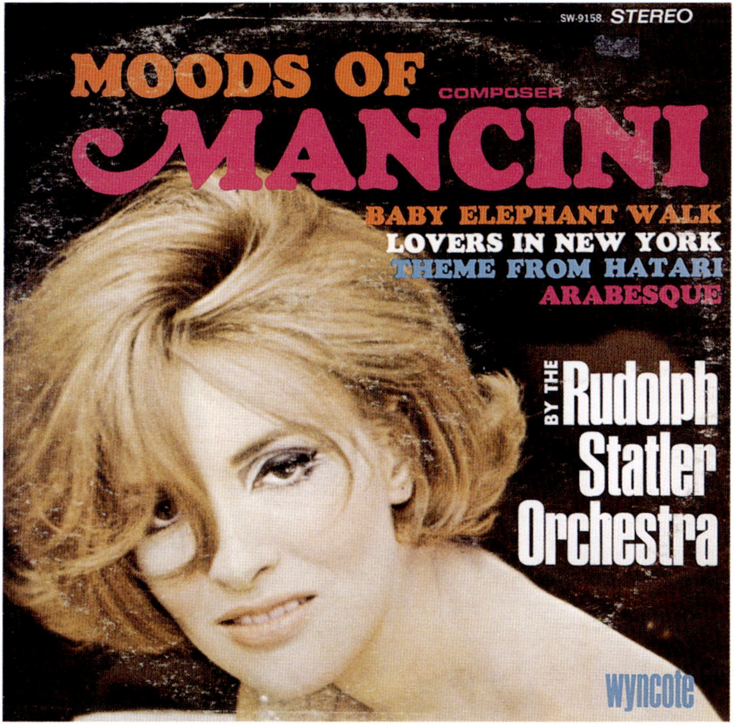

A vixen can be wild or cool, sometimes both in the same night.

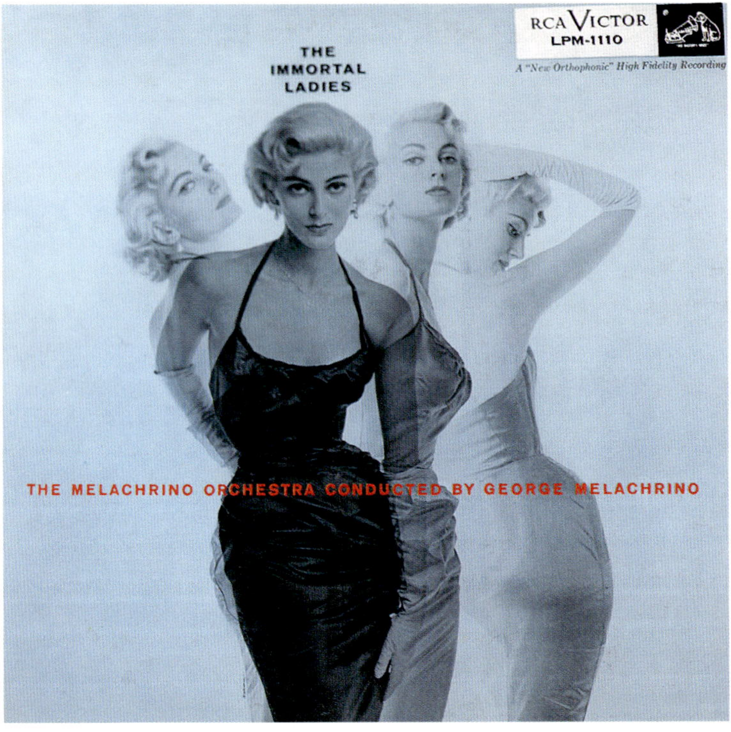
RCA VICTOR
LPM-1110
A "New Orthophonic" High Fidelity Recording
THE
IMMORTAL
LADIES
THE MELACHRINO ORCHESTRA CONDUCTED BY GEORGE MELACHRINO

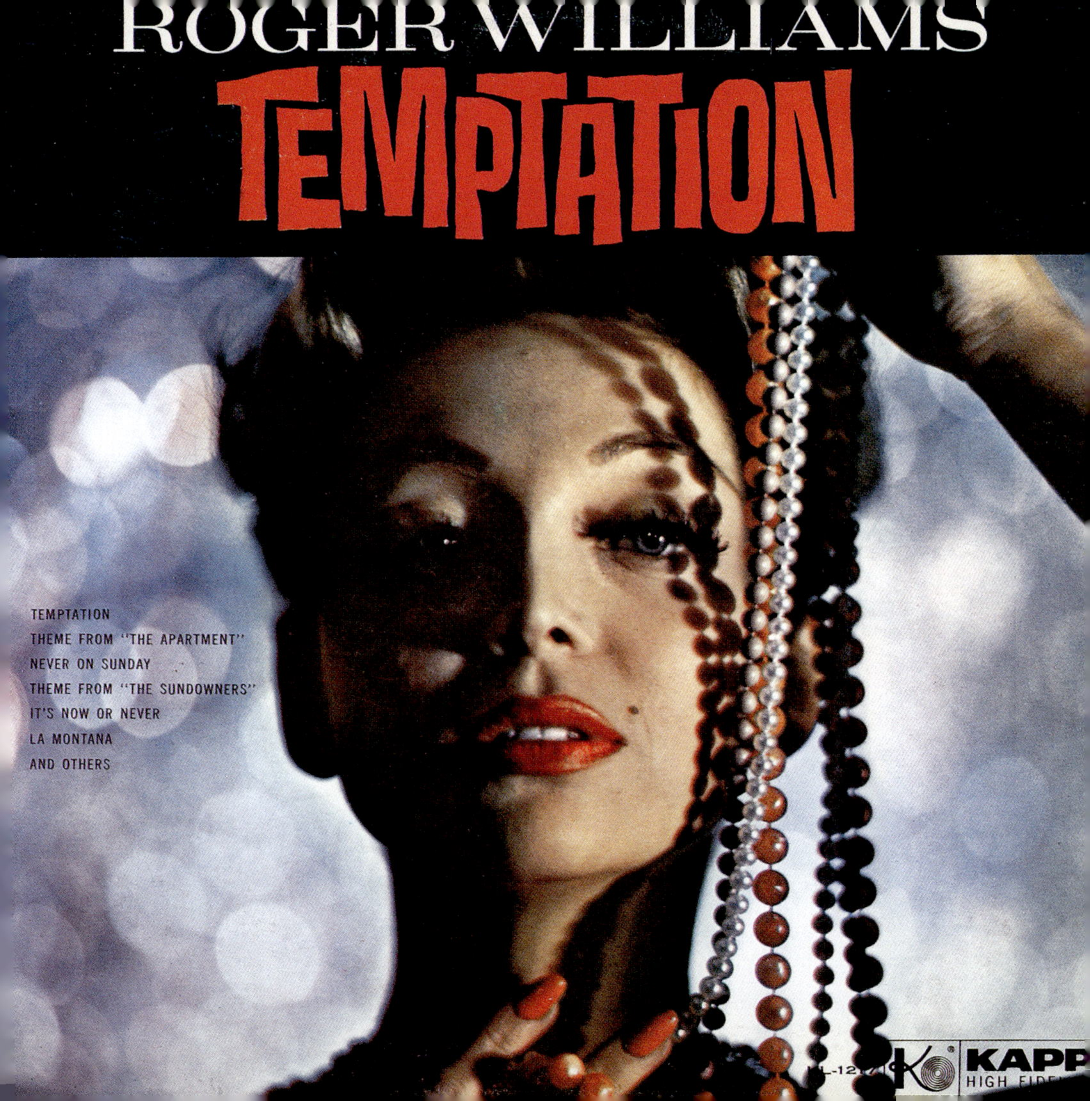
ROGER WILLIAMS
TEMPTATION
TEMPTATION
THEME FROM "THE APARTMENT"
NEVER ON SUNDAY
THEME FROM "THE SUNDOWNERS"
IT'S NOW OR NEVER
LA MONTANA
AND OTHERS
KAPP

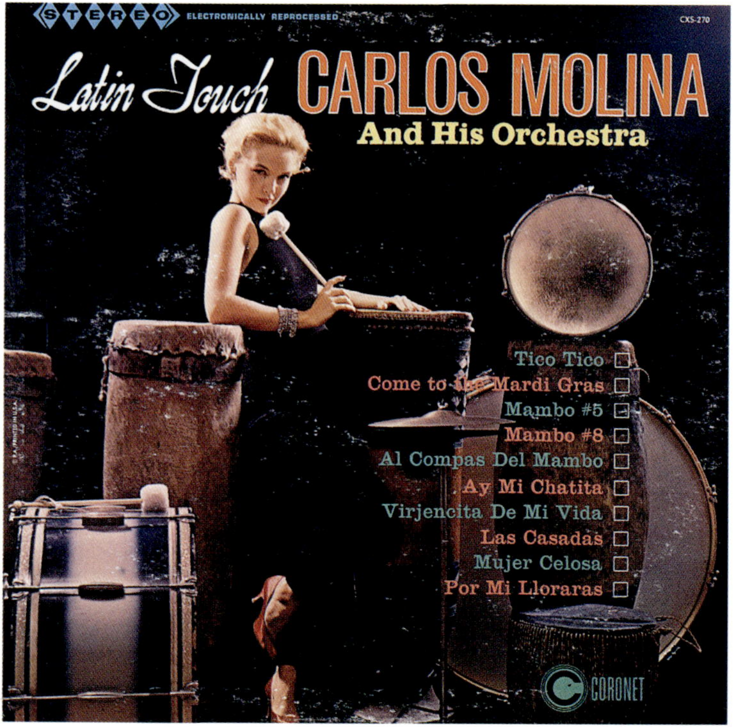
STEREO
ELECTRONICALLY REPROCESSED
CXS-270
Latin Touch
CARLOS MOLINA
And His Orchestra
Tico Tico
Come to the Mardi Gras
Mambo #5
Mambo #8
Al Compas Del Mambo
Ay Mi Chatita
Virjencita De Mi Vida
Las Casadas
Mujer Celosa
Por Mi Lloraras
CORONET

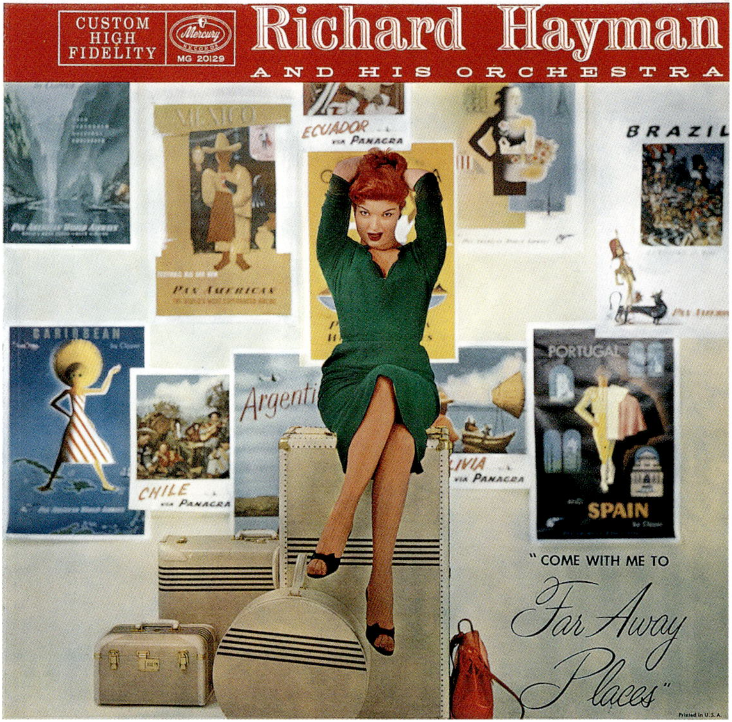
CUSTOM
HIGH
FIDELITY
Mercury
MG 20129
Richard Hayman
AND HIS ORCHESTRA
ECUADOR
via PANAGRA
BRAZIL
PAN AMERICAN
CARIBBEAN
CHILE
via PANAGRA
Argenti
LIVIA
via PANAGRA
PORTUGAL
SPAIN
"COME WITH ME TO
Far Away
Places"
Printed in U.S.A.

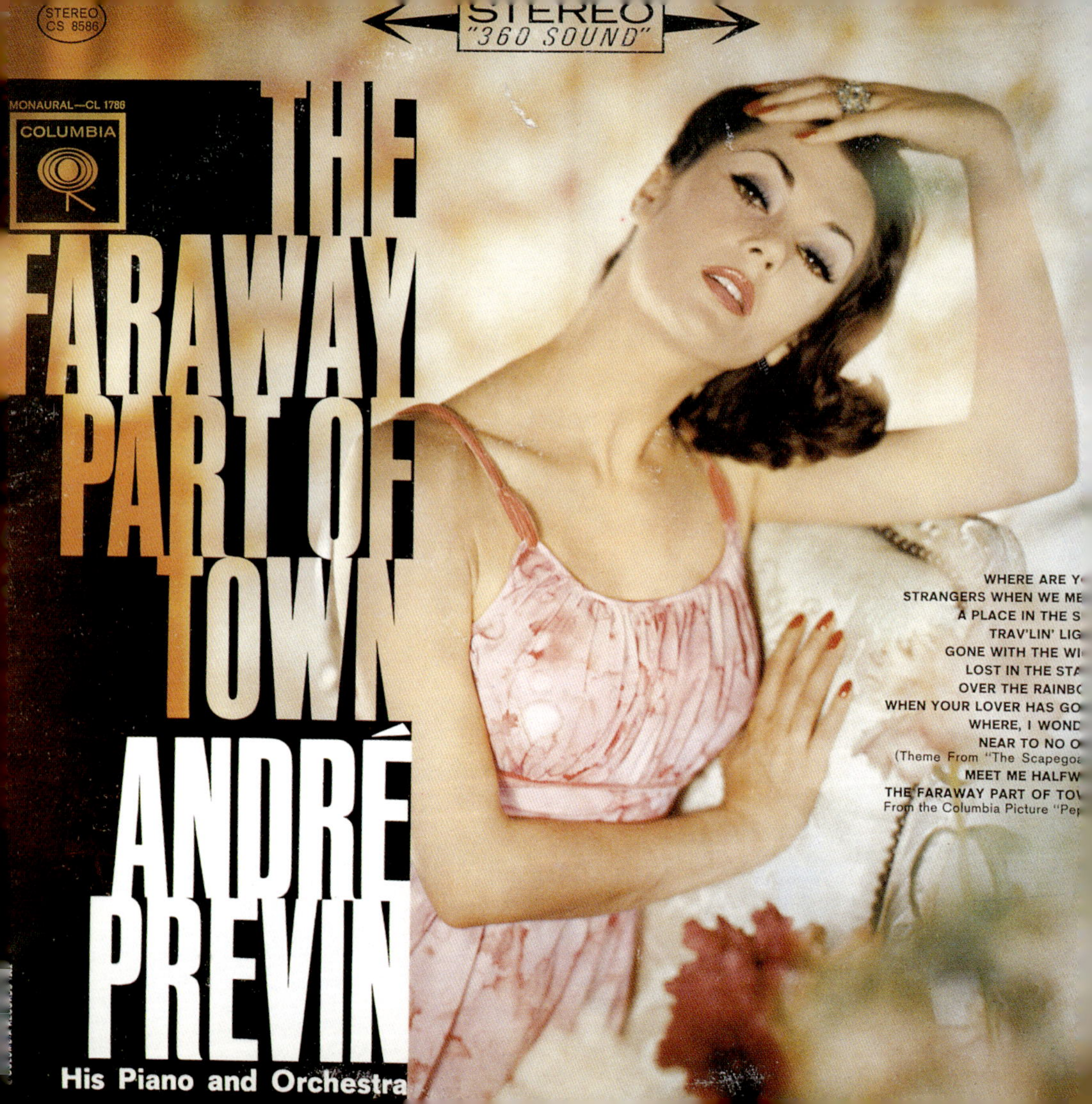
STEREO
CS 8586
STEREO
"360 SOUND"
MONAURAL—CL 1786
COLUMBIA
THE FARAWAY PART OF TOWN
ANDRÉ PREVIN
His Piano and Orchestra
WHERE ARE Y
STRANGERS WHEN WE ME
A PLACE IN THE S
TRAV'LIN' LIG
GONE WITH THE WI
LOST IN THE STA
OVER THE RAINBO
WHEN YOUR LOVER HAS GO
WHERE, I WOND
NEAR TO NO O
(Theme From "The Scapegoa
MEET ME HALFW
THE FARAWAY PART OF TO
From the Columbia Picture "Pe

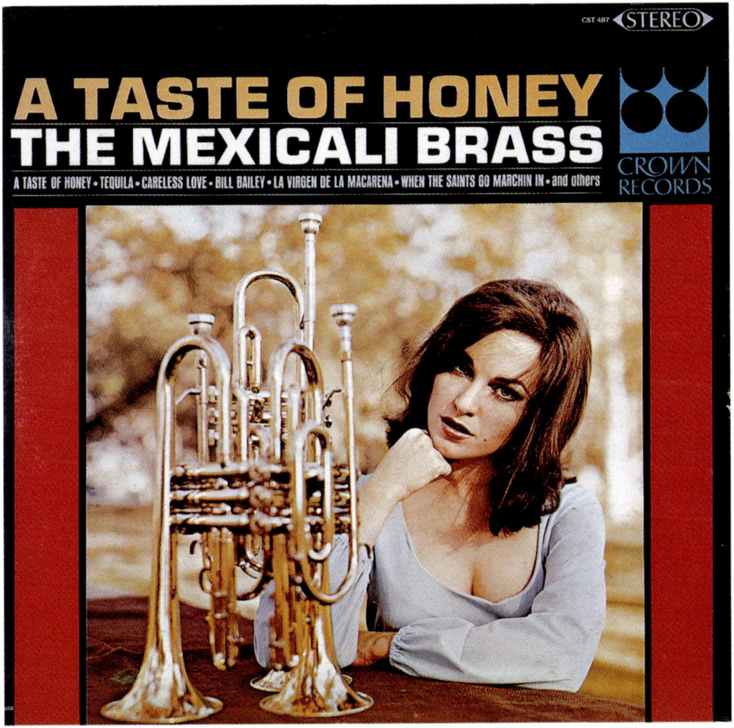
CST 487
STEREO
A TASTE OF HONEY
THE MEXICALI BRASS
A TASTE OF HONEY • TEQUILA • CARELESS LOVE • BILL BAILEY • LA VIRGEN DE LA MACARENA • WHEN THE SAINTS GO MARCHIN IN • and others
CROWN RECORDS

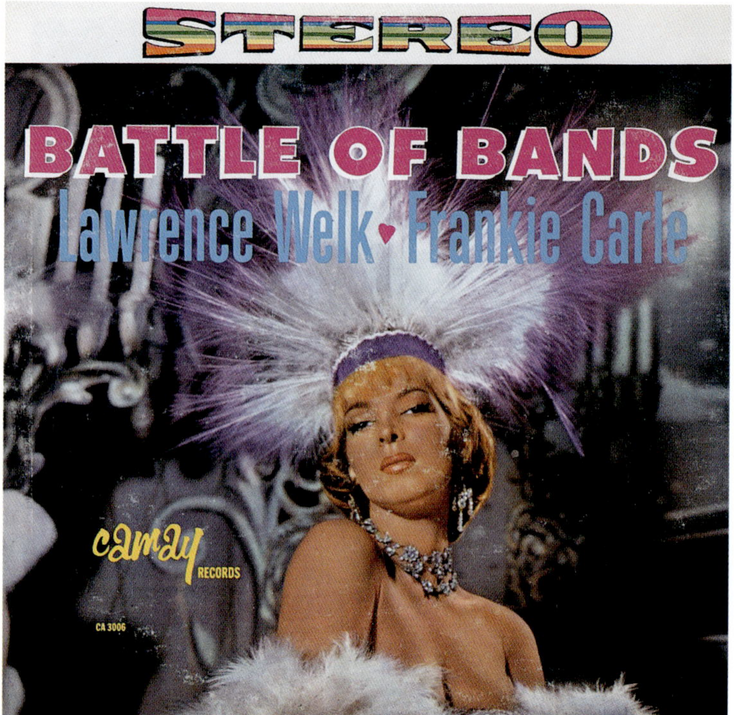
STEREO
BATTLE OF BANDS
Lawrence Welk • Frankie Carle
camay
RECORDS
CA 3006

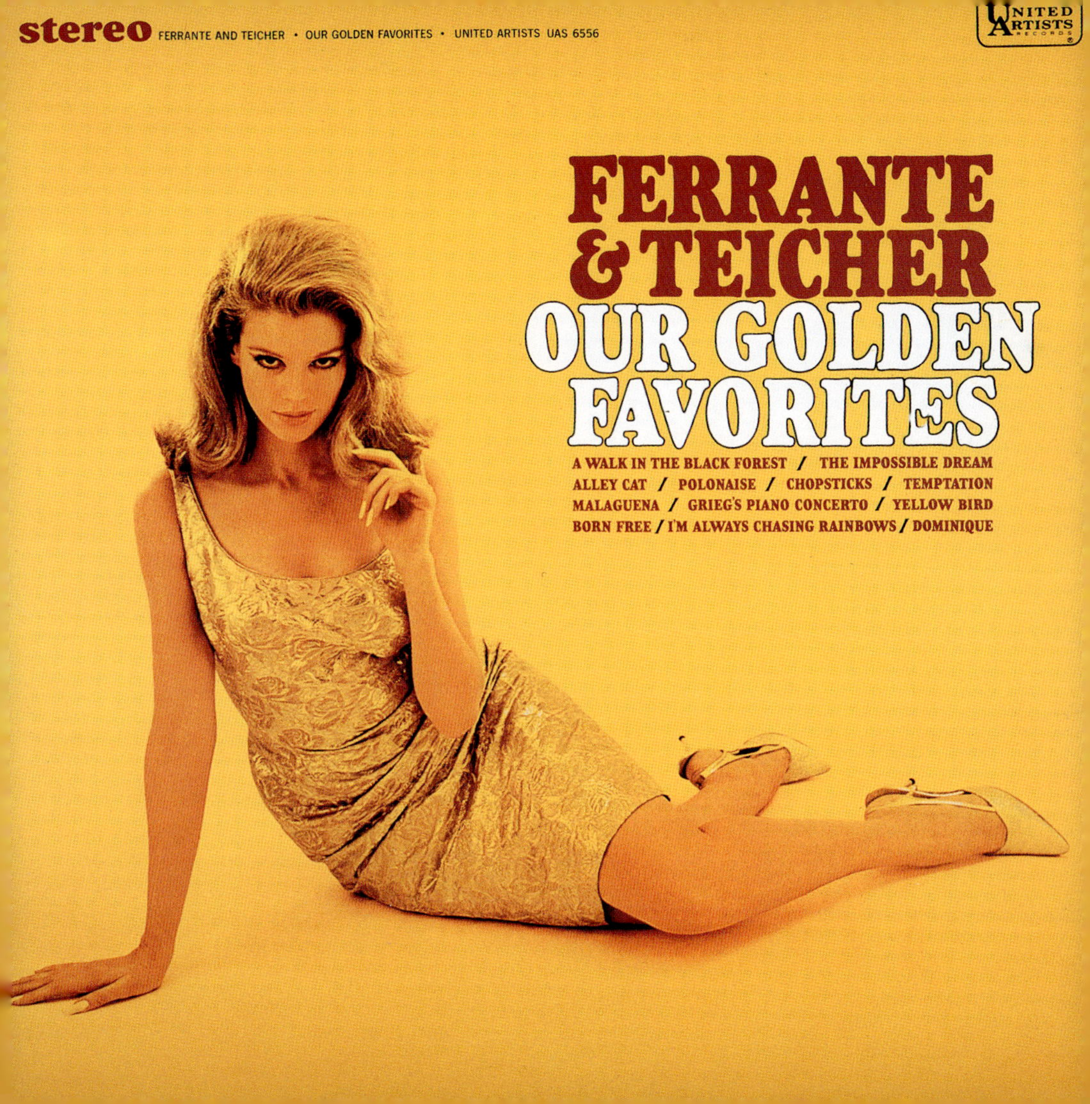
stereo FERRANTE AND TEICHER • OUR GOLDEN FAVORITES • UNITED ARTISTS UAS 6556
UNITED ARTISTS RECORDS
FERRANTE & TEICHER
OUR GOLDEN FAVORITES
A WALK IN THE BLACK FOREST / THE IMPOSSIBLE DREAM
ALLEY CAT / POLONAISE / CHOPSTICKS / TEMPTATION
MALAGUENA / GRIEG'S PIANO CONCERTO / YELLOW BIRD
BORN FREE / I'M ALWAYS CHASING RAINBOWS / DOMINIQUE

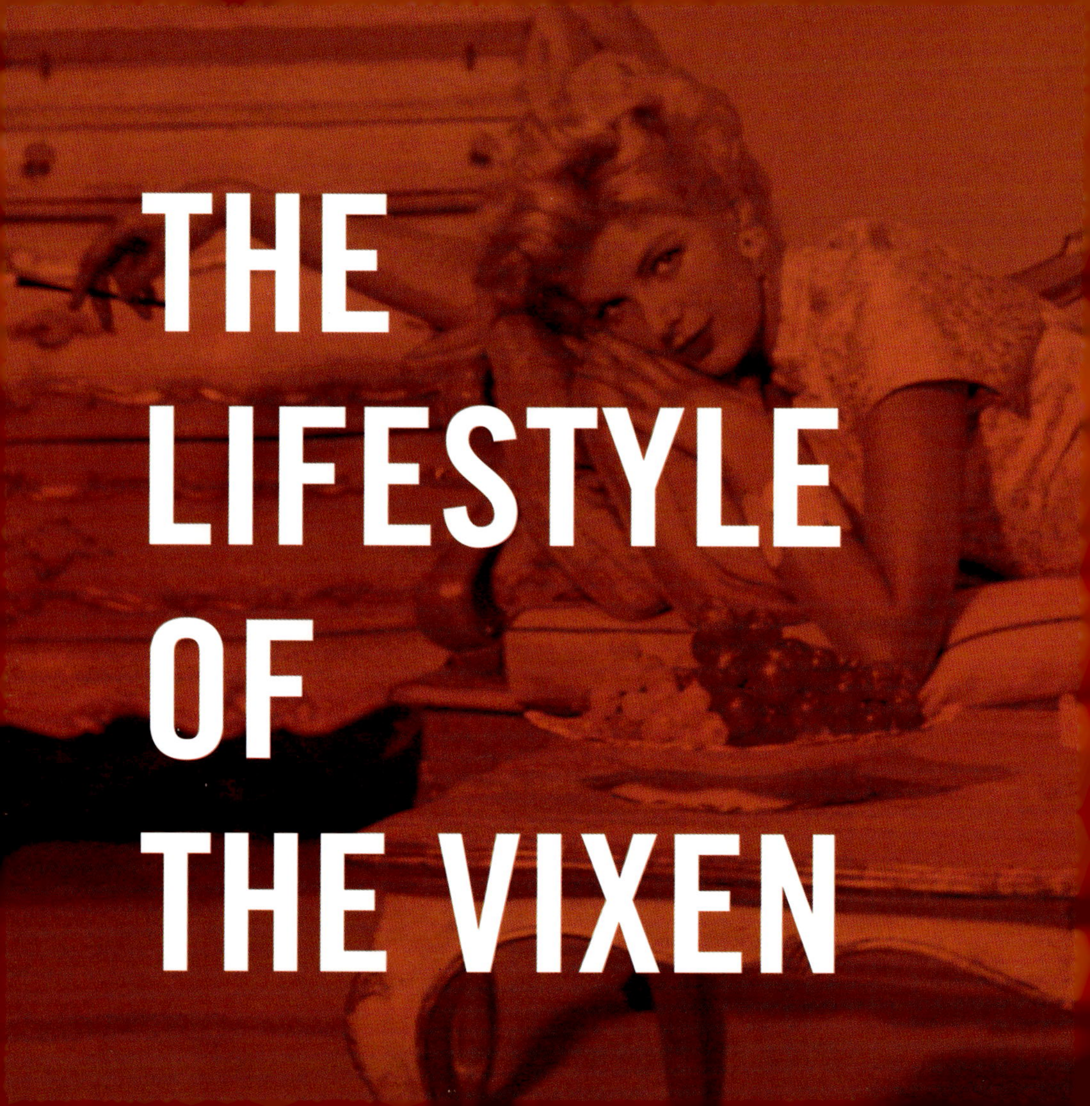

THE LIFESTYLE OF THE VIXEN

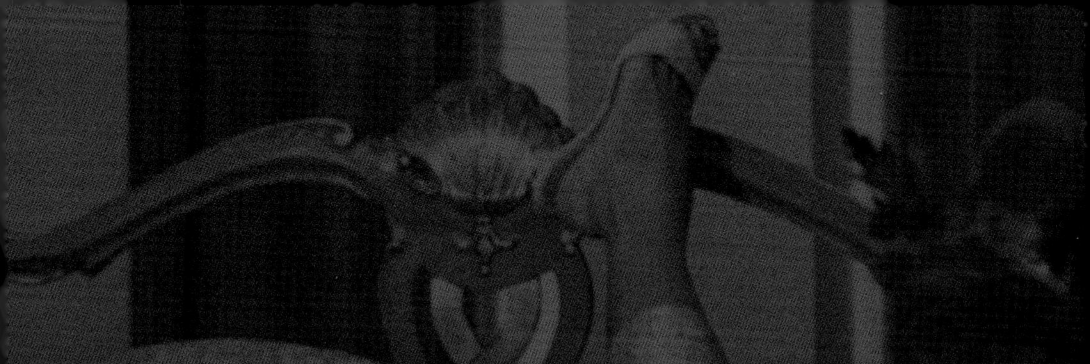

The vixen is a sensualist, a lover of life, an unrepentant indulger in all the pleasures the world has to offer. The vixen loves big cities, nightclubs, hot jazz, and cool cats. The motto of the vixen is "Laissez les bon temps roulez!"

You can learn a lot from her lifestyle by the examples set on the album covers. When a vixen wakes up in the afternoon, she rolls off her satin sheets, slips on a semitransparent silk dressing gown, and lights a cigarette. The vixen will generally spend her days lounging on the divan, talking on the telephone, or, most preferably, being held in the arms of her paramour.

If a vixen works at something (other than vixenism, that is), she usually models for album covers or plays the tambourine or maracas at her current guy's gig.

As the evening approaches, the vixen will wrap herself in something low-cut and satin and prepare for cocktails and dinner with her guy and then a show or a nightclub. Very soon into the evening he wants to go back to her place, but she wants to enjoy everything the night has to offer. Only afterward, as dawn starts to creep up the skyscrapers, will she retire.

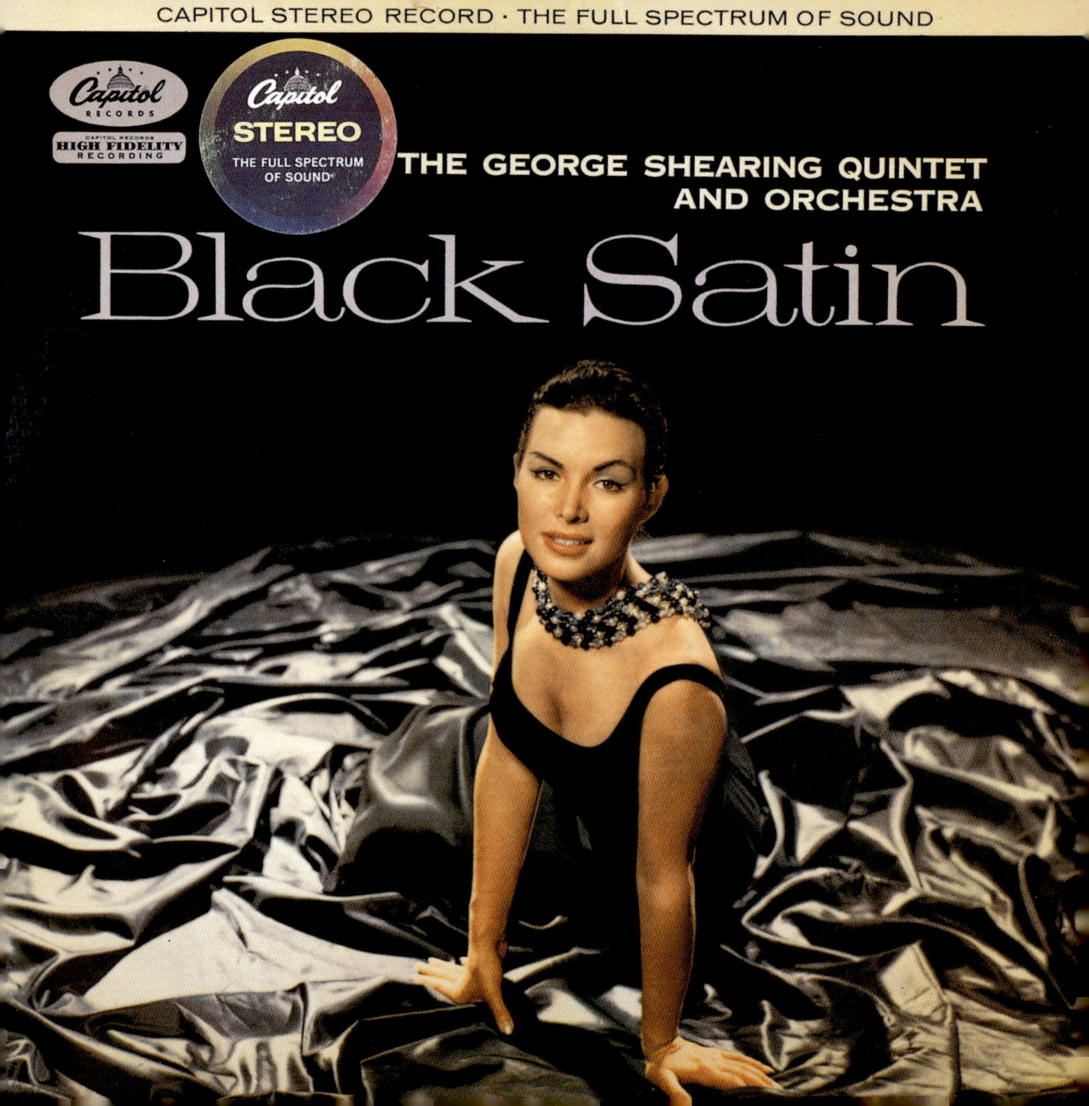
CAPITOL STEREO RECORD · THE FULL SPECTRUM OF SOUND
Capitol RECORDS
CAPITOL RECORDS HIGH FIDELITY RECORDING
Capitol STEREO THE FULL SPECTRUM OF SOUND
THE GEORGE SHEARING QUINTET AND ORCHESTRA
Black Satin

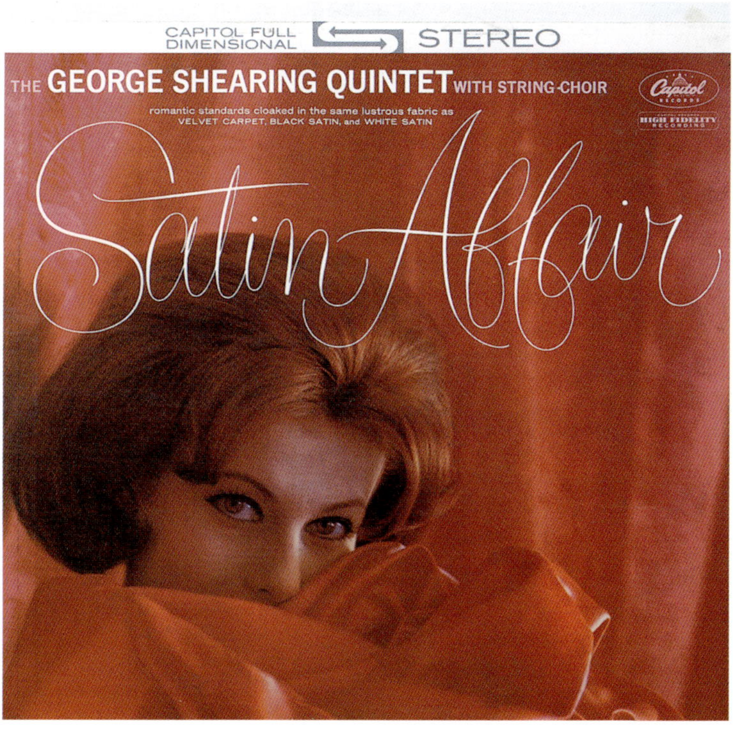
CAPITOL FULL DIMENSIONAL STEREO
THE GEORGE SHEARING QUINTET WITH STRING-CHOIR
Capitol RECORDS
romantic standards cloaked in the same lustrous fabric as
VELVET CARPET, BLACK SATIN, and WHITE SATIN
HIGH FIDELITY RECORDING
Satin Affair

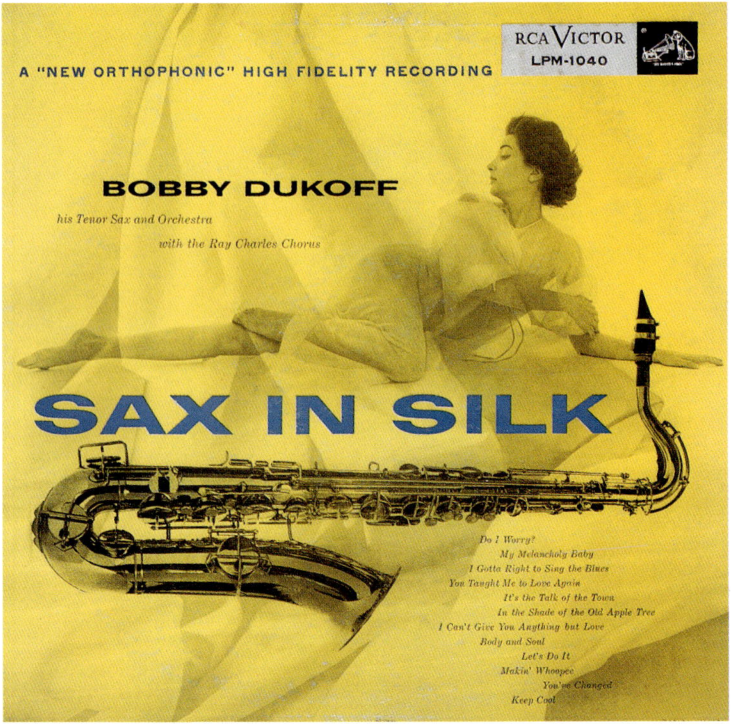

RCA VICTOR
LPM-1040
A "NEW ORTHOPHONIC" HIGH FIDELITY RECORDING
BOBBY DUKOFF
his Tenor Sax and Orchestra
with the Ray Charles Chorus
SAX IN SILK
Do I Worry?
My Melancholy Baby
I Gotta Right to Sing the Blues
You Taught Me to Love Again
It's the Talk of the Town
In the Shade of the Old Apple Tree
I Can't Give You Anything but Love
Body and Soul
Let's Do It
Makin' Whoopee
You've Changed
Keep Cool

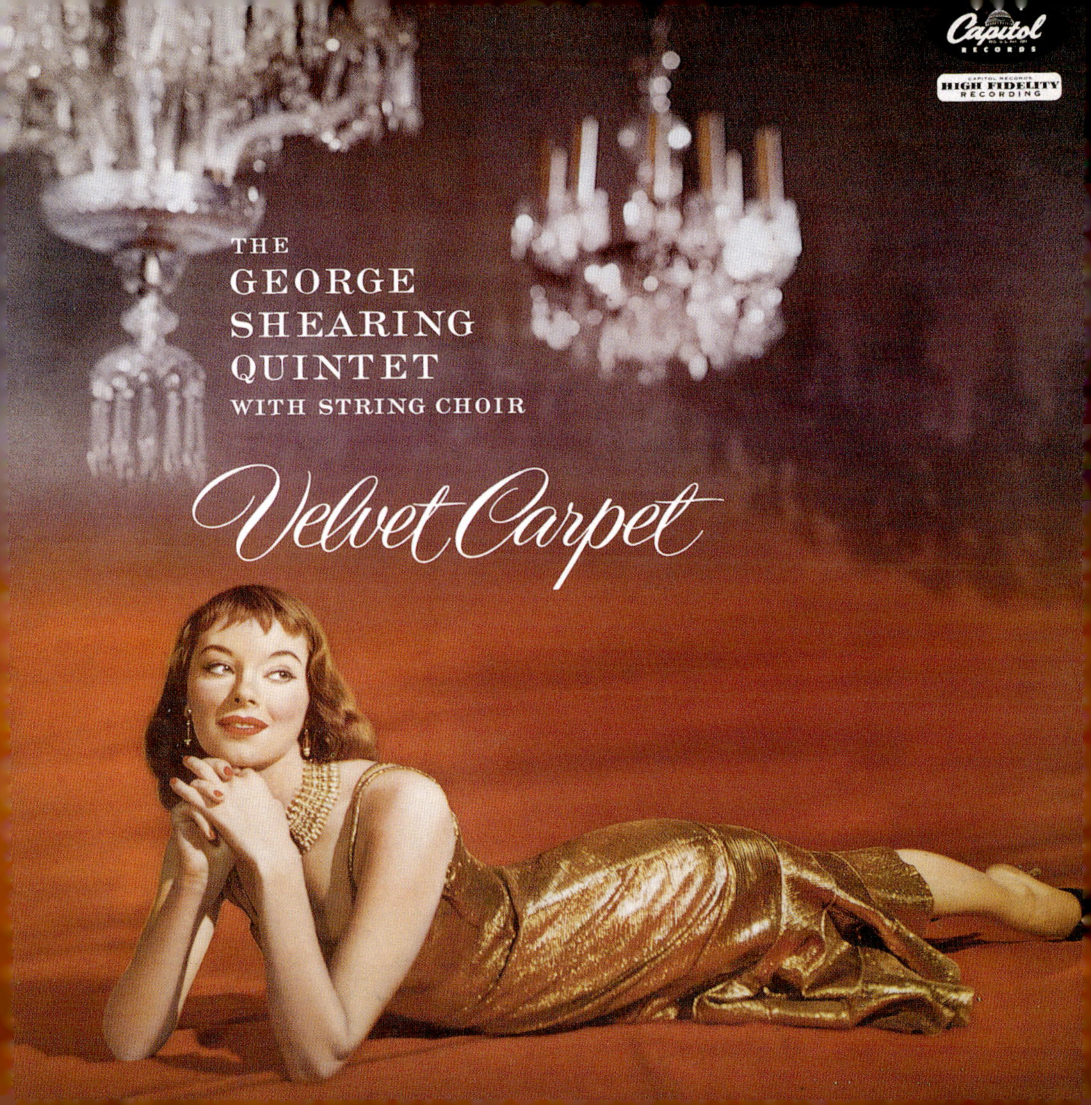
Capitol
RECORDS
CAPITOL RECORDS
HIGH FIDELITY
RECORDING
THE
GEORGE
SHEARING
QUINTET
WITH STRING CHOIR
Velvet Carpet

A "NEW ORTHOPHONIC" HIGH FIDELITY RECORDING

RCA VICTOR
LPM-1064

Frankie Carle plays Cole Porter

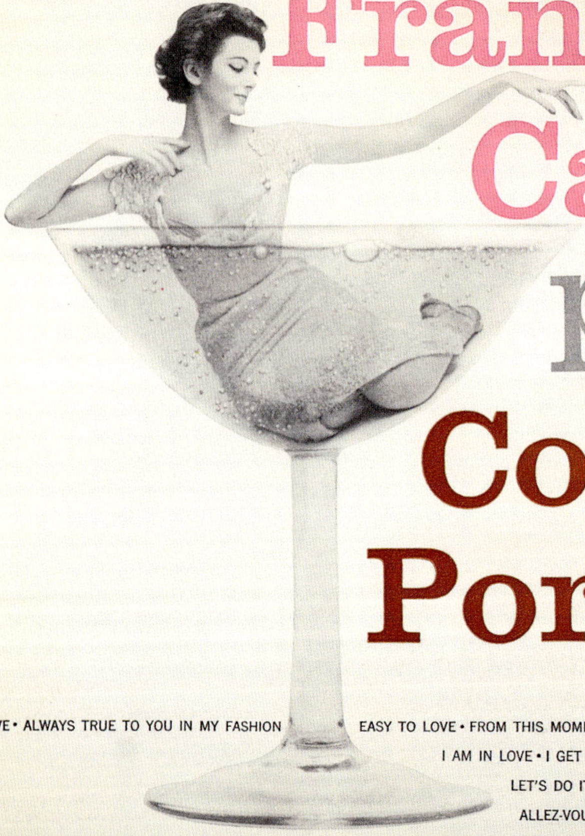

SO IN LOVE • ALWAYS TRUE TO YOU IN MY FASHION • EASY TO LOVE • FROM THIS MOMENT ON

I AM IN LOVE • I GET A KICK OUT OF YOU

LET'S DO IT • LOVE FOR SALE

ALLEZ-VOUS EN • C'EST MAGNIFIQUE

I LOVE PARIS • IT'S ALL RIGHT WITH ME

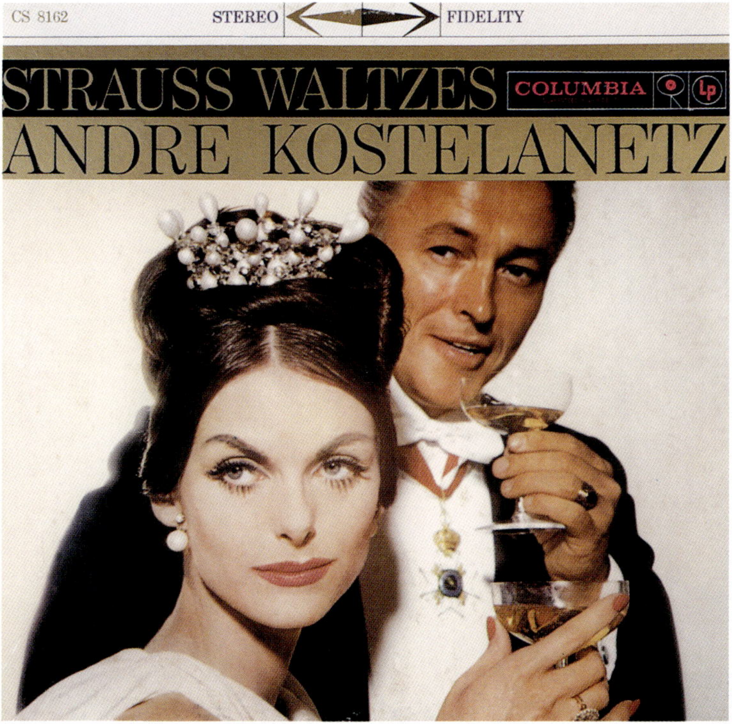

The vixen loves Champagne (French, with a capital C). When she's down on her luck, she drinks Manhattans.

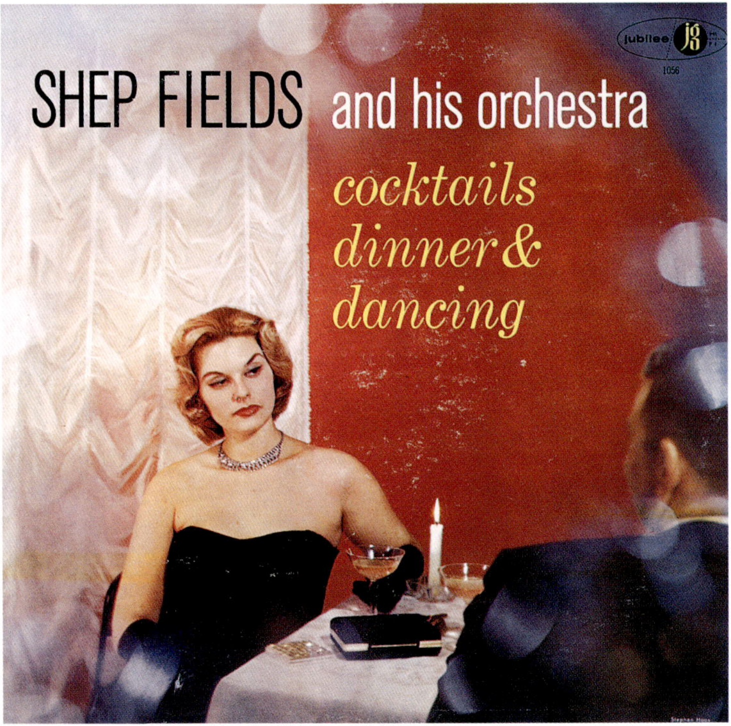
jubilee
jg
1056
SHEP FIELDS and his orchestra
cocktails
dinner &
dancing

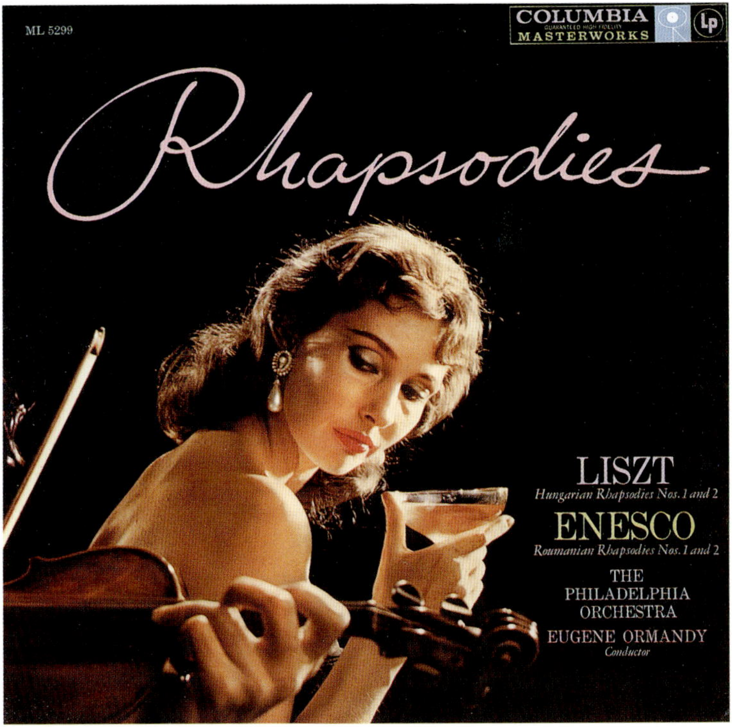
ML 5299
COLUMBIA
GUARANTEED HIGH FIDELITY
MASTERWORKS
Lp
Rhapsodies
LISZT
Hungarian Rhapsodies Nos. 1 and 2
ENESCO
Roumanian Rhapsodies Nos. 1 and 2
THE
PHILADELPHIA
ORCHESTRA
EUGENE ORMANDY
Conductor

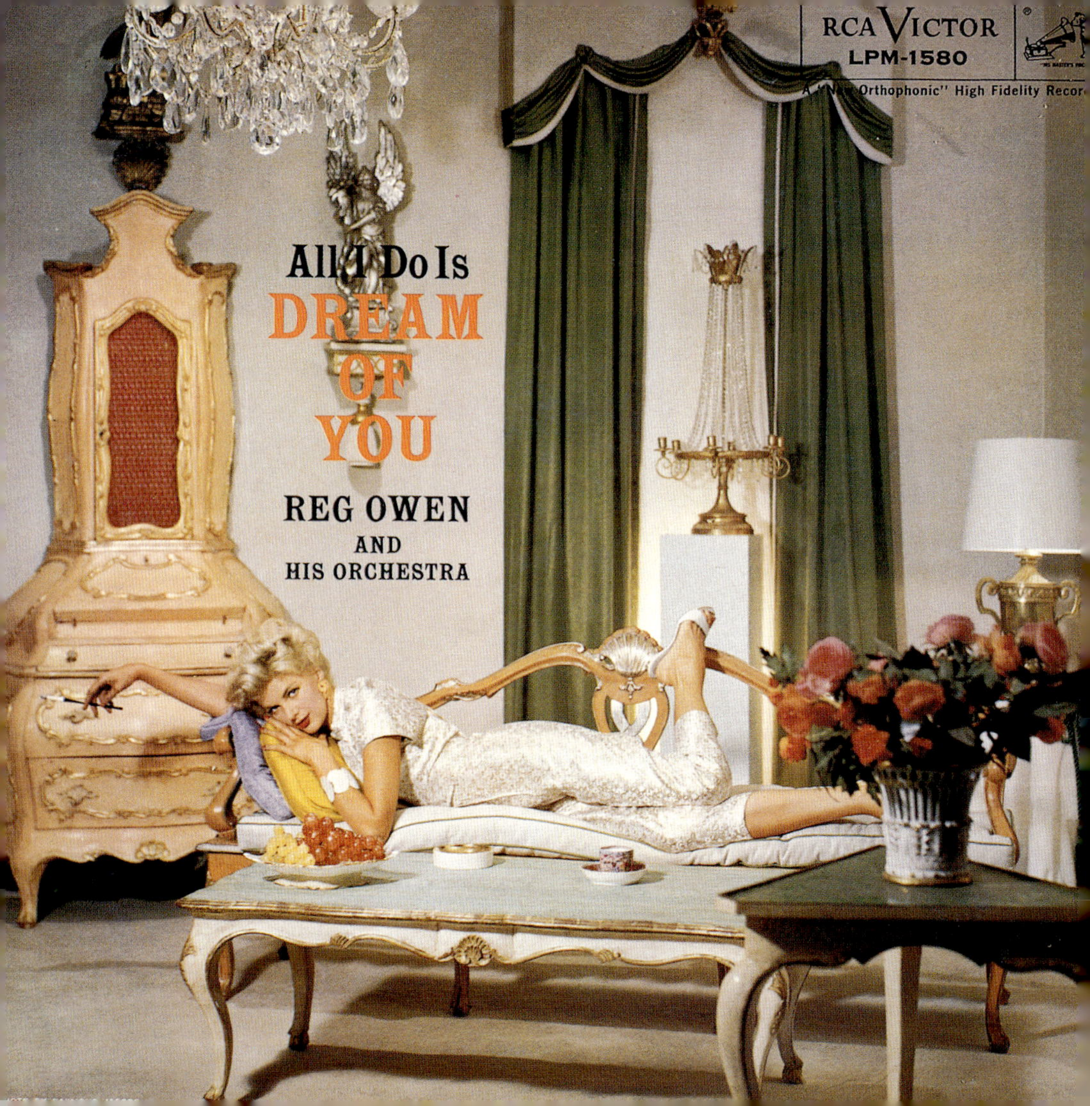
RCA VICTOR
LPM-1580
A "New Orthophonic" High Fidelity Recor
All I Do Is
DREAM
OF
YOU
REG OWEN
AND
HIS ORCHESTRA

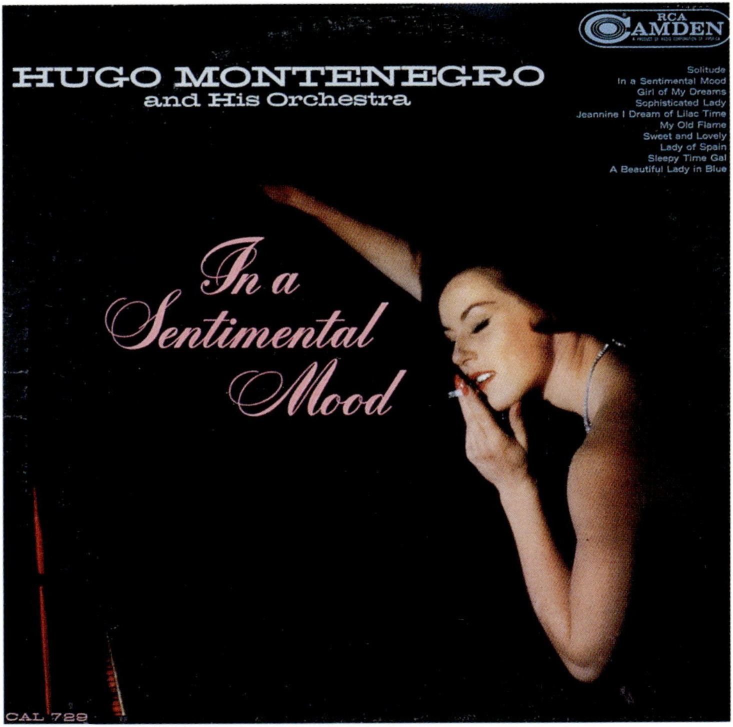

A vixen smoking a cigarette: She makes it a luxurious sin; she makes it look illegal.

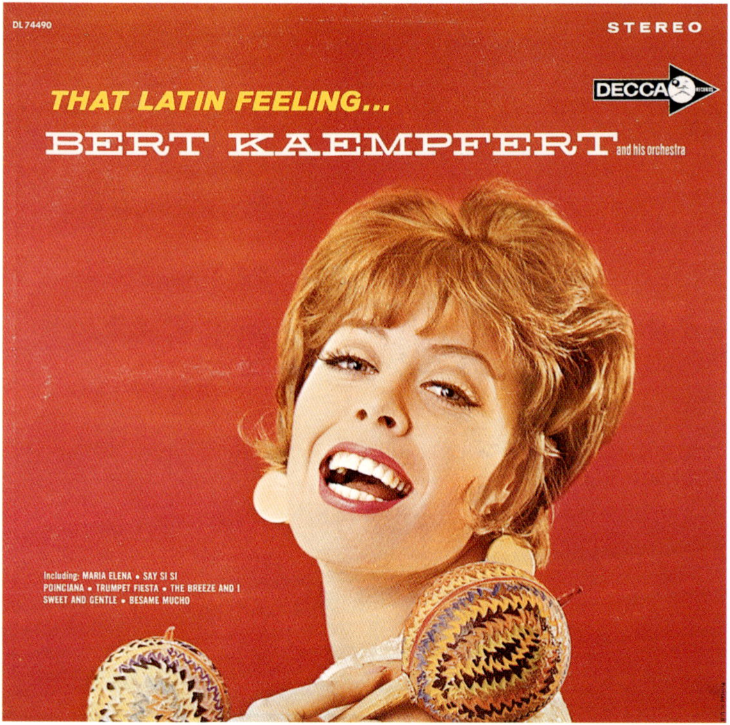
DL 74490
STEREO
DECCA
THAT LATIN FEELING...
BERT KAEMPFERT and his orchestra
Including: MARIA ELENA • SAY SI SI
POINCIANA • TRUMPET FIESTA • THE BREEZE AND I
SWEET AND GENTLE • BESAME MUCHO

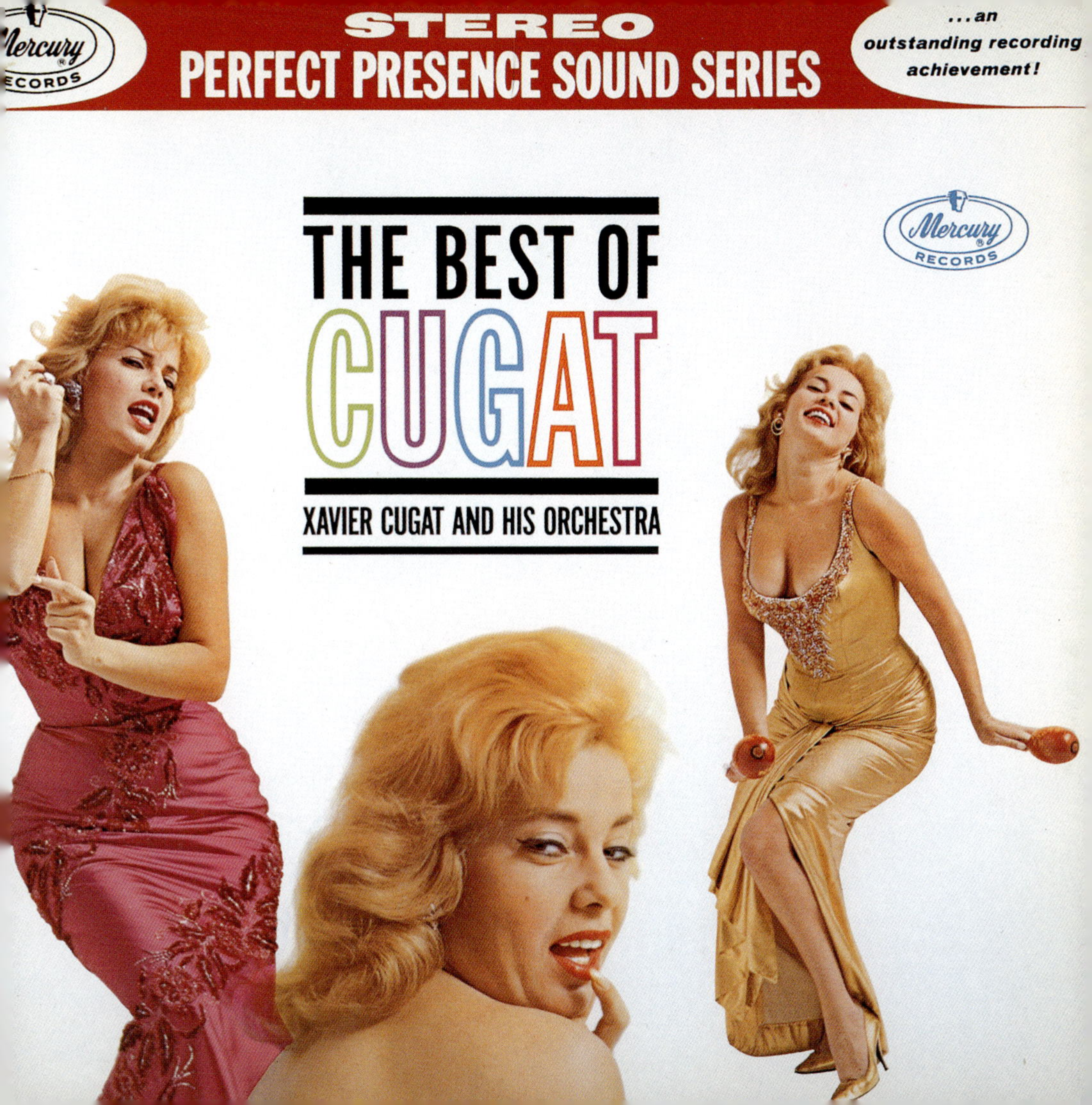
Mercury RECORDS
STEREO
PERFECT PRESENCE SOUND SERIES
...an outstanding recording achievement!
THE BEST OF
CUGAT
XAVIER CUGAT AND HIS ORCHESTRA
Mercury RECORDS

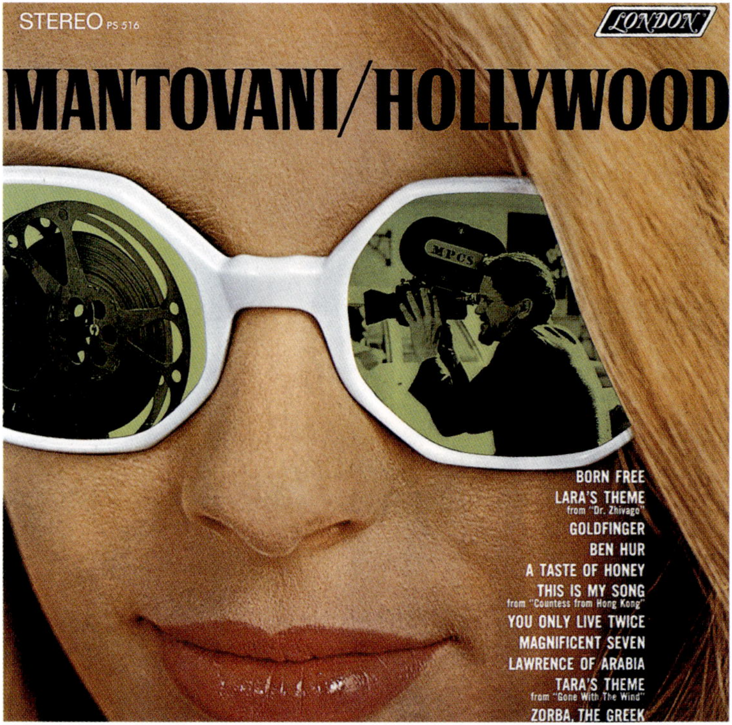

If a vixen does go outside in the daytime, she'll arm herself for this unnatural event with a large pair of sunglasses.

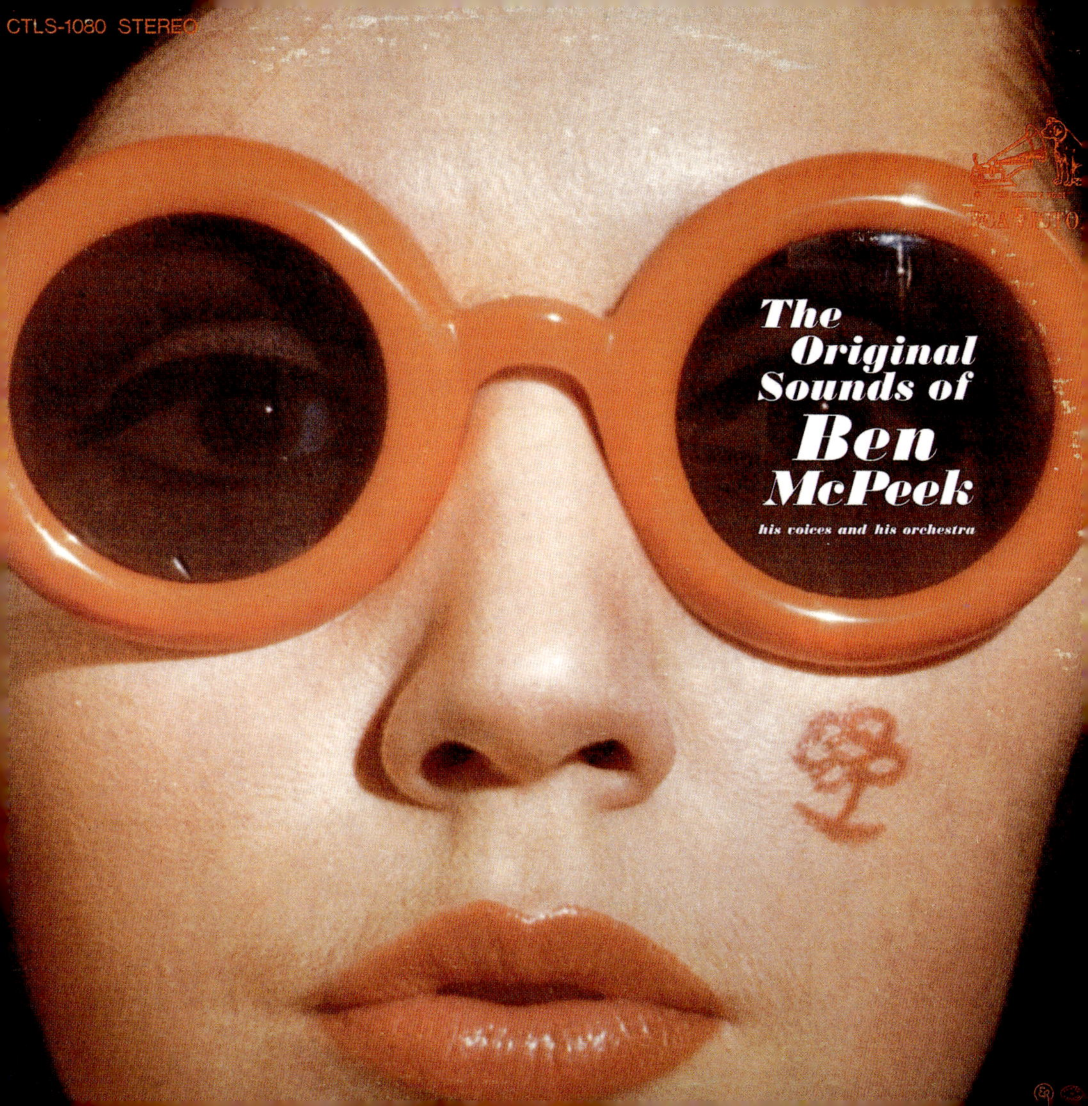
CTLS-1080 STEREO
The Original Sounds of
Ben McPeek
his voices and his orchestra

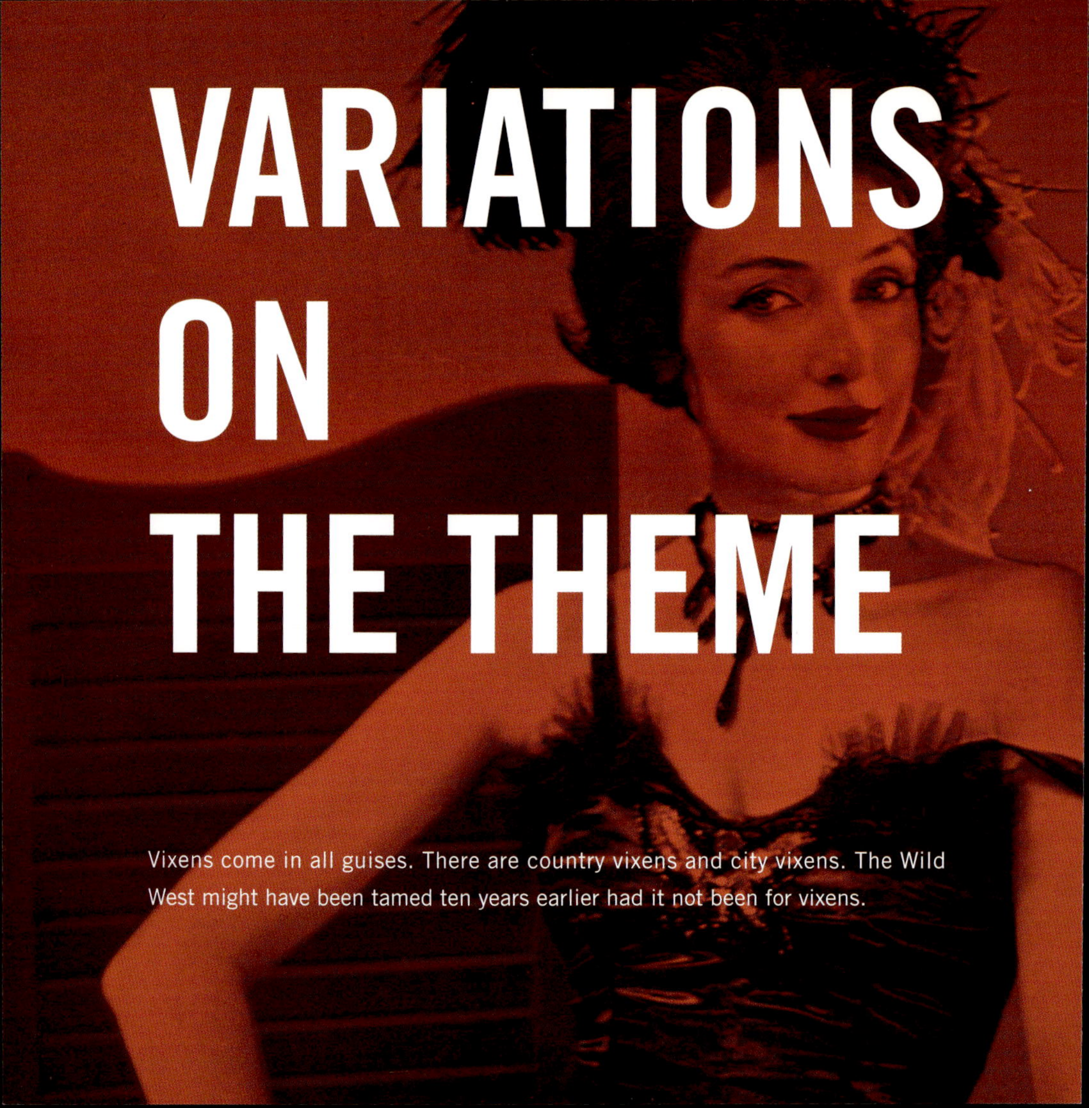

VARIATIONS ON THE THEME

Vixens come in all guises. There are country vixens and city vixens. The Wild West might have been tamed ten years earlier had it not been for vixens.

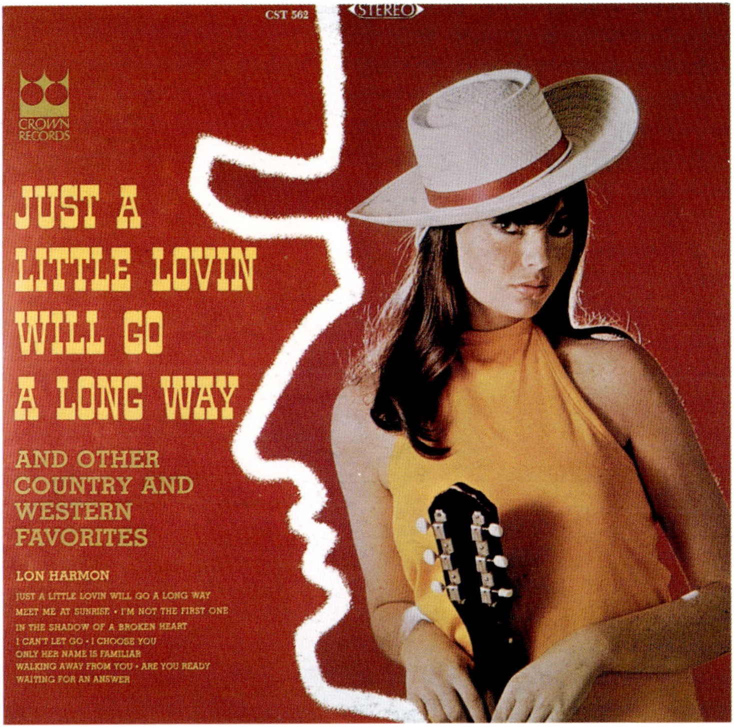
CST 562
STEREO
CROWN RECORDS
JUST A LITTLE LOVIN WILL GO A LONG WAY
AND OTHER COUNTRY AND WESTERN FAVORITES
LON HARMON
JUST A LITTLE LOVIN WILL GO A LONG WAY
MEET ME AT SUNRISE • I'M NOT THE FIRST ONE
IN THE SHADOW OF A BROKEN HEART
I CAN'T LET GO • I CHOOSE YOU
ONLY HER NAME IS FAMILIAR
WALKING AWAY FROM YOU • ARE YOU READY
WAITING FOR AN ANSWER

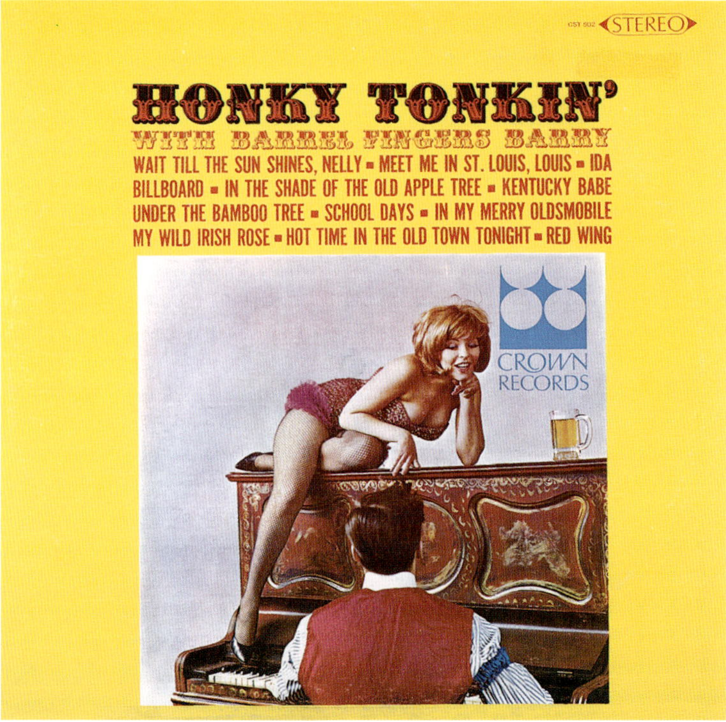
CST 502 STEREO
HONKY TONKIN'
WITH BARREL FINGERS BARRY
WAIT TILL THE SUN SHINES, NELLY ■ MEET ME IN ST. LOUIS, LOUIS ■ IDA
BILLBOARD ■ IN THE SHADE OF THE OLD APPLE TREE ■ KENTUCKY BABE
UNDER THE BAMBOO TREE ■ SCHOOL DAYS ■ IN MY MERRY OLDSMOBILE
MY WILD IRISH ROSE ■ HOT TIME IN THE OLD TOWN TONIGHT ■ RED WING
CROWN
RECORDS

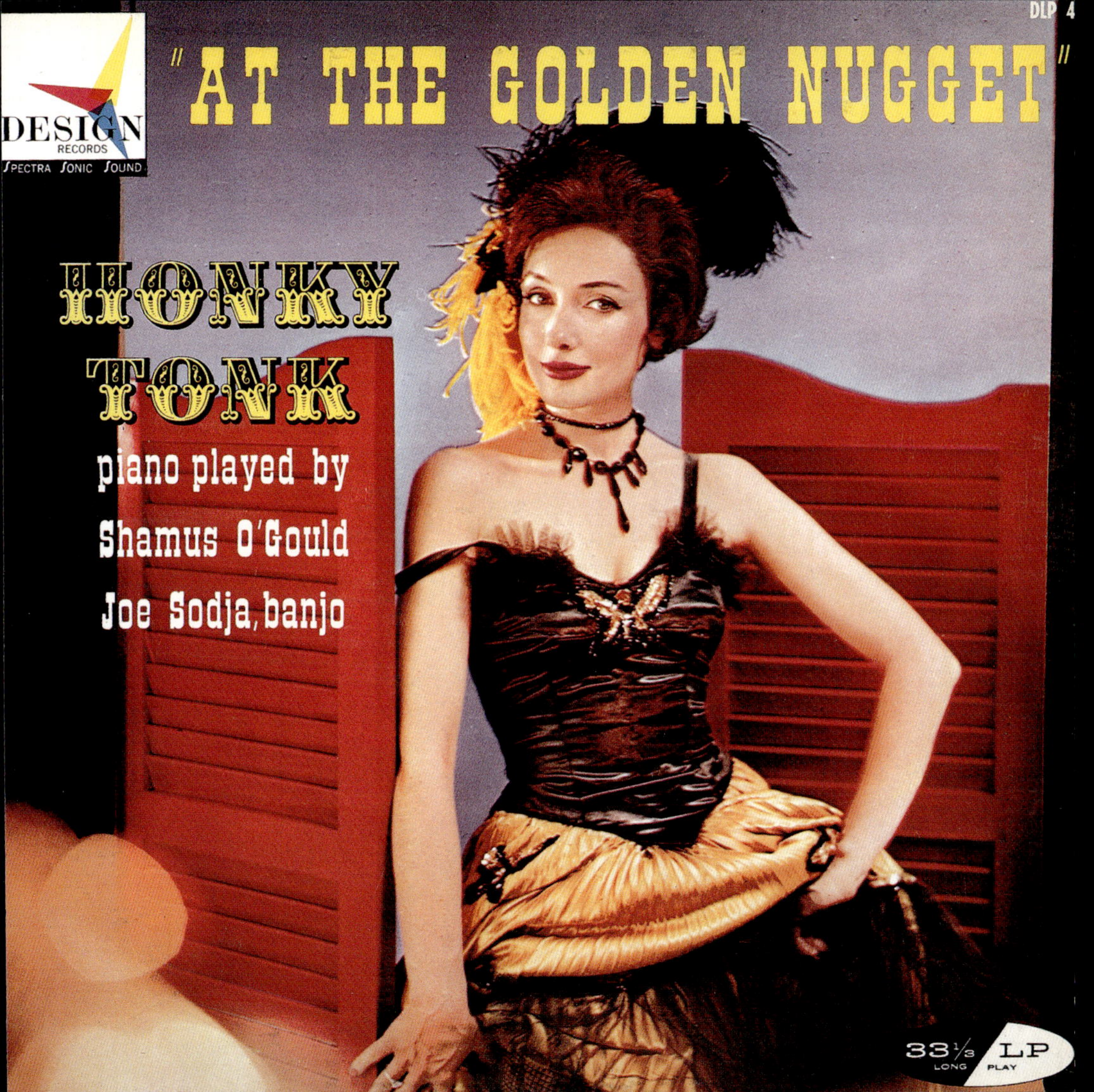
DLP 4
"AT THE GOLDEN NUGGET"
DESIGN
RECORDS
SPECTRA SONIC SOUND
HONKY
TONK
piano played by
Shamus O'Gould
Joe Sodja, banjo
33 1/3 LP
LONG PLAY

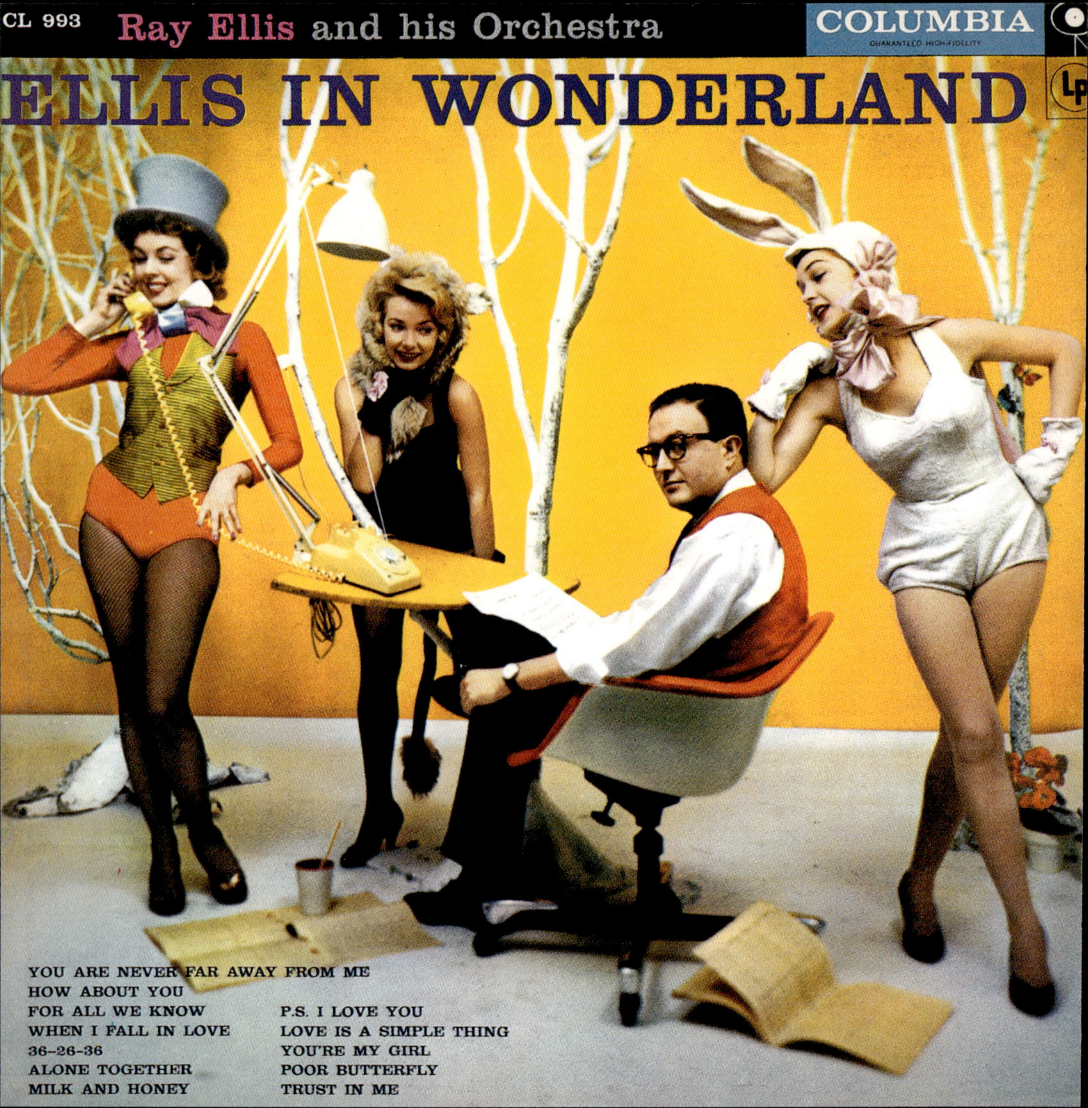
CL 993
Ray Ellis and his Orchestra
COLUMBIA
GUARANTEED HIGH-FIDELITY
LP
ELLIS IN WONDERLAND
YOU ARE NEVER FAR AWAY FROM ME
HOW ABOUT YOU
FOR ALL WE KNOW
WHEN I FALL IN LOVE
36-26-36
ALONE TOGETHER
MILK AND HONEY
P.S. I LOVE YOU
LOVE IS A SIMPLE THING
YOU'RE MY GIRL
POOR BUTTERFLY
TRUST IN ME

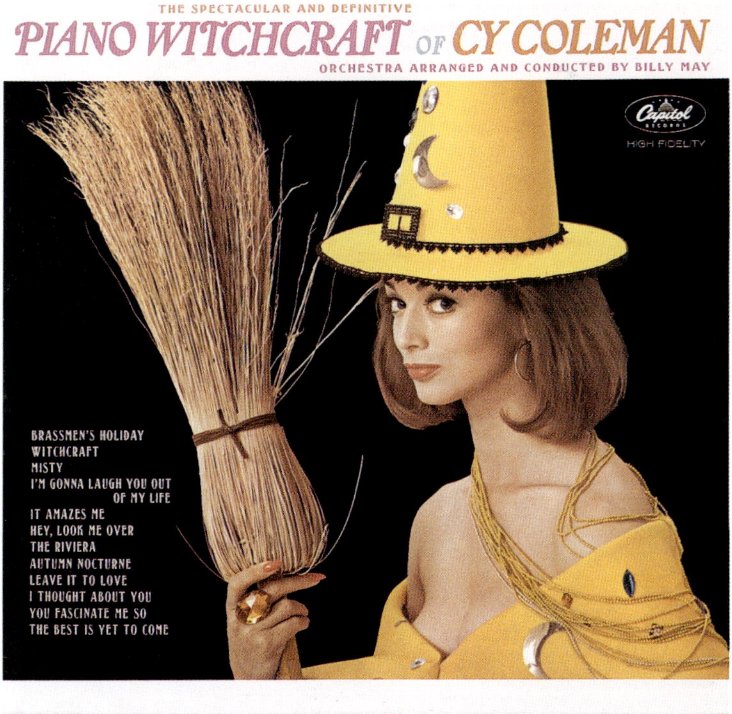

Vixens love to dress up . . .

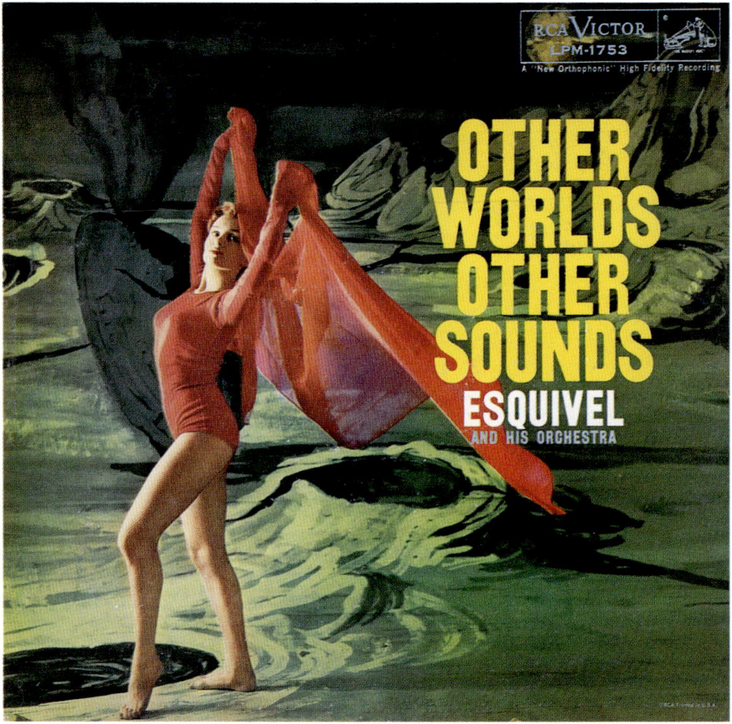

Could there really be vixens in outer space? If there's any intelligent life out there at all, you bet.

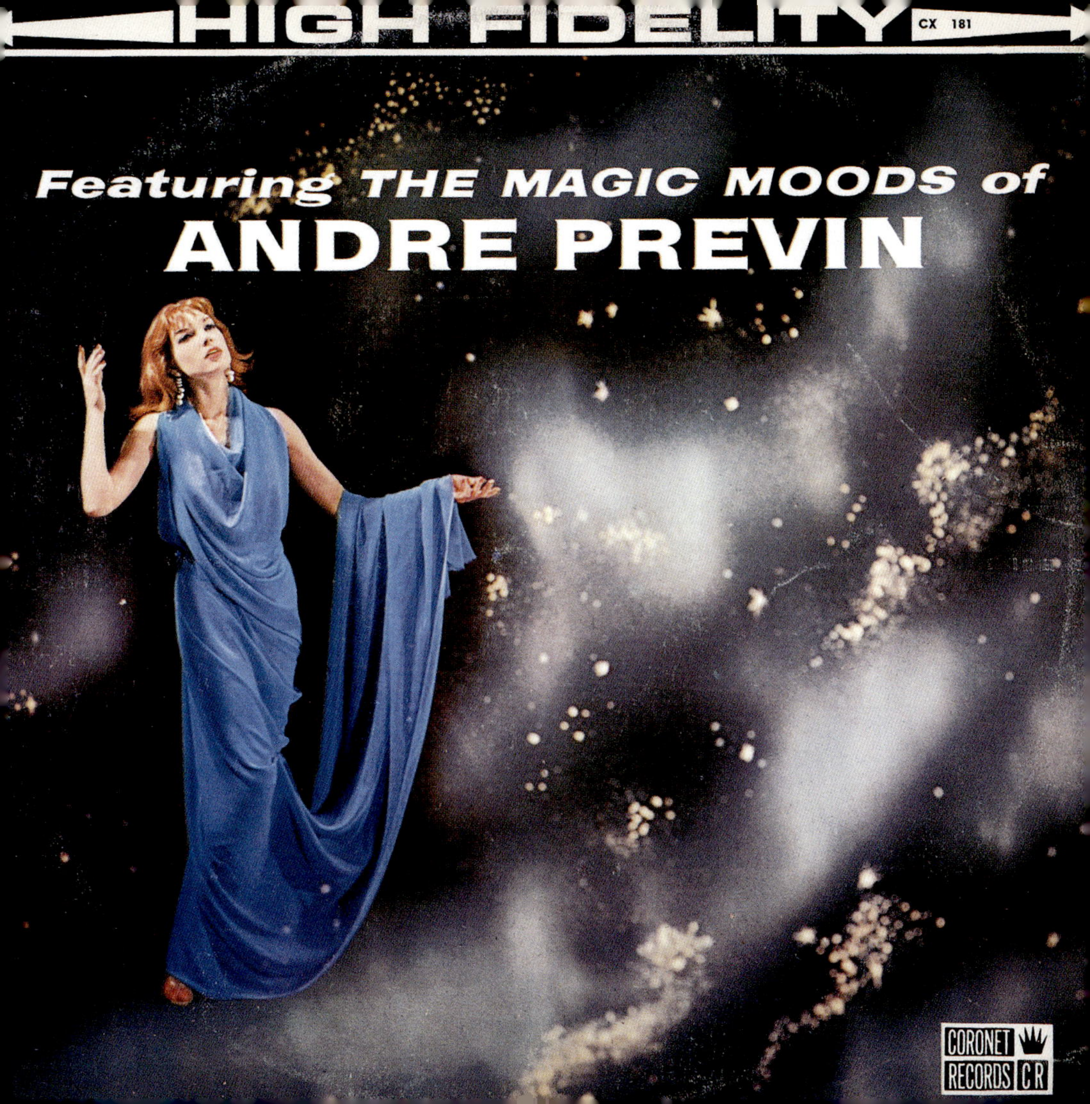
HIGH FIDELITY
CX 181
Featuring THE MAGIC MOODS of
ANDRE PREVIN
CORONET
RECORDS
CR

INTER-NATIONAL VIXENISM

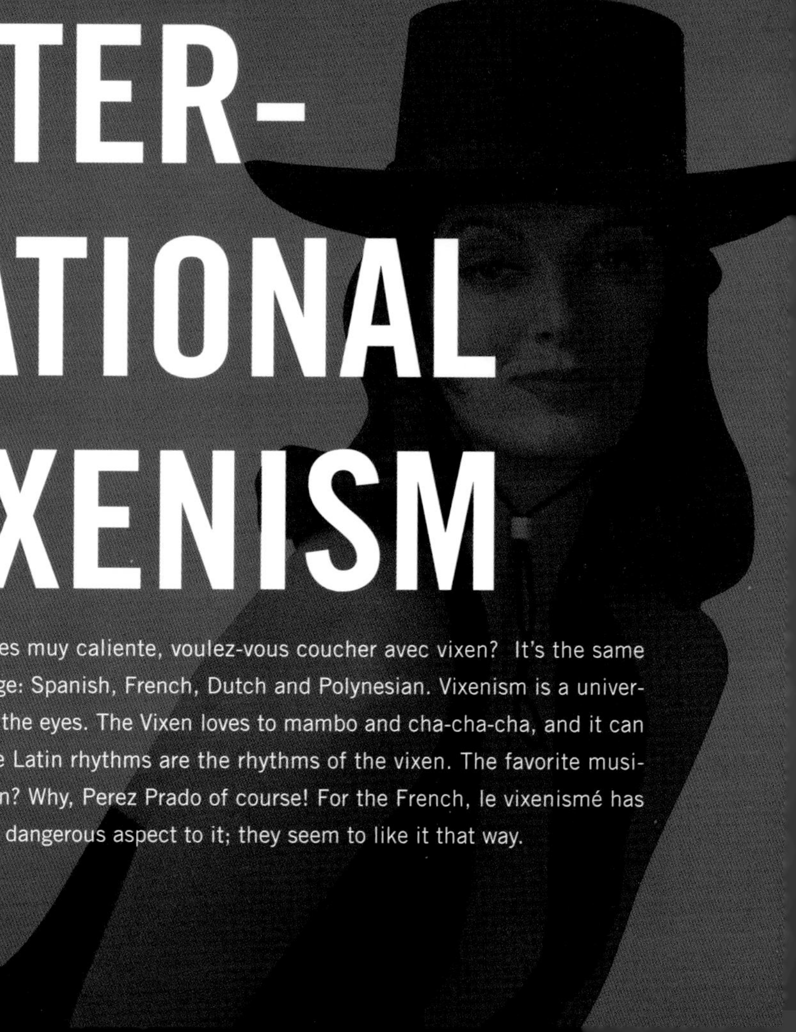

Vixen, la vixen es muy caliente, voulez-vous coucher avec vixen? It's the same in every language: Spanish, French, Dutch and Polynesian. Vixenism is a universal language of the eyes. The Vixen loves to mambo and cha-cha-cha, and it can be said that the Latin rhythms are the rhythms of the vixen. The favorite musician of the vixen? Why, Perez Prado of course! For the French, le vixenismé has a sharper, more dangerous aspect to it; they seem to like it that way.

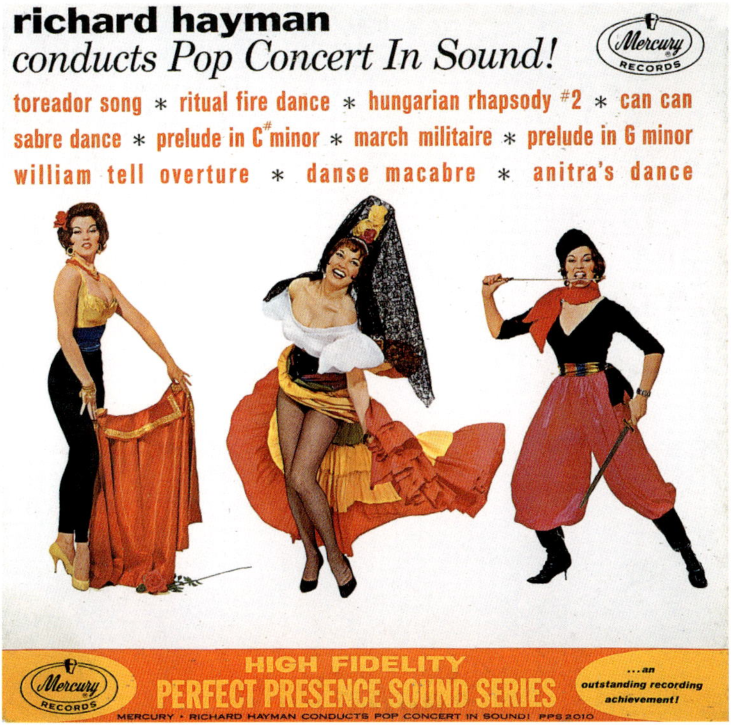
richard hayman
conducts Pop Concert In Sound!
Mercury RECORDS
toreador song * ritual fire dance * hungarian rhapsody #2 * can can
sabre dance * prelude in C# minor * march militaire * prelude in G minor
william tell overture * danse macabre * anitra's dance
Mercury RECORDS
HIGH FIDELITY
PERFECT PRESENCE SOUND SERIES
...an outstanding recording achievement!
MERCURY · RICHARD HAYMAN CONDUCTS POP CONCERT IN SOUND! PPS 2010

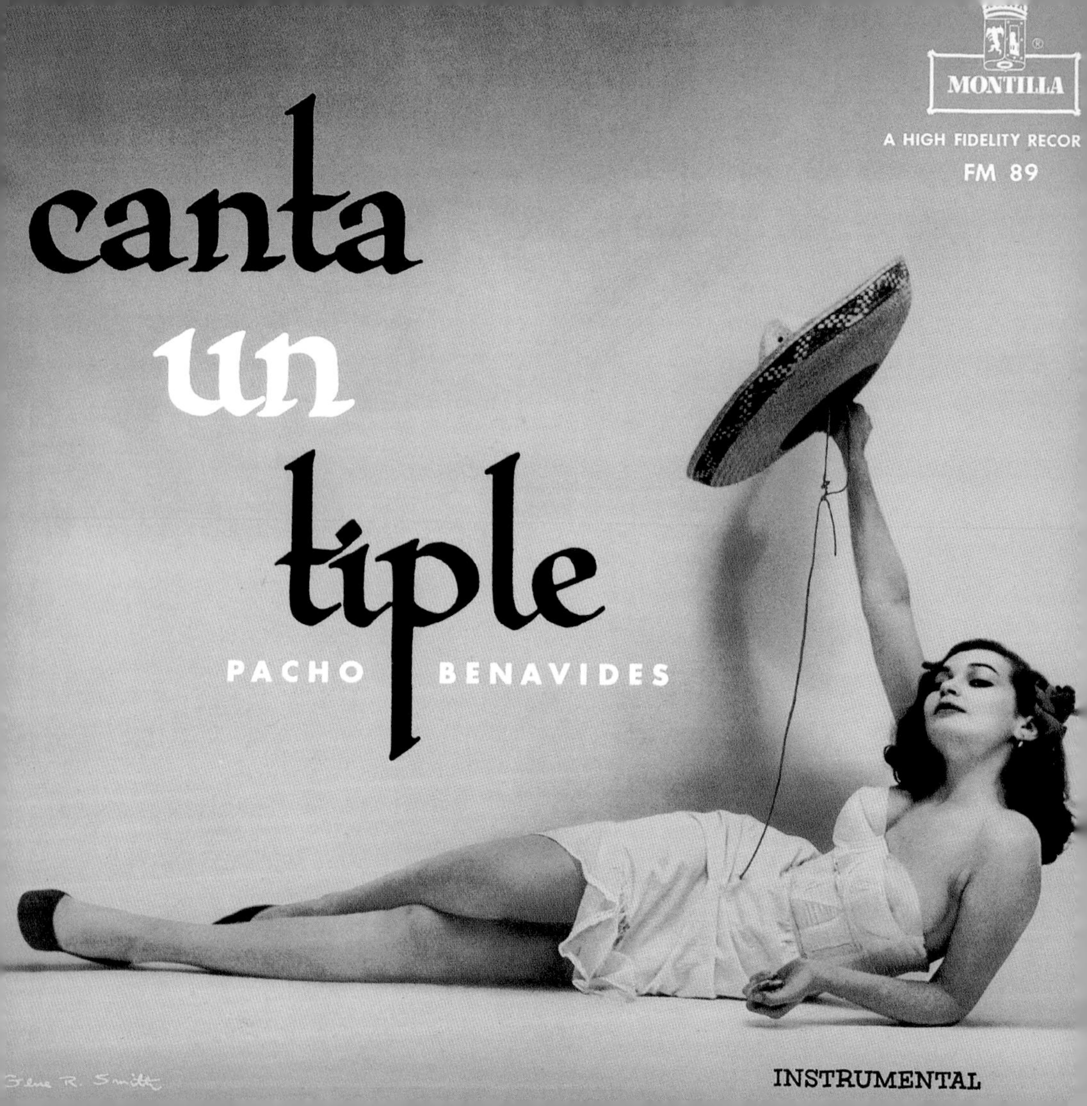
MONTILLA
A HIGH FIDELITY RECOR
FM 89
canta
un
tiple
PACHO BENAVIDES
INSTRUMENTAL

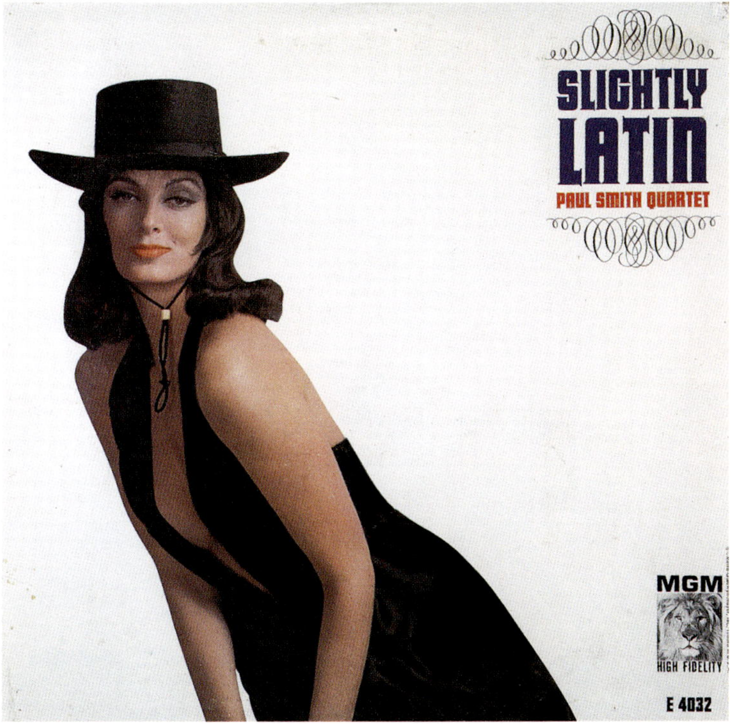
SLIGHTLY
LATIN
PAUL SMITH QUARTET
MGM
HIGH FIDELITY
E 4032

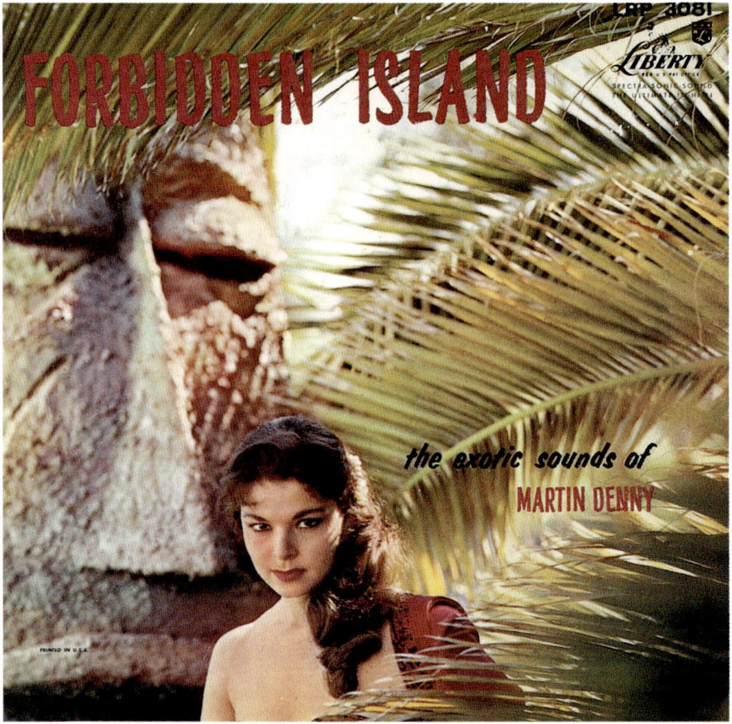
LRP 3081
LIBERTY
FORBIDDEN ISLAND
the exotic sounds of
MARTIN DENNY
PRINTED IN U.S.A.

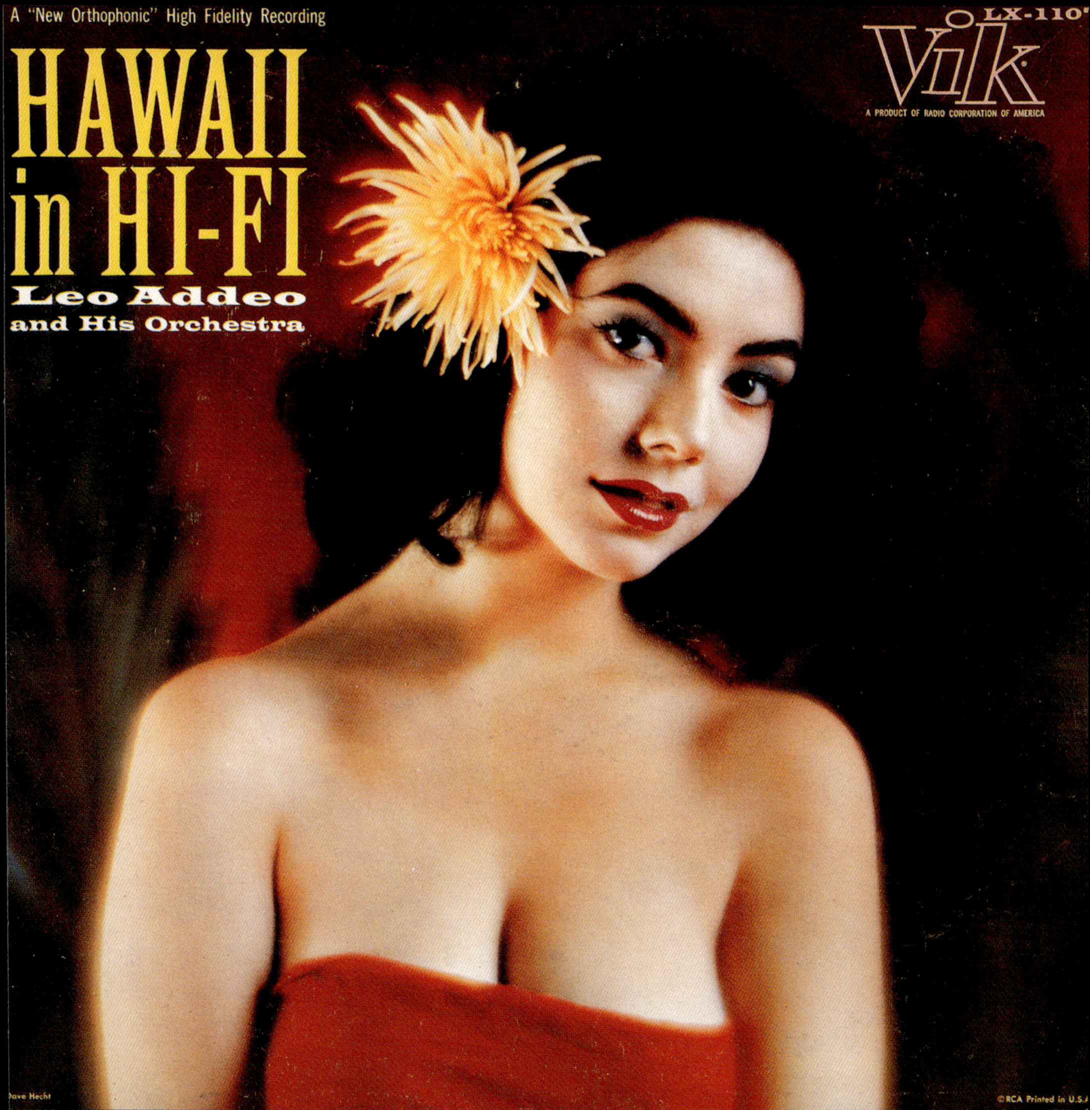
A "New Orthophonic" High Fidelity Recording
HAWAII in HI-FI
Leo Addeo
and His Orchestra
LX-110
Vik
A PRODUCT OF RADIO CORPORATION OF AMERICA
Dave Hecht
©RCA Printed in U.S.

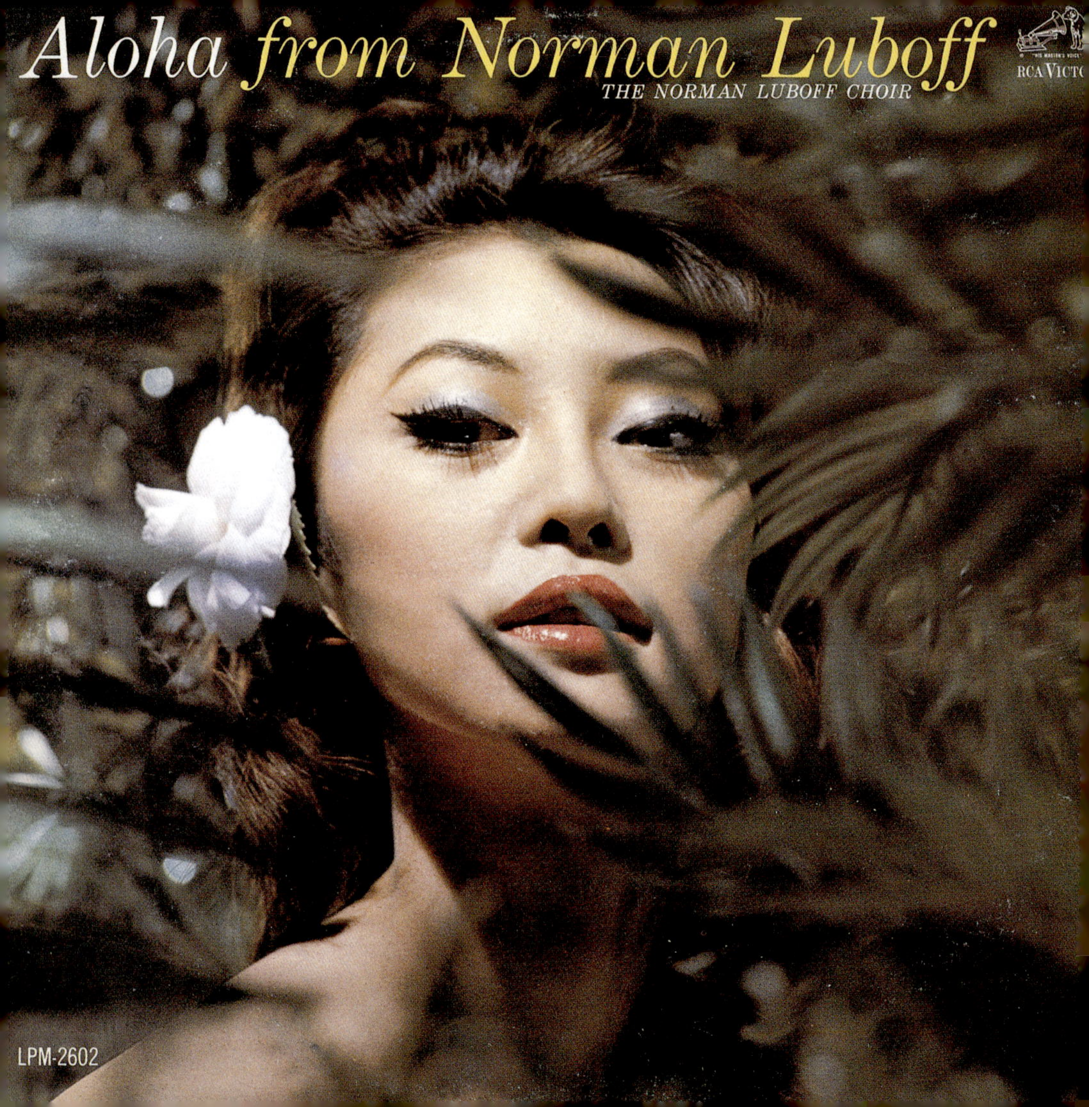
Aloha from Norman Luboff
THE NORMAN LUBOFF CHOIR
LPM-2602

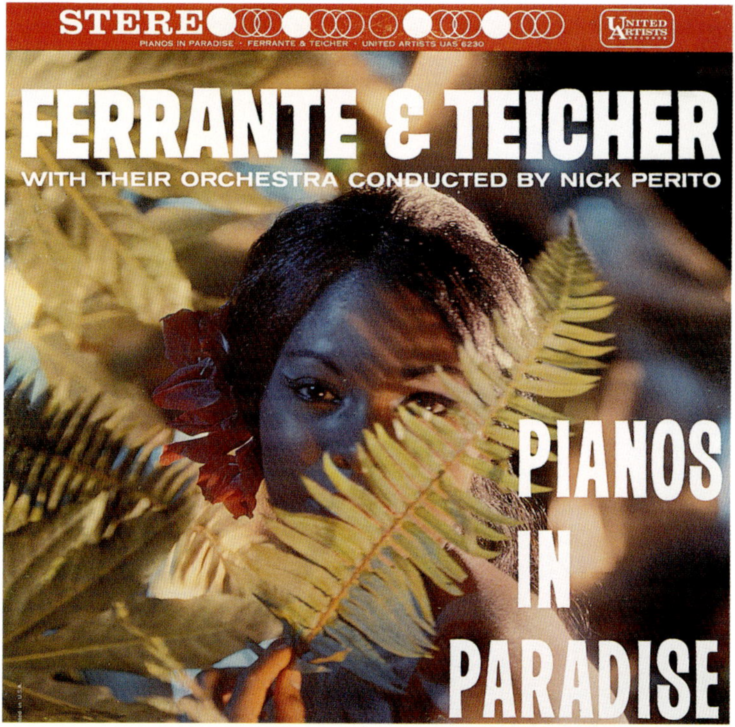
STEREO
PIANOS IN PARADISE · FERRANTE & TEICHER · UNITED ARTISTS UAS 6230
UNITED ARTISTS RECORDS
FERRANTE & TEICHER
WITH THEIR ORCHESTRA CONDUCTED BY NICK PERITO
PIANOS IN PARADISE

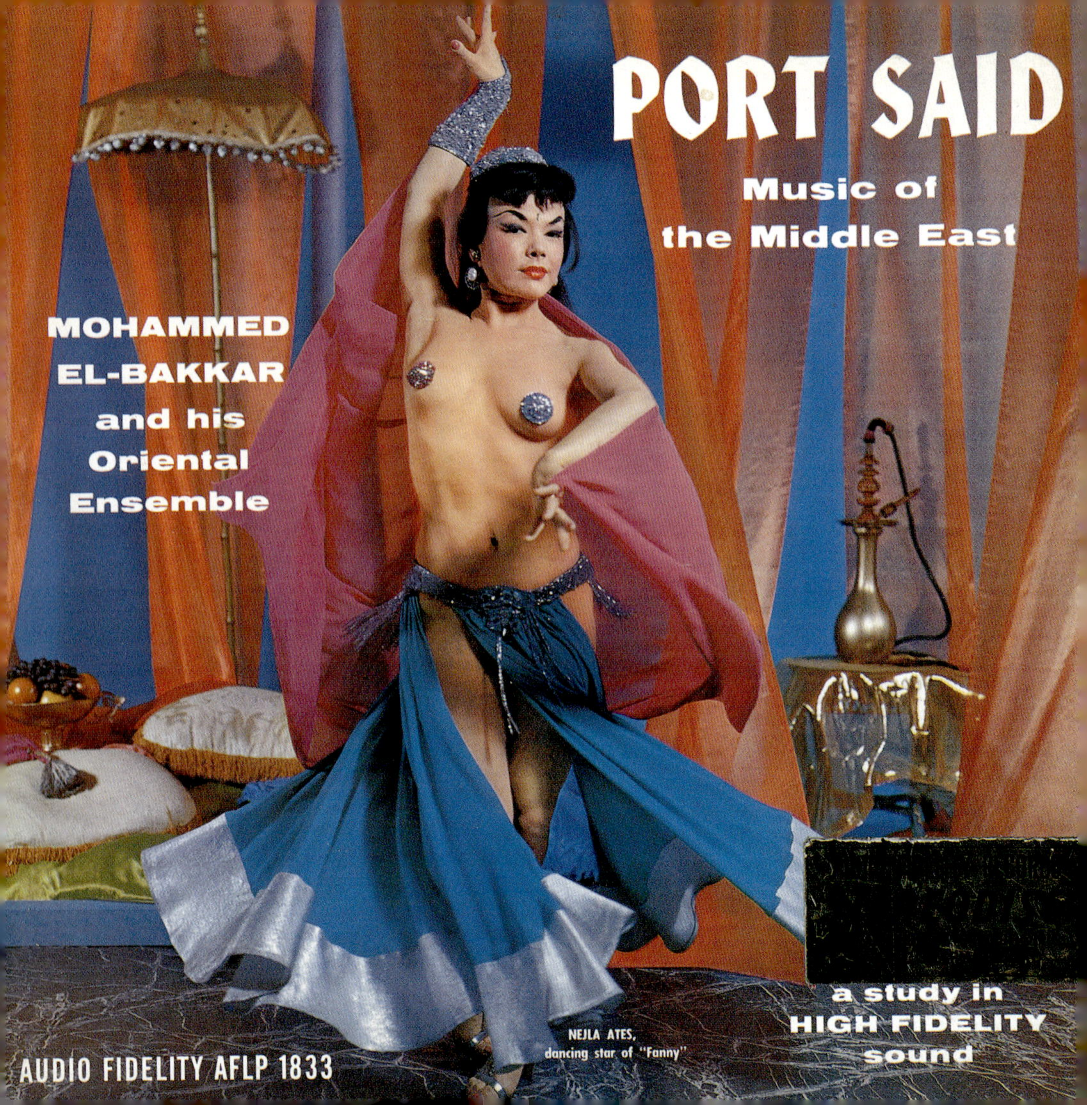

PORT SAID
Music of the Middle East
MOHAMMED EL-BAKKAR and his Oriental Ensemble
a study in HIGH FIDELITY sound
NEJLA ATES, dancing star of "Fanny"
AUDIO FIDELITY AFLP 1833

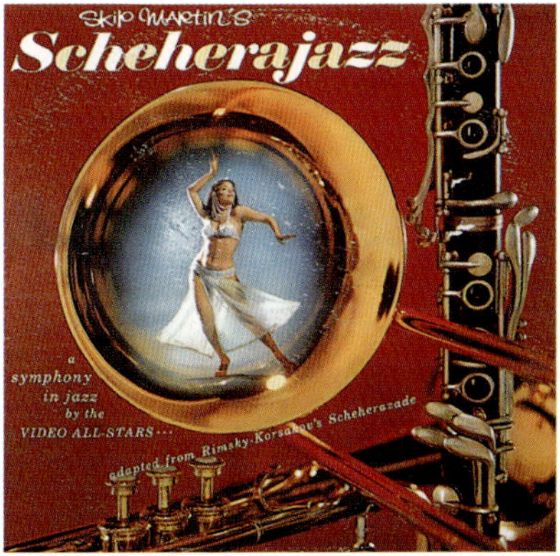

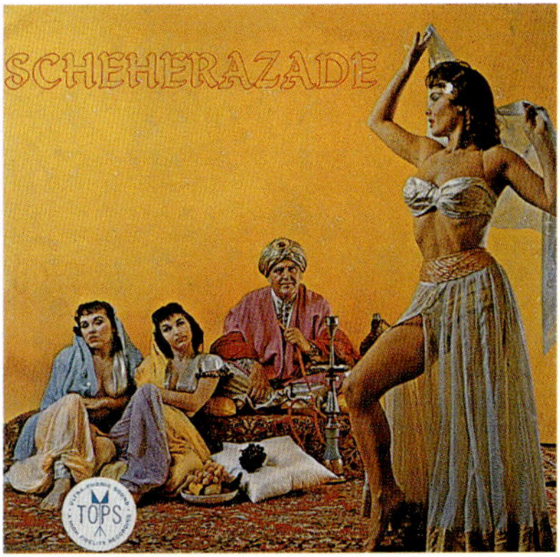

ABOVE LEFT *Liner Note:* . . . as we listened to a recording and Skip analyzed the original Rimsky-Korsakov score, he became so carried away with the idea that he swore off "straight booze and girls of questionable morals" until the score was completed . . .

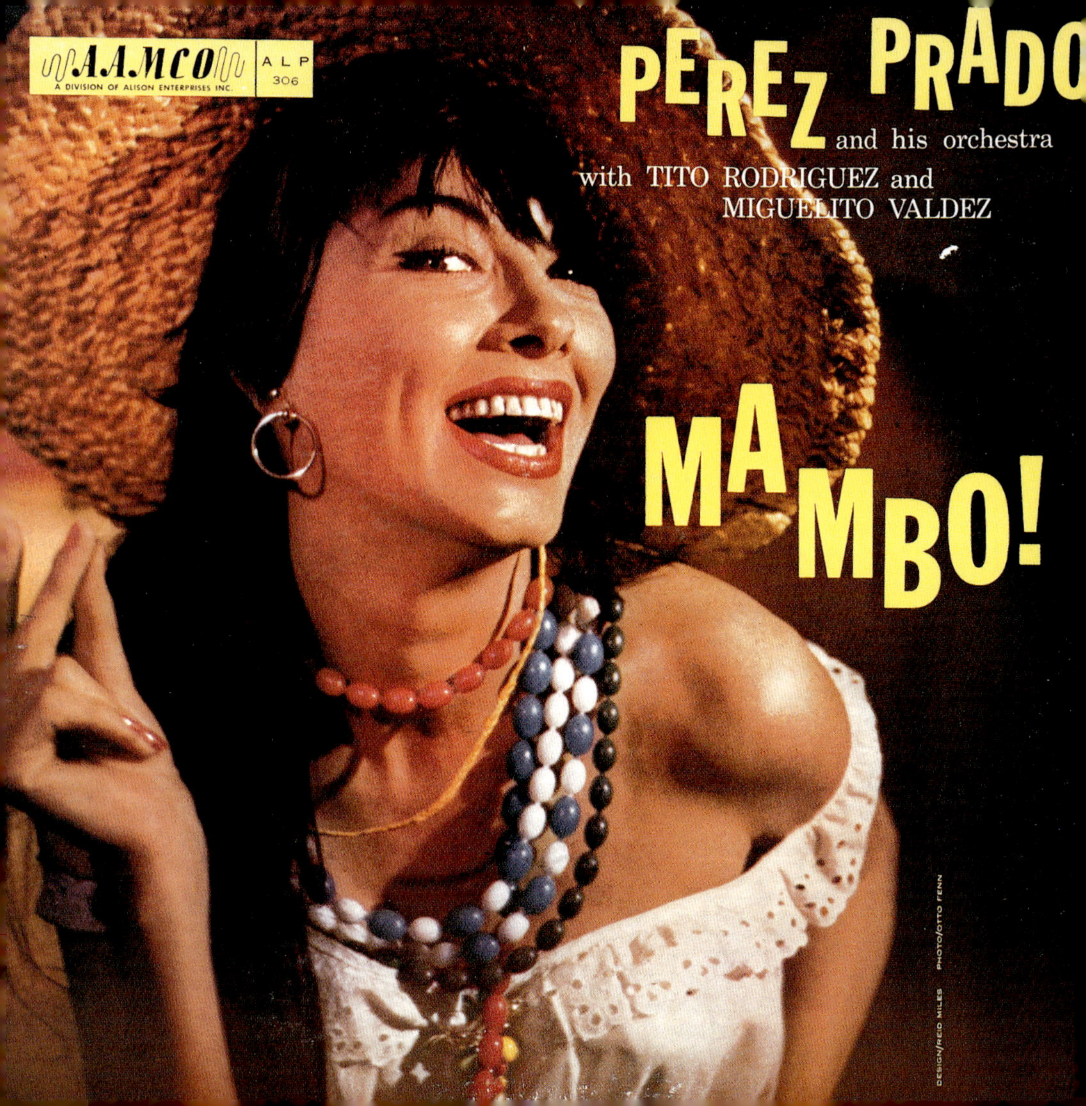

AAMCO
A DIVISION OF ALISON ENTERPRISES INC.
ALP 306
PEREZ PRADO
and his orchestra
with TITO RODRIGUEZ and
MIGUELITO VALDEZ
MAMBO!
DESIGN/REID MILES
PHOTO/OTTO FENN

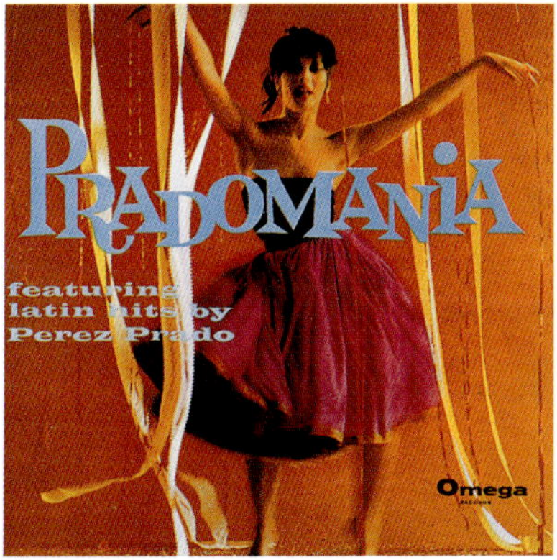
PRADOMANIA
featuring
latin hits by
Perez Prado
Omega

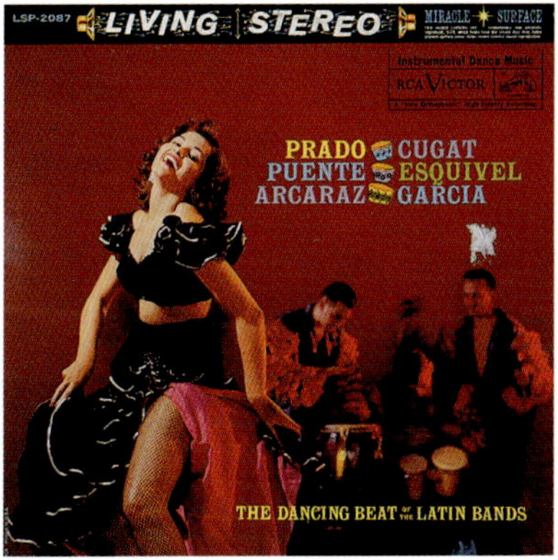
LSP-2087
LIVING STEREO
MIRACLE SURFACE
Instrumental Dance Music
RCA VICTOR
PRADO CUGAT
PUENTE ESQUIVEL
ARCARAZ GARCIA
THE DANCING BEAT OF THE LATIN BANDS

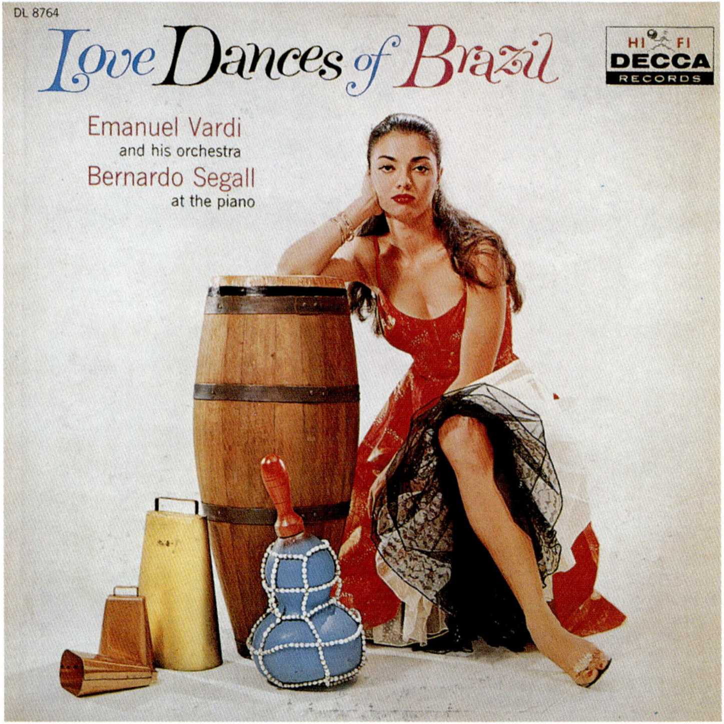

RIGHT *Liner Note*: Love and the soft sands of the shore . . . the warm, caressing night and the creamy surf . . . the exotic fragrance of strange and wonderful flowers . . . and a girl with long hair and deep, promising eyes.

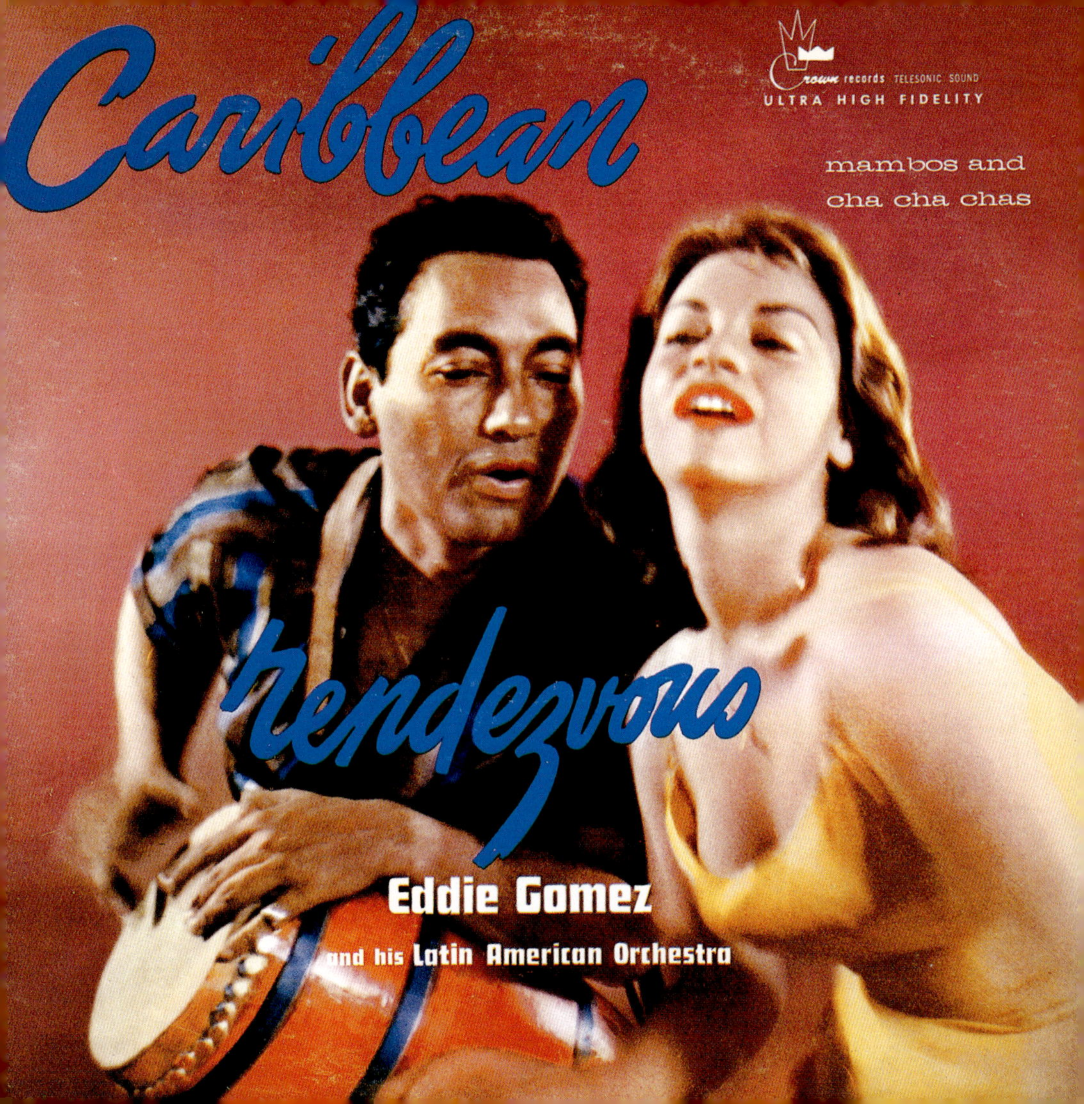
Caribbean
Crown records TELESONIC SOUND
ULTRA HIGH FIDELITY
mambos and
cha cha chas
rendezvous
Eddie Gomez
and his Latin American Orchestra

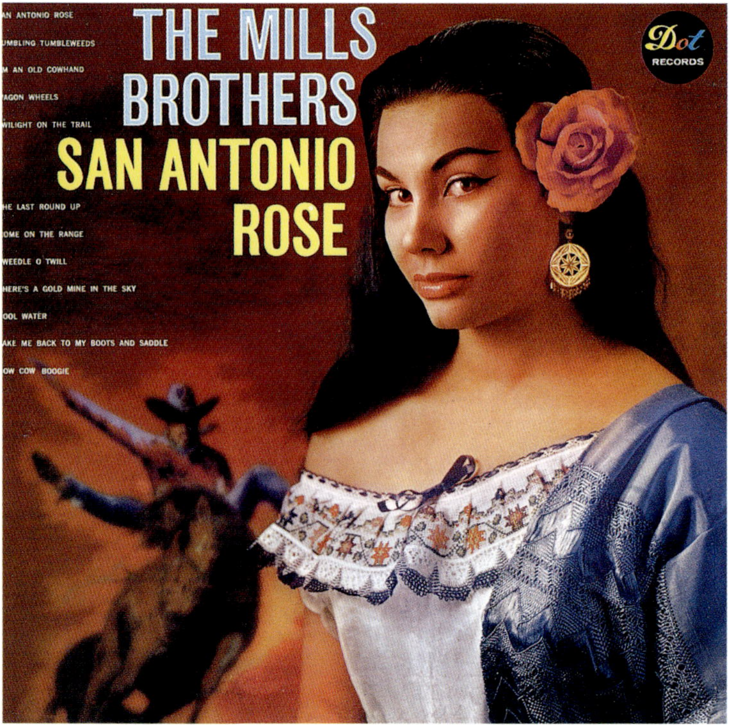
THE MILLS BROTHERS
SAN ANTONIO ROSE
Dot RECORDS
AN ANTONIO ROSE
UMBLING TUMBLEWEEDS
M AN OLD COWHAND
AGON WHEELS
WILIGHT ON THE TRAIL
HE LAST ROUND UP
OME ON THE RANGE
WEEDLE O TWILL
HERE'S A GOLD MINE IN THE SKY
OOL WATER
AKE ME BACK TO MY BOOTS AND SADDLE
OW COW BOOGIE

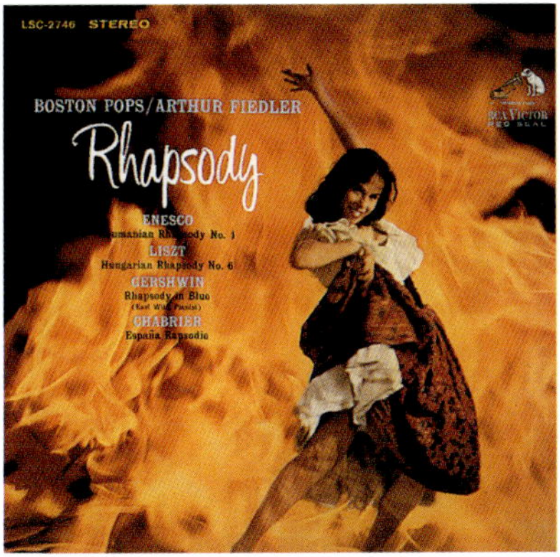
LSC-2746 STEREO
BOSTON POPS/ARTHUR FIEDLER
Rhapsody
RCA VICTOR
RED SEAL
ENESCO
LISZT
Hungarian Rhapsody No. 6
GERSHWIN
Rhapsody in Blue
CHABRIER
España Rapsodie

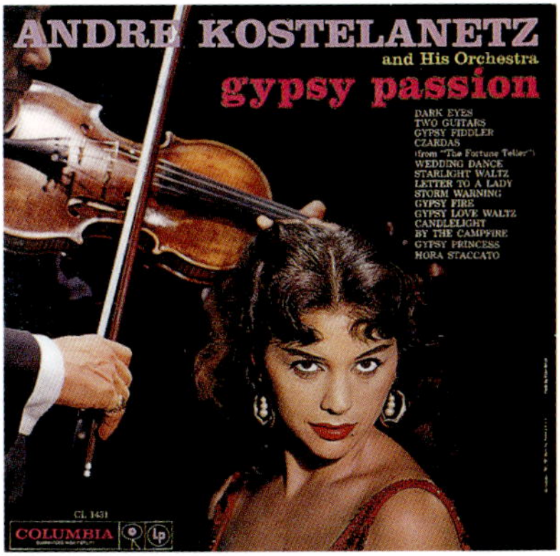
ANDRE KOSTELANETZ
and His Orchestra
gypsy passion
DARK EYES
TWO GUITARS
GYPSY FIDDLER
CZARDAS
(from "The Fortune Teller")
WEDDING DANCE
STARLIGHT WALTZ
LETTER TO A LADY
STORM WARNING
GYPSY FIRE
GYPSY LOVE WALTZ
CANDLELIGHT
BY THE CAMPFIRE
GYPSY PRINCESS
HORA STACCATO
CL 1431
COLUMBIA

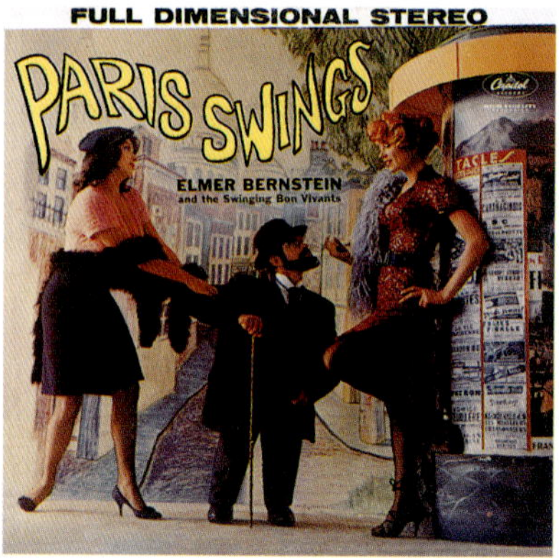
FULL DIMENSIONAL STEREO
PARIS SWINGS
ELMER BERNSTEIN
and the Swinging Bon Vivants

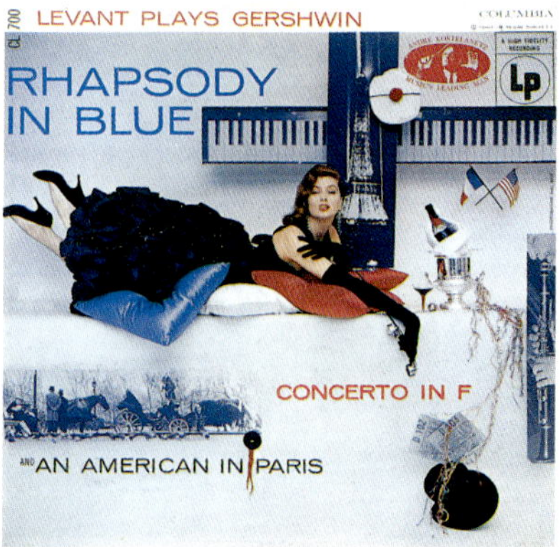
CL 700
LEVANT PLAYS GERSHWIN
COLUMBIA
RHAPSODY
IN BLUE
LP
CONCERTO IN F
AND AN AMERICAN IN PARIS

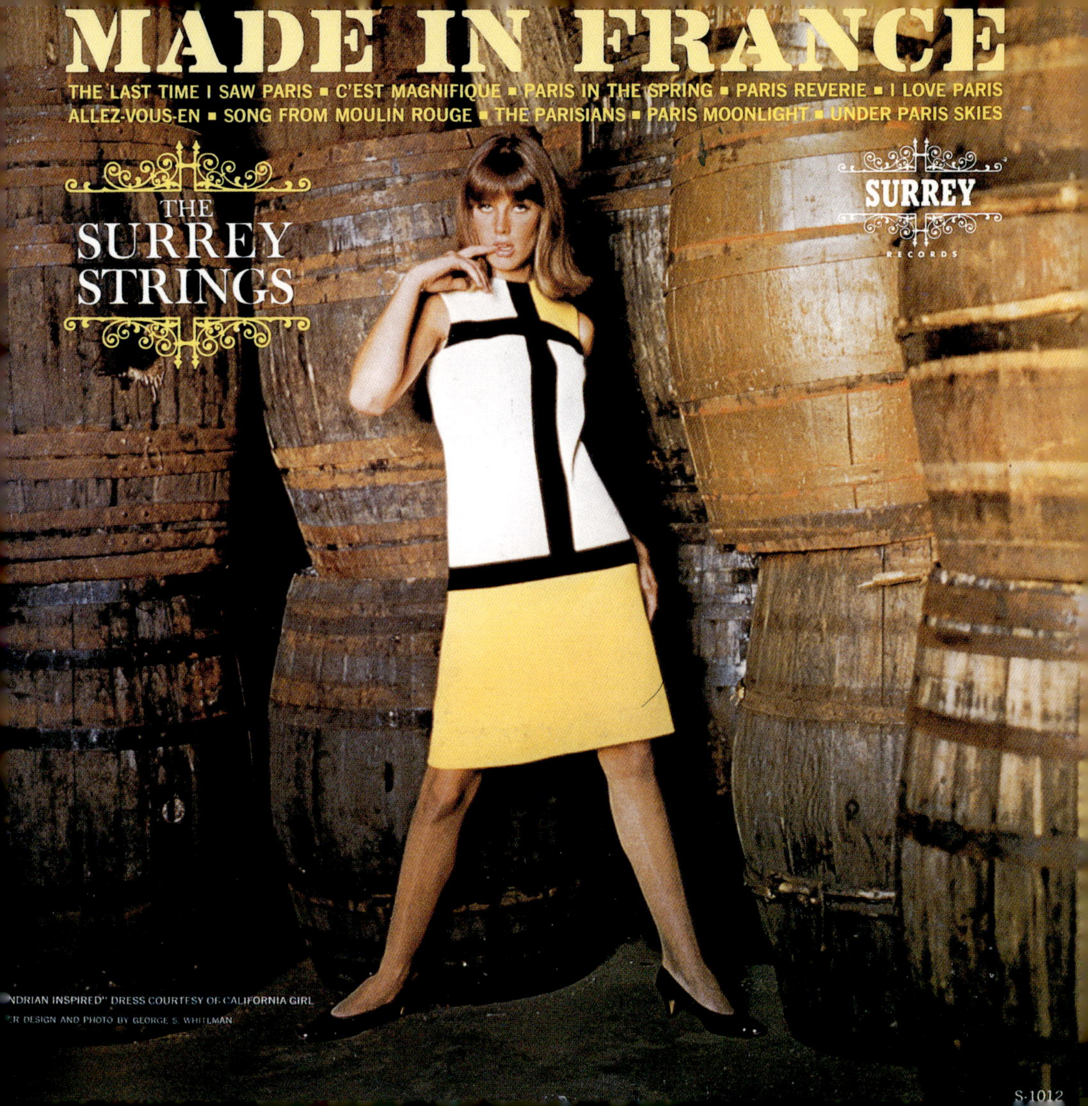

MADE IN FRANCE
THE LAST TIME I SAW PARIS ▪ C'EST MAGNIFIQUE ▪ PARIS IN THE SPRING ▪ PARIS REVERIE ▪ I LOVE PARIS
ALLEZ-VOUS-EN ▪ SONG FROM MOULIN ROUGE ▪ THE PARISIANS ▪ PARIS MOONLIGHT ▪ UNDER PARIS SKIES
THE SURREY STRINGS
SURREY
RECORDS
NDRIAN INSPIRED" DRESS COURTESY OF CALIFORNIA GIRL
ER DESIGN AND PHOTO BY GEORGE S. WHITLMAN
S-1012

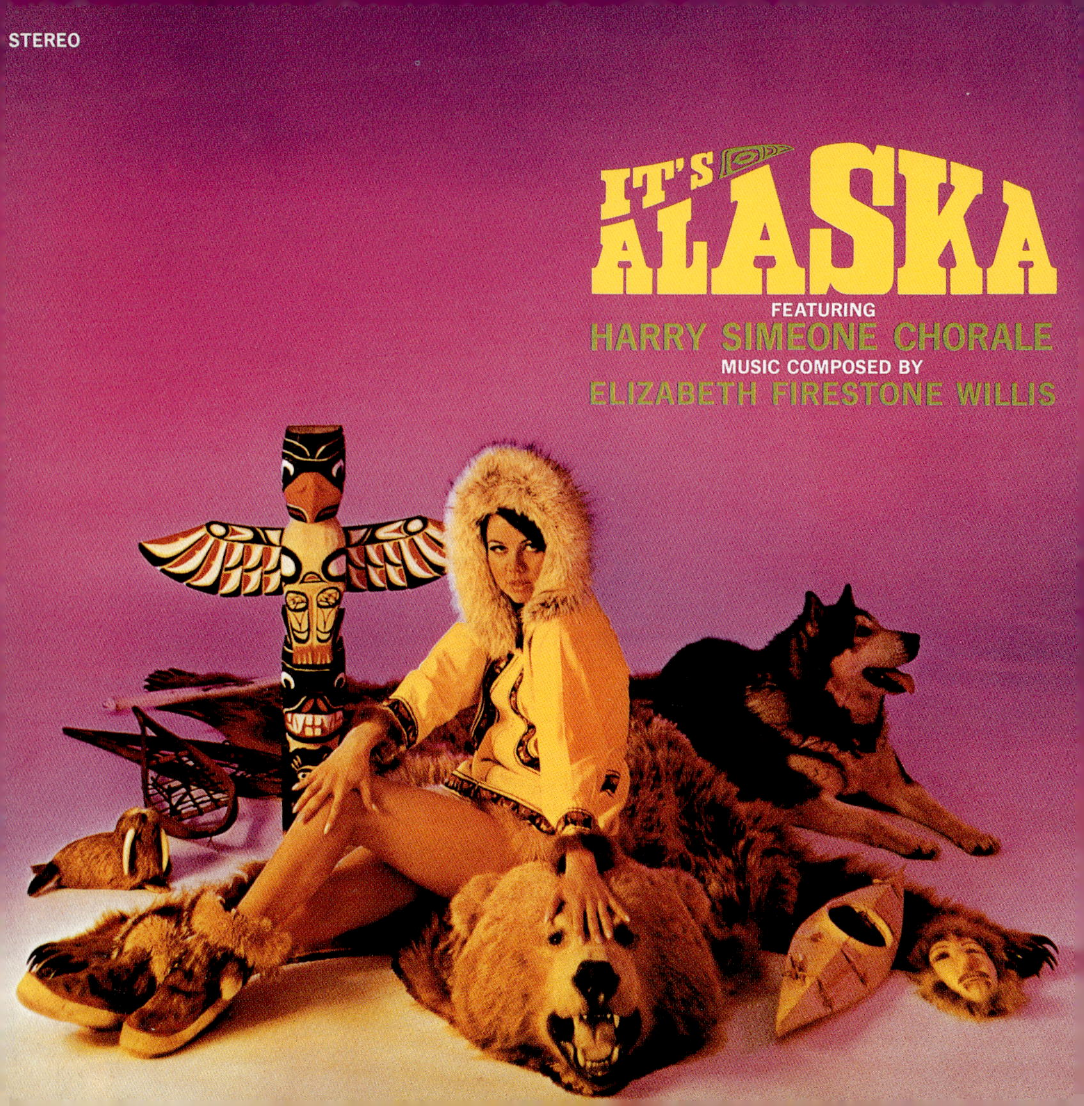
STEREO
IT'S ALASKA
FEATURING
HARRY SIMEONE CHORALE
MUSIC COMPOSED BY
ELIZABETH FIRESTONE WILLIS

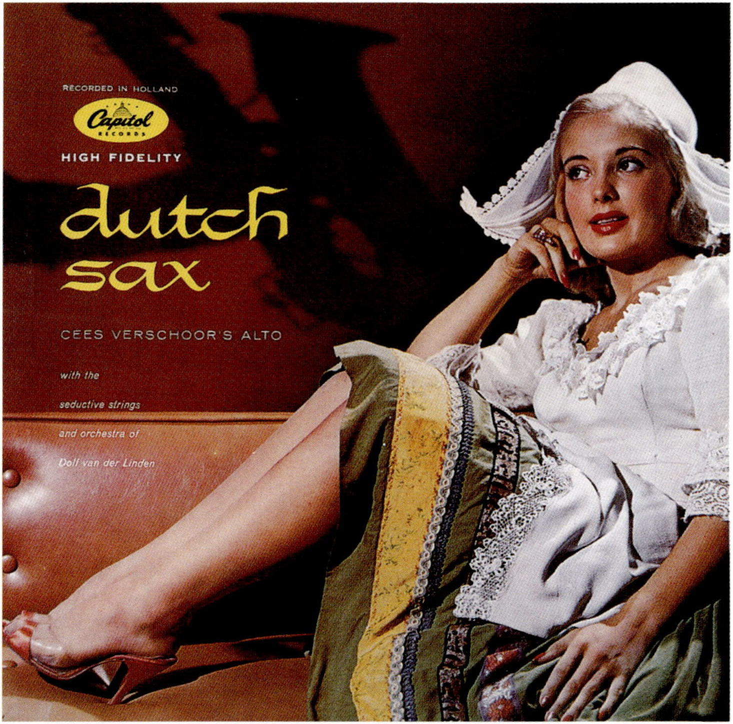
RECORDED IN HOLLAND
Capitol RECORDS
HIGH FIDELITY
dutch sax
CEES VERSCHOOR'S ALTO
with the
seductive strings
and orchestra of
Dolf van der Linden

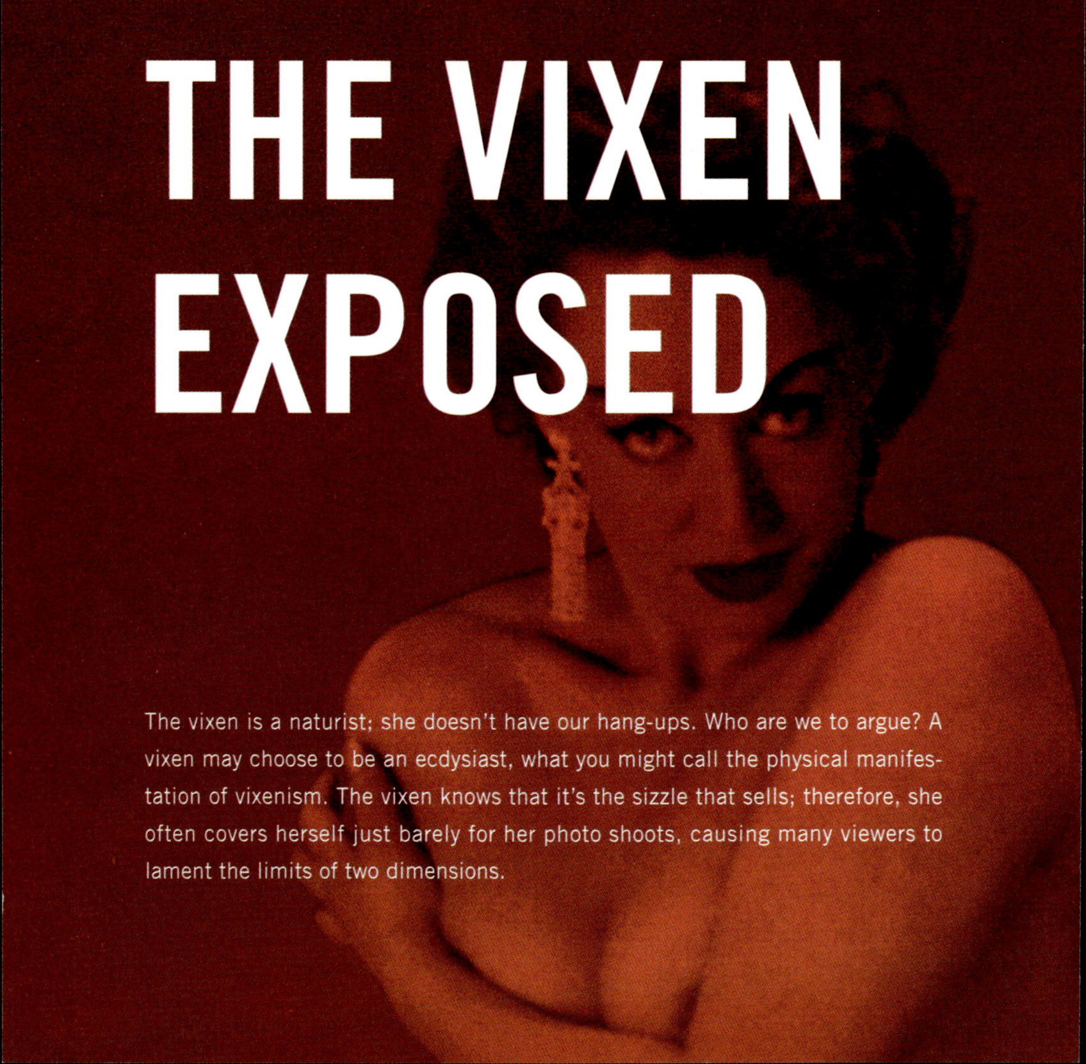

THE VIXEN EXPOSED

The vixen is a naturist; she doesn't have our hang-ups. Who are we to argue? A vixen may choose to be an ecdysiast, what you might call the physical manifestation of vixenism. The vixen knows that it's the sizzle that sells; therefore, she often covers herself just barely for her photo shoots, causing many viewers to lament the limits of two dimensions.

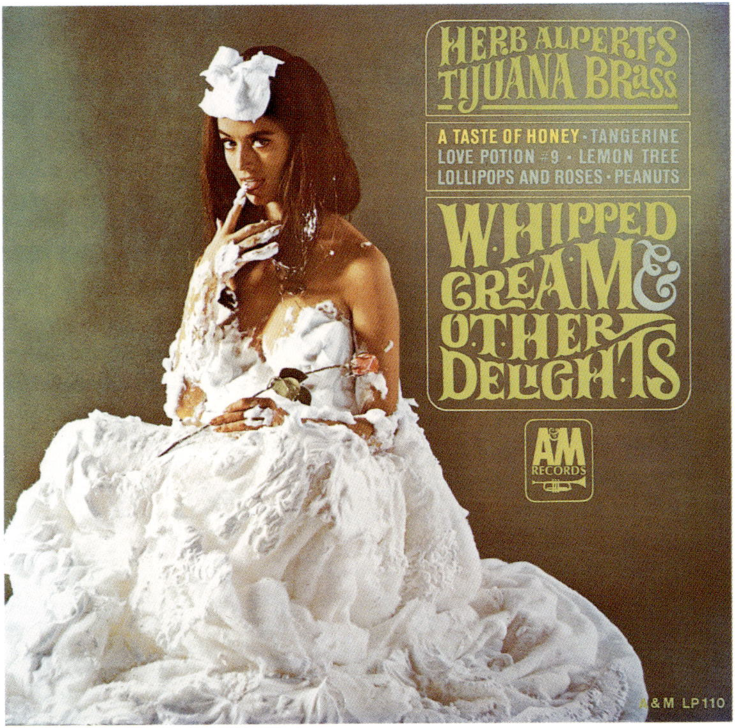
HERB ALPERT'S
TIJUANA BRASS
A TASTE OF HONEY · TANGERINE
LOVE POTION #9 · LEMON TREE
LOLLIPOPS AND ROSES · PEANUTS
WHIPPED
CREAM&
OTHER
DELIGHTS
A&M
RECORDS
A&M LP110

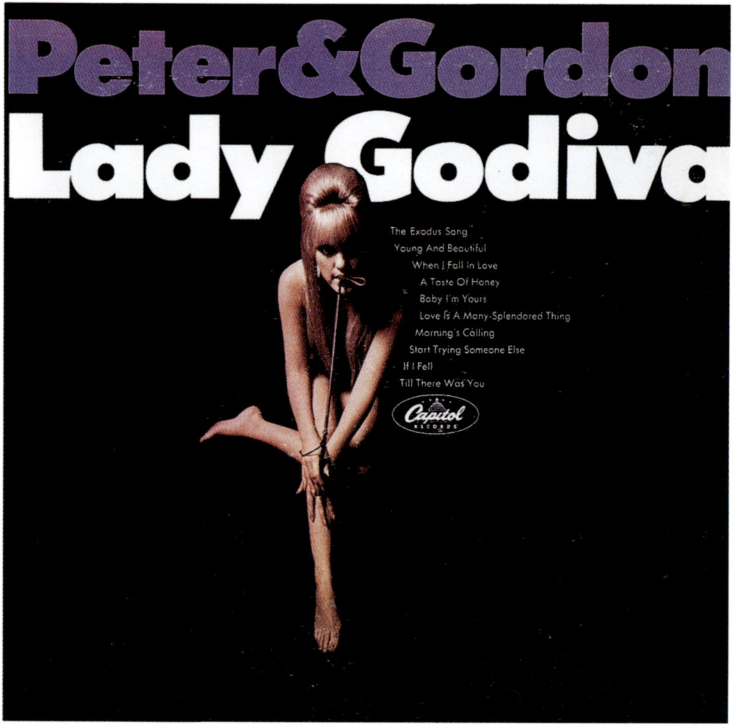
Peter&Gordon
Lady Godiva
The Exodus Song
Young And Beautiful
When I Fall In Love
A Taste Of Honey
Baby I'm Yours
Love Is A Many-Splendored Thing
Morning's Calling
Start Trying Someone Else
If I Fell
Till There Was You
Capitol
RECORDS

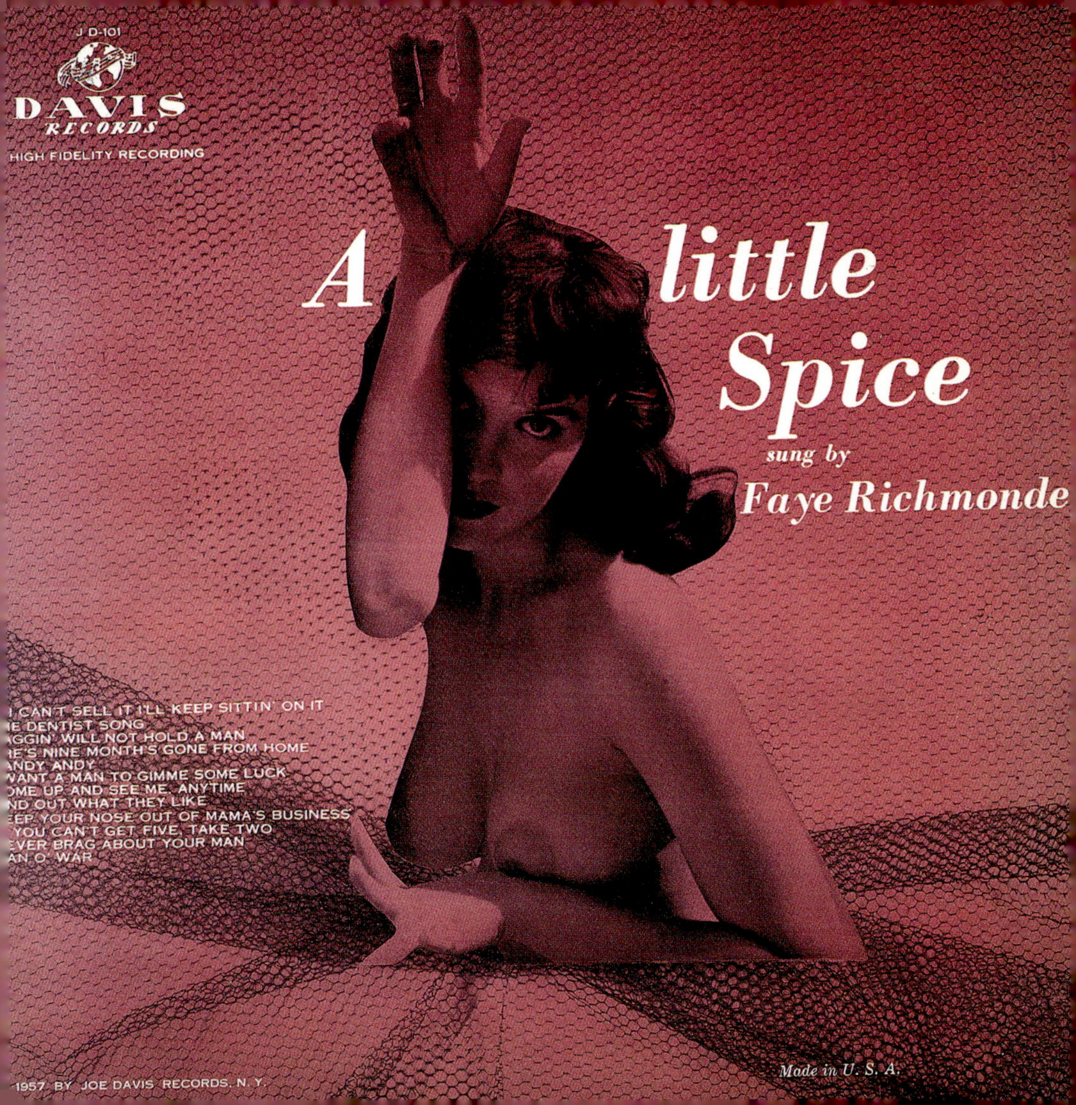

J D-101
DAVIS
RECORDS
HIGH FIDELITY RECORDING
A little Spice
sung by
Faye Richmonde
I CAN'T SELL IT I'LL KEEP SITTIN' ON IT
E DENTIST SONG
GGIN' WILL NOT HOLD A MAN
E'S NINE MONTH'S GONE FROM HOME
NDY ANDY
WANT A MAN TO GIMME SOME LUCK
OME UP AND SEE ME, ANYTIME
ND OUT WHAT THEY LIKE
EEP YOUR NOSE OUT OF MAMA'S BUSINESS
YOU CAN'T GET FIVE, TAKE TWO
EVER BRAG ABOUT YOUR MAN
AN O' WAR
1957 BY JOE DAVIS RECORDS, N. Y.
Made in U. S. A.

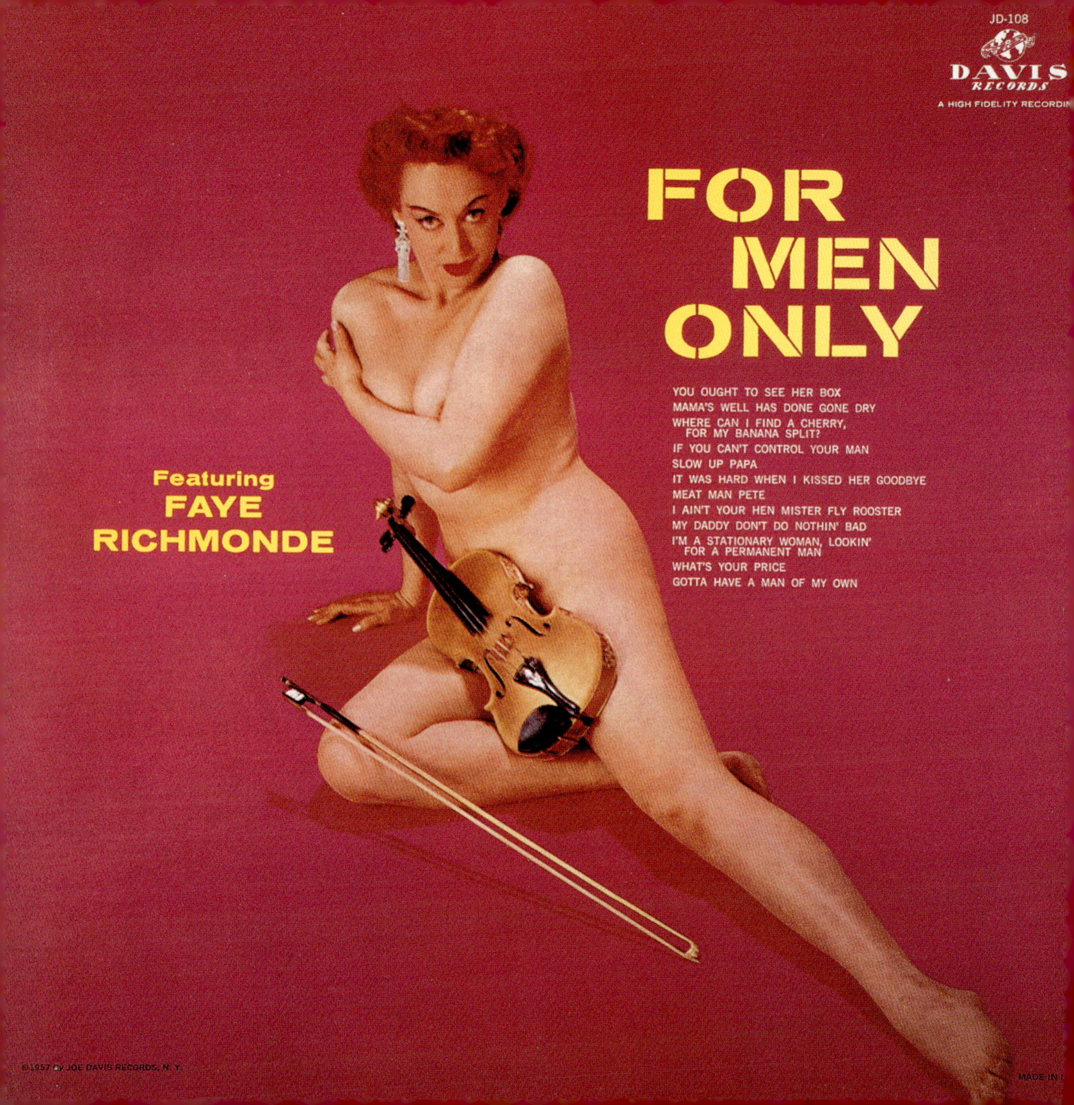
JD-108
DAVIS
RECORDS
A HIGH FIDELITY RECORDIN
FOR
MEN
ONLY
YOU OUGHT TO SEE HER BOX
MAMA'S WELL HAS DONE GONE DRY
WHERE CAN I FIND A CHERRY, FOR MY BANANA SPLIT?
IF YOU CAN'T CONTROL YOUR MAN
SLOW UP PAPA
IT WAS HARD WHEN I KISSED HER GOODBYE
MEAT MAN PETE
I AIN'T YOUR HEN MISTER FLY ROOSTER
MY DADDY DON'T DO NOTHIN' BAD
I'M A STATIONARY WOMAN, LOOKIN' FOR A PERMANENT MAN
WHAT'S YOUR PRICE
GOTTA HAVE A MAN OF MY OWN
Featuring
FAYE
RICHMONDE
©1957 by JOE DAVIS RECORDS, N. Y.
MADE IN

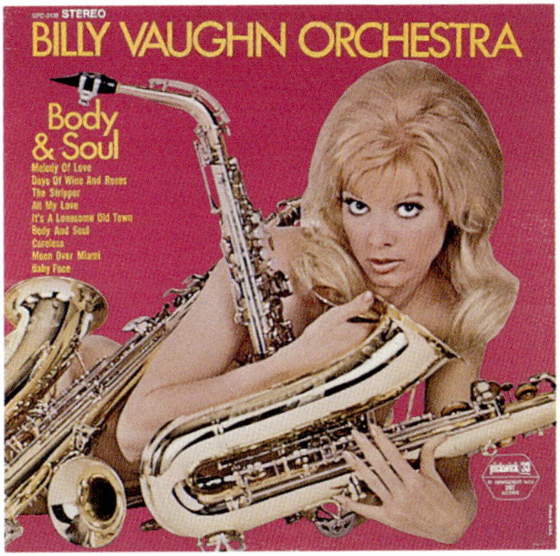
STEREO
BILLY VAUGHN ORCHESTRA
Body & Soul
Melody Of Love
Days Of Wine And Roses
The Stripper
All My Love
It's A Lonesome Old Town
Body And Soul
Careless
Moon Over Miami
Baby Face

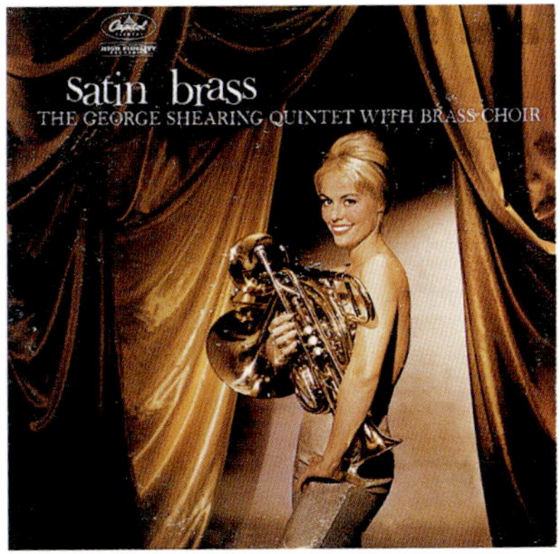
satin brass
THE GEORGE SHEARING QUINTET WITH BRASS CHOIR

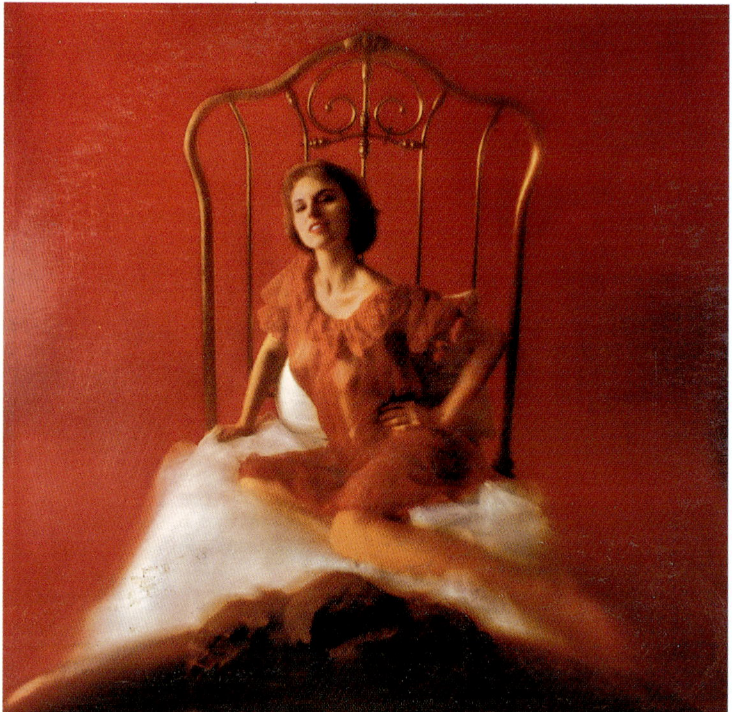

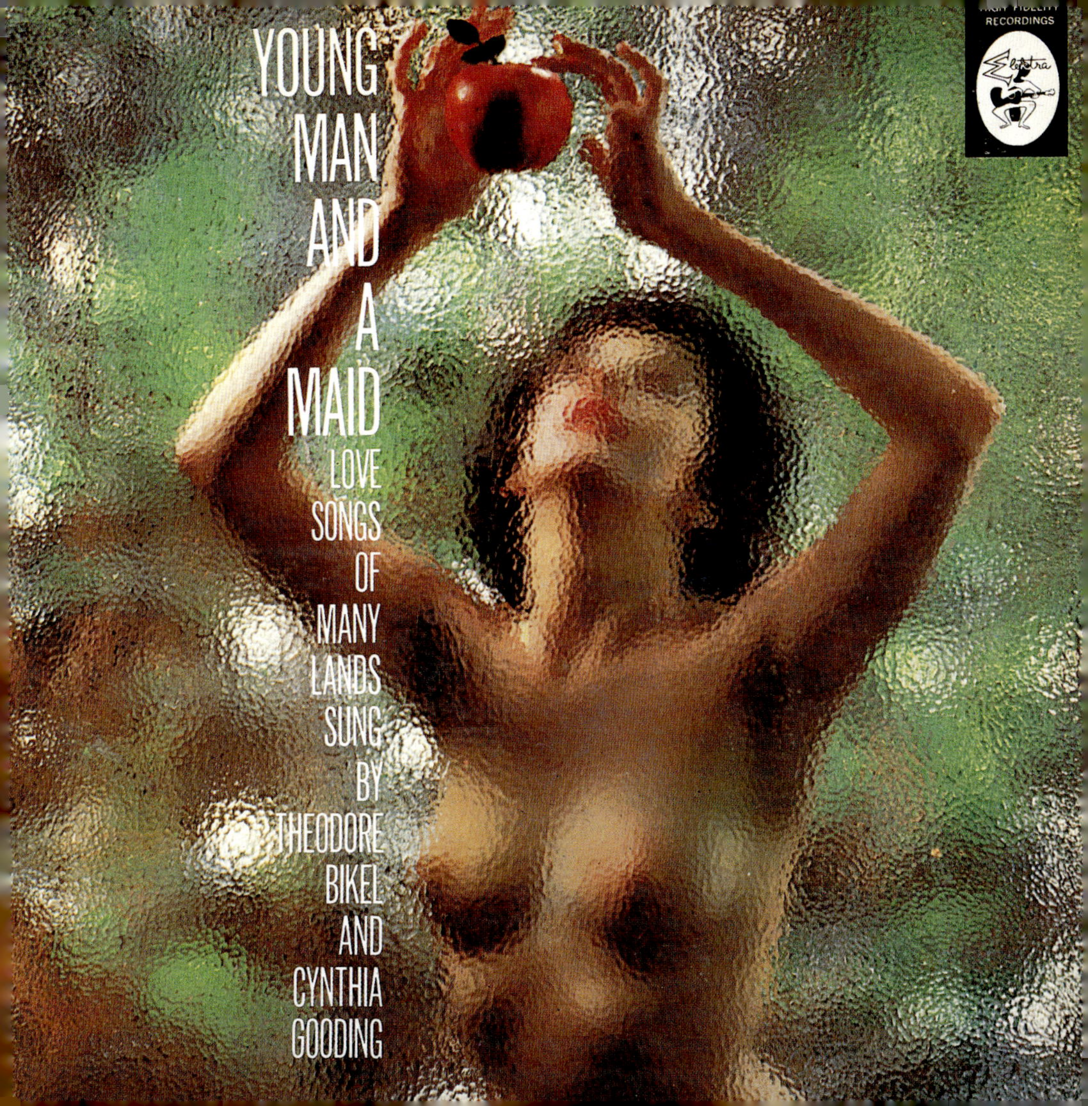
YOUNG MAN AND A MAID
LOVE SONGS OF MANY LANDS SUNG BY THEODORE BIKEL AND CYNTHIA GOODING
RECORDINGS
Elektra

YOUR GIRL FOR THE NIGHT

LYNN ROBINSON

Sings

A TRIP AROUND THE WORLD

PETTING MY PUSSY

I'M A GIRL WHO LIKES TO EAT

HE'S UP IN THE MORNING

IT'S HARD TO EAT IT WHEN IT'S SOFT

GIVE IT TO ME BABY PLEASE

HE'S SIXTY INCHES LONG

THE PLUMBER'S SNAKE

COME INTO MY CAVE

HOT ROD HENRY

UP THE CANAL

HOW FAR CAN I GO

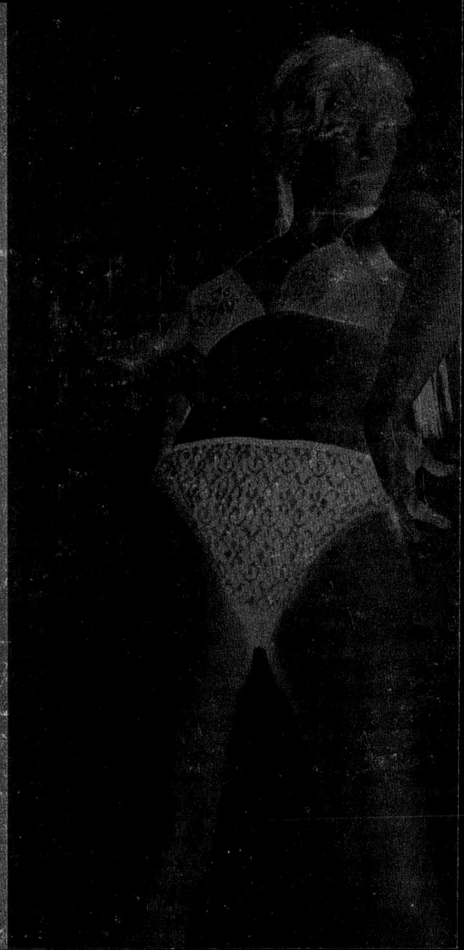

HA HA RECORDS

FOR ADULTS ONLY

CENSORED/NOT FOR AIR PLAY

NO-33

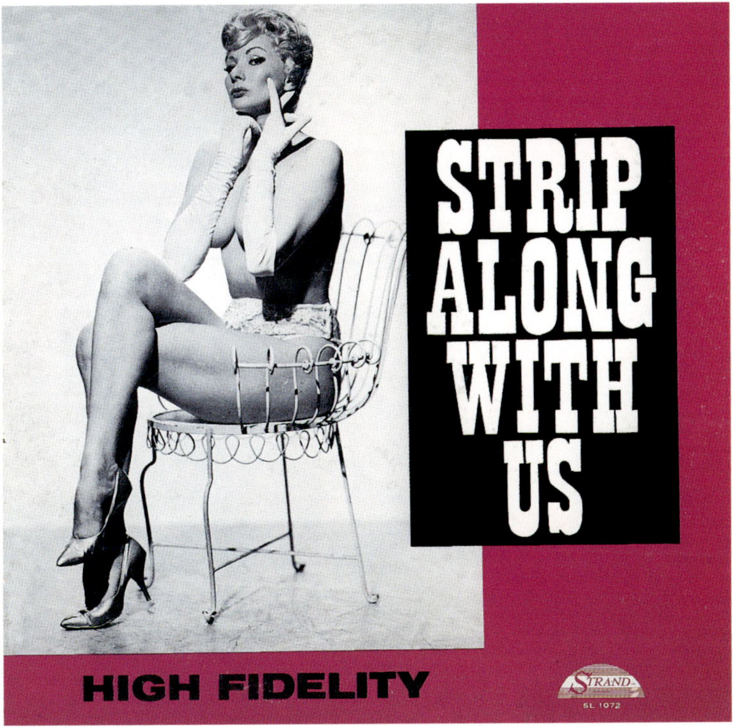

Liner Note: The cover photo was used with the permission of one of the country's foremost performers, Miss Libby Jones, The Park Avenue Playgirl.

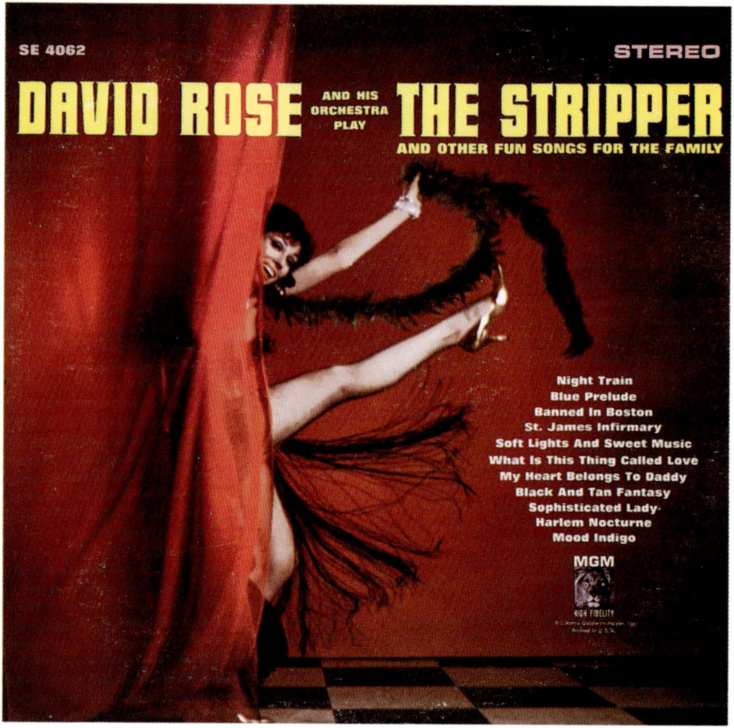
SE 4062
STEREO
DAVID ROSE
AND HIS ORCHESTRA PLAY
THE STRIPPER
AND OTHER FUN SONGS FOR THE FAMILY
Night Train
Blue Prelude
Banned In Boston
St. James Infirmary
Soft Lights And Sweet Music
What Is This Thing Called Love
My Heart Belongs To Daddy
Black And Tan Fantasy
Sophisticated Lady
Harlem Nocturne
Mood Indigo
MGM
HIGH FIDELITY

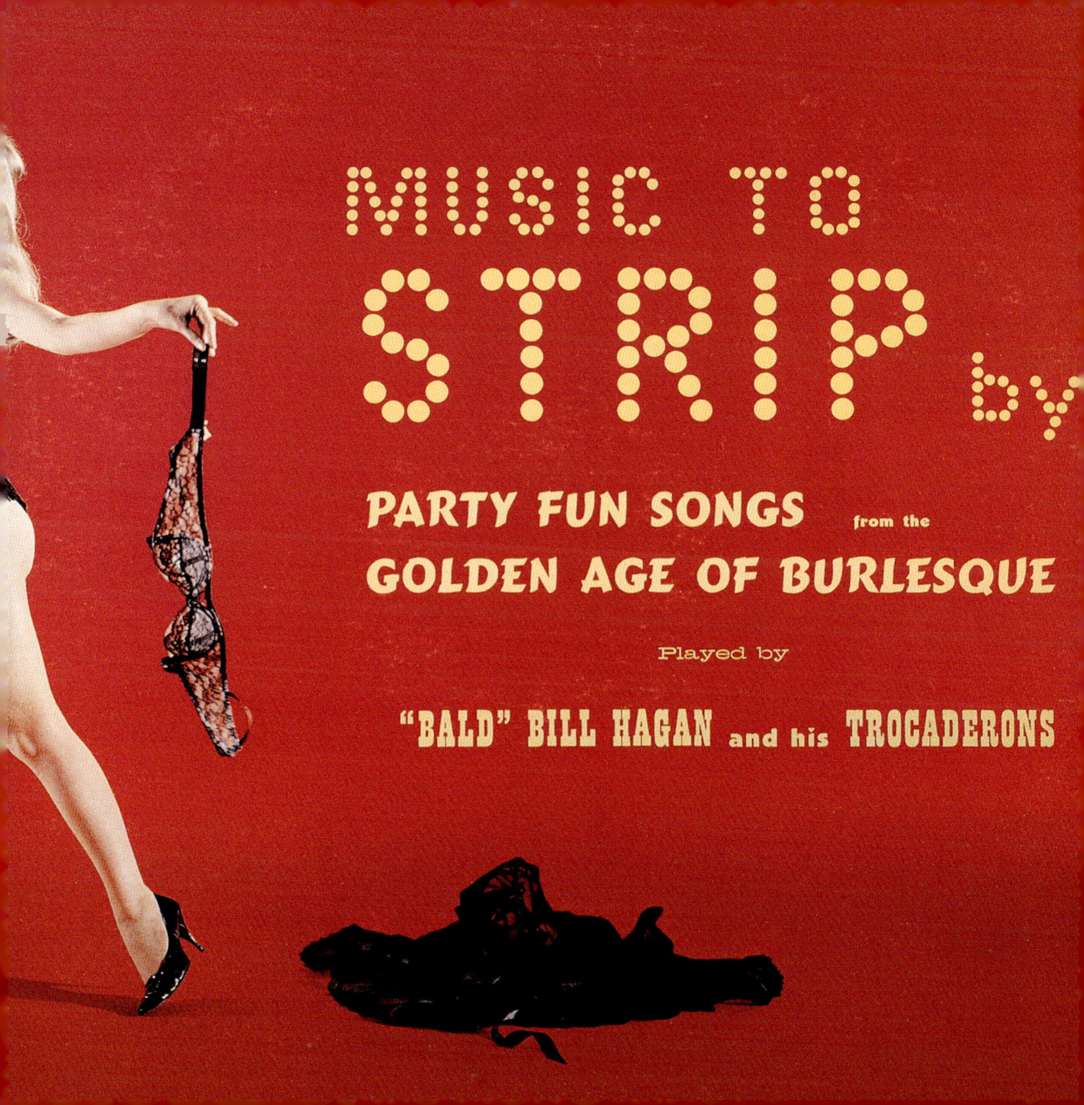
MUSIC TO
STRIP by
PARTY FUN SONGS from the
GOLDEN AGE OF BURLESQUE
Played by
"BALD" BILL HAGAN and his TROCADERONS

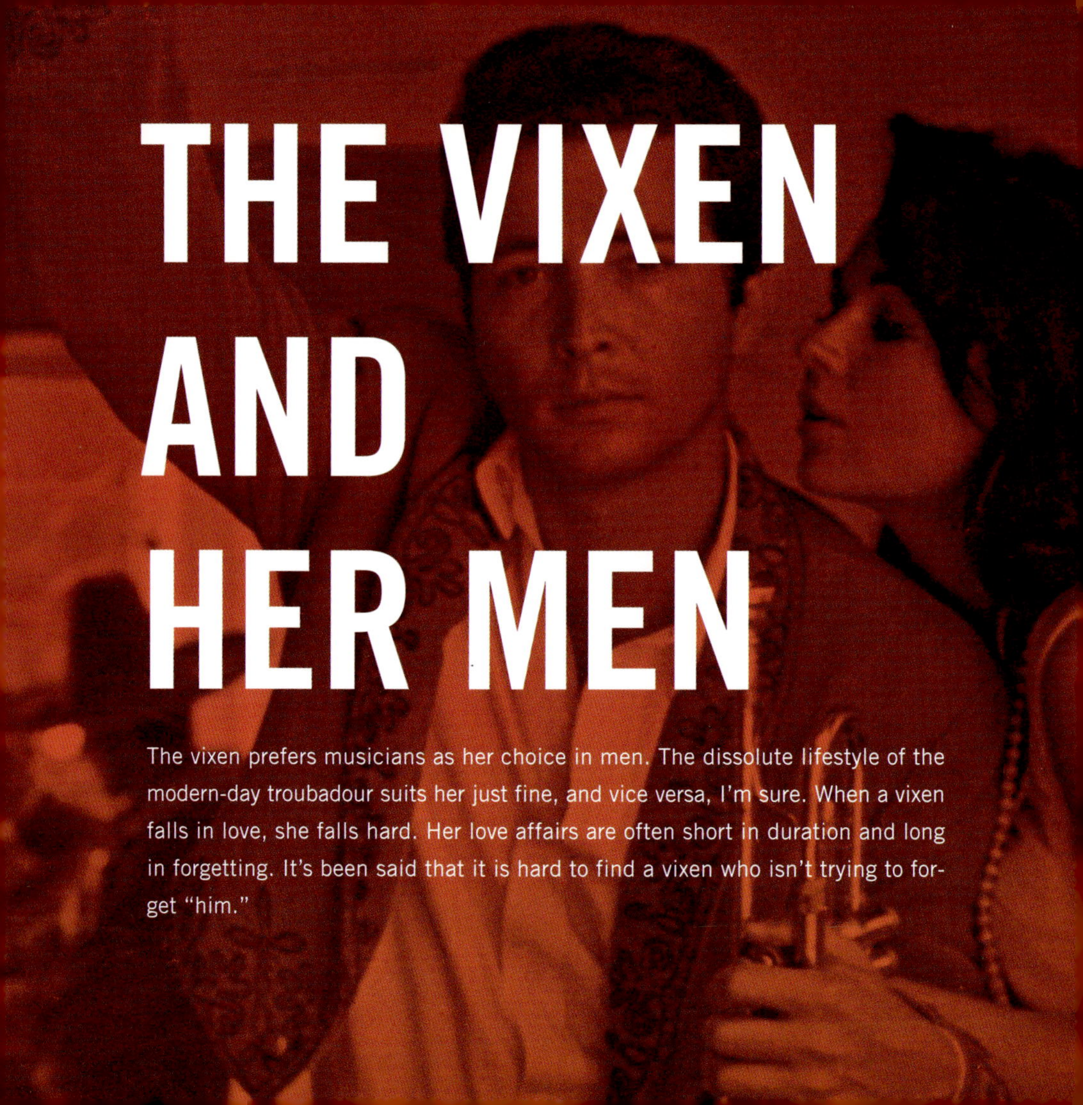

THE VIXEN AND HER MEN

The vixen prefers musicians as her choice in men. The dissolute lifestyle of the modern-day troubadour suits her just fine, and vice versa, I'm sure. When a vixen falls in love, she falls hard. Her love affairs are often short in duration and long in forgetting. It's been said that it is hard to find a vixen who isn't trying to forget "him."

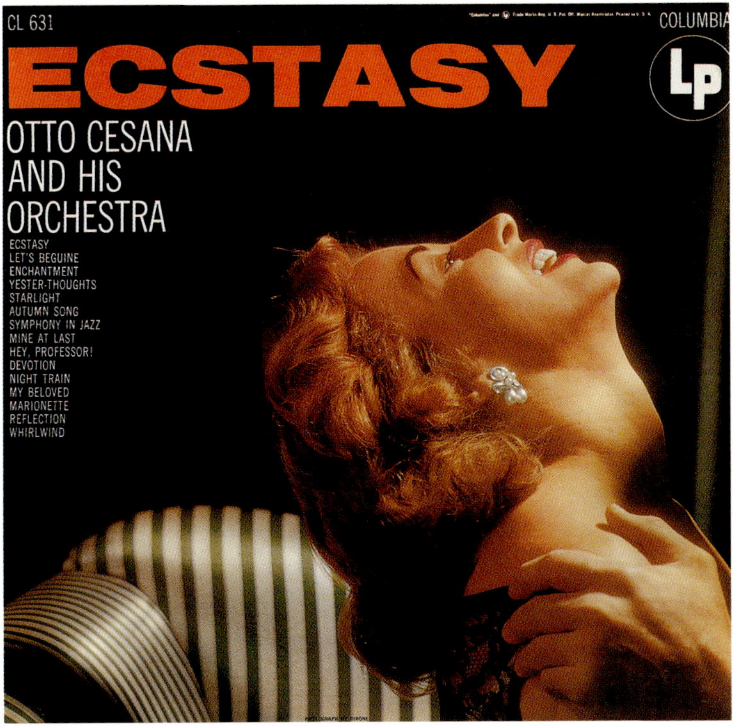
CL 631
COLUMBIA
LP
ECSTASY
OTTO CESANA
AND HIS
ORCHESTRA
ECSTASY
LET'S BEGUINE
ENCHANTMENT
YESTER-THOUGHTS
STARLIGHT
AUTUMN SONG
SYMPHONY IN JAZZ
MINE AT LAST
HEY, PROFESSOR!
DEVOTION
NIGHT TRAIN
MY BELOVED
MARIONETTE
REFLECTION
WHIRLWIND

Mercury RECORDS

HI-FI STEREO

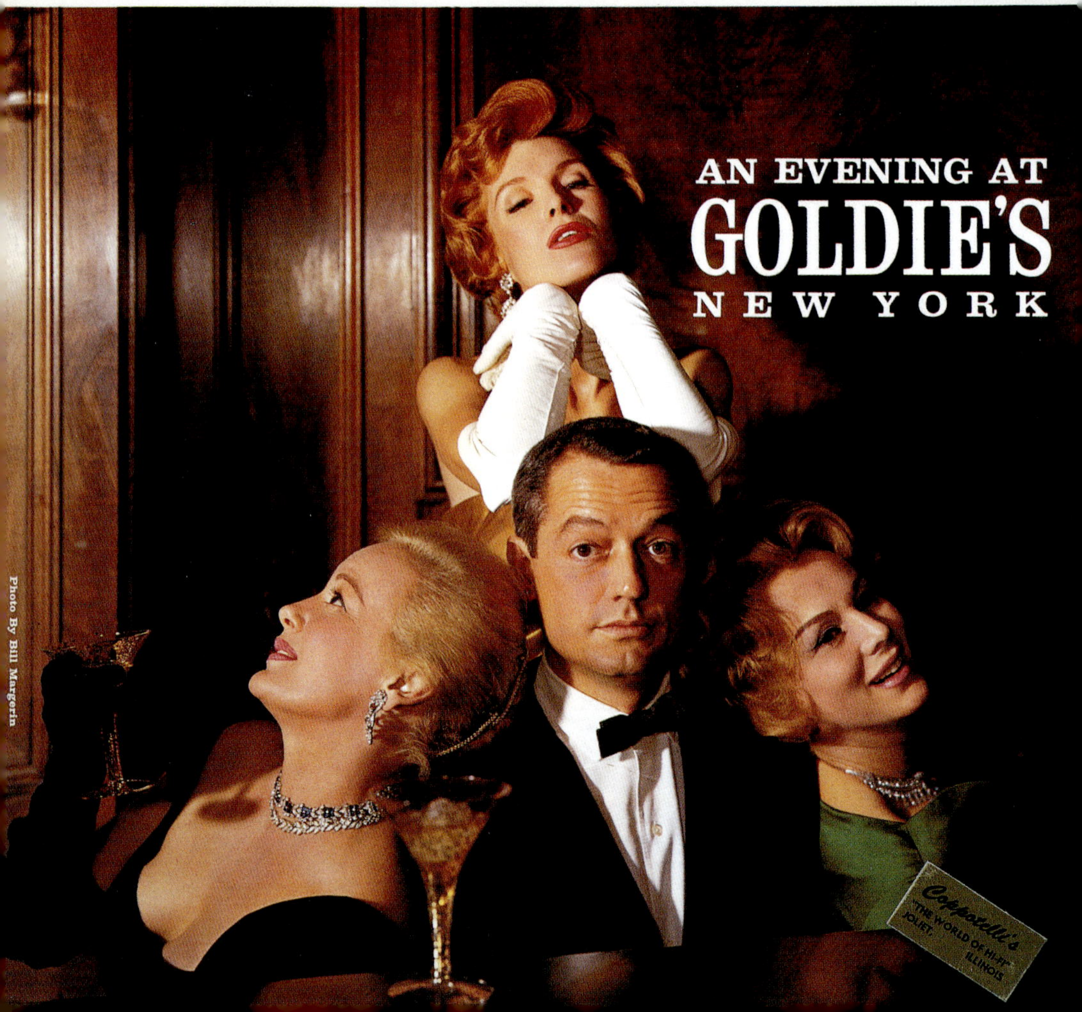

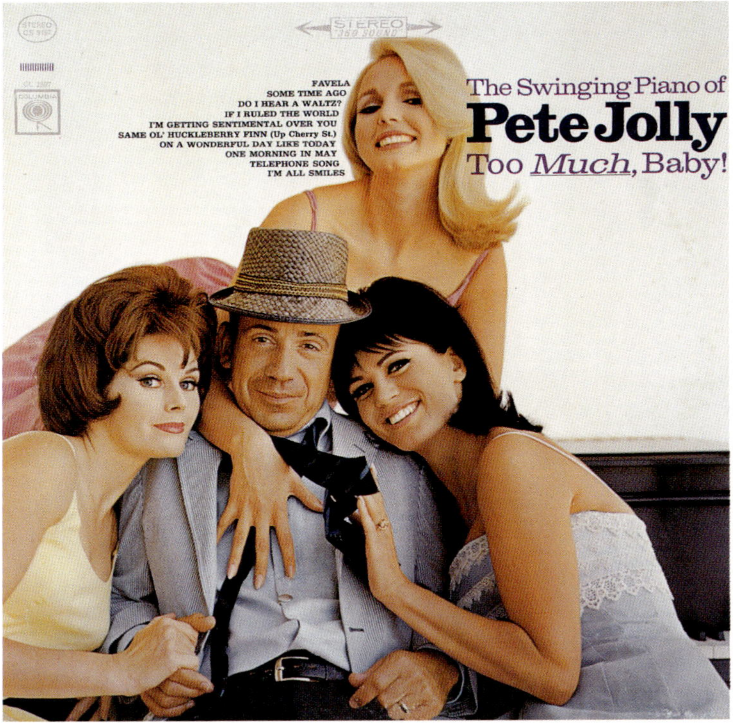
STEREO
360 SOUND
FAVELA
SOME TIME AGO
DO I HEAR A WALTZ?
IF I RULED THE WORLD
I'M GETTING SENTIMENTAL OVER YOU
SAME OL' HUCKLEBERRY FINN (Up Cherry St.)
ON A WONDERFUL DAY LIKE TODAY
ONE MORNING IN MAY
TELEPHONE SONG
I'M ALL SMILES
The Swinging Piano of
Pete Jolly
Too Much, Baby!

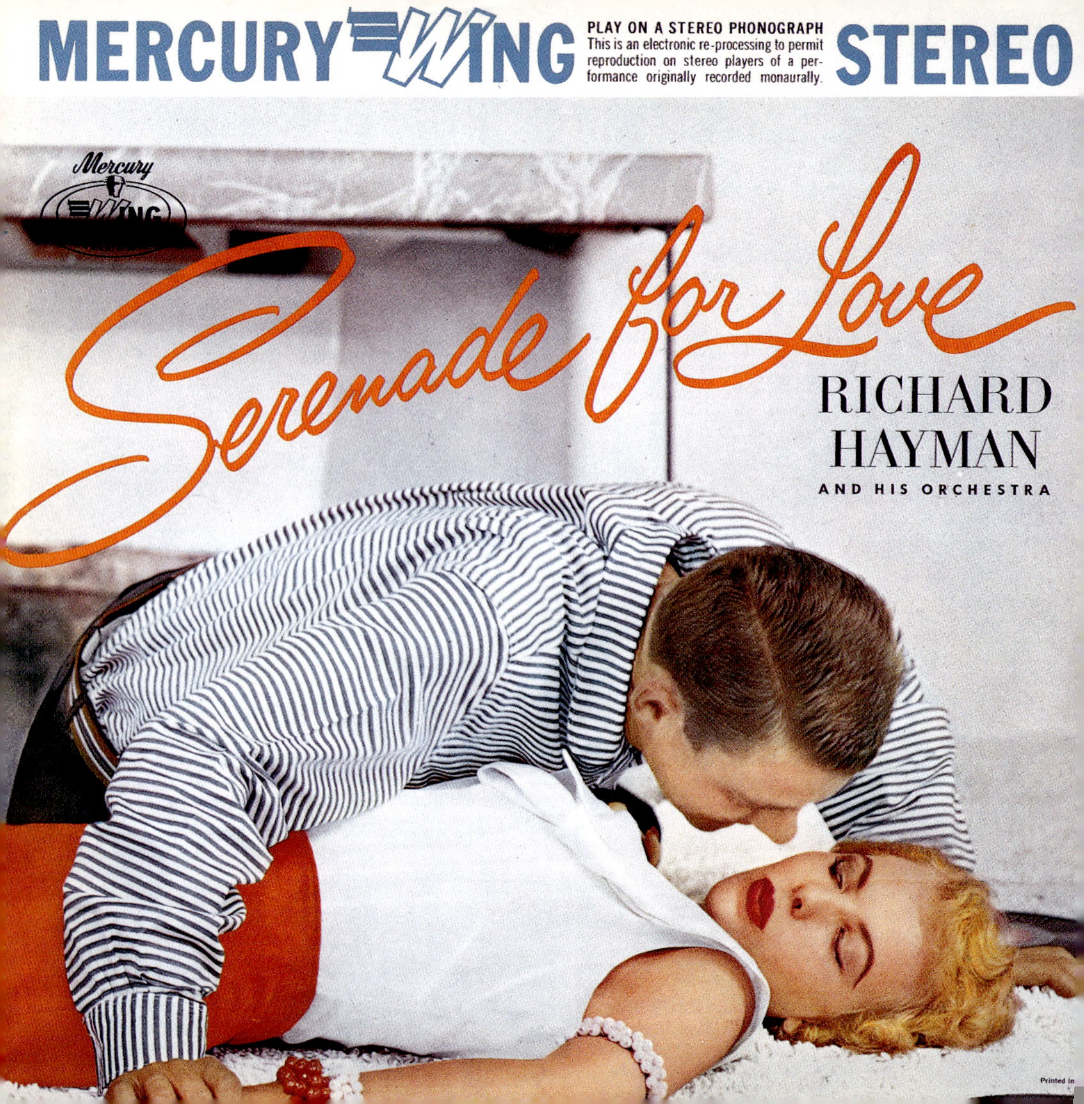
MERCURY WING
PLAY ON A STEREO PHONOGRAPH
This is an electronic re-processing to permit reproduction on stereo players of a performance originally recorded monaurally.
STEREO
Mercury WING
Serenade for Love
RICHARD HAYMAN
AND HIS ORCHESTRA
Printed in

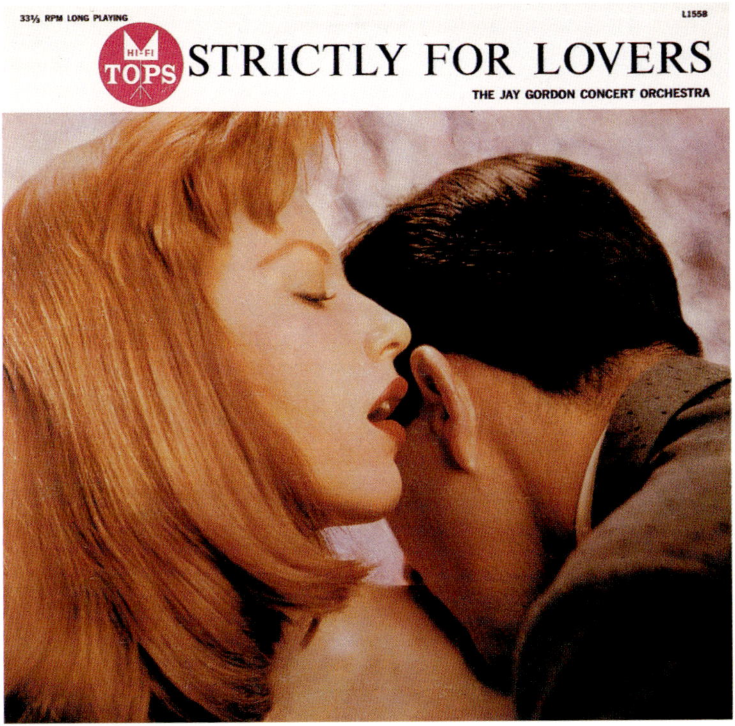
33⅓ RPM LONG PLAYING
L1558
HI-FI
TOPS
STRICTLY FOR LOVERS
THE JAY GORDON CONCERT ORCHESTRA

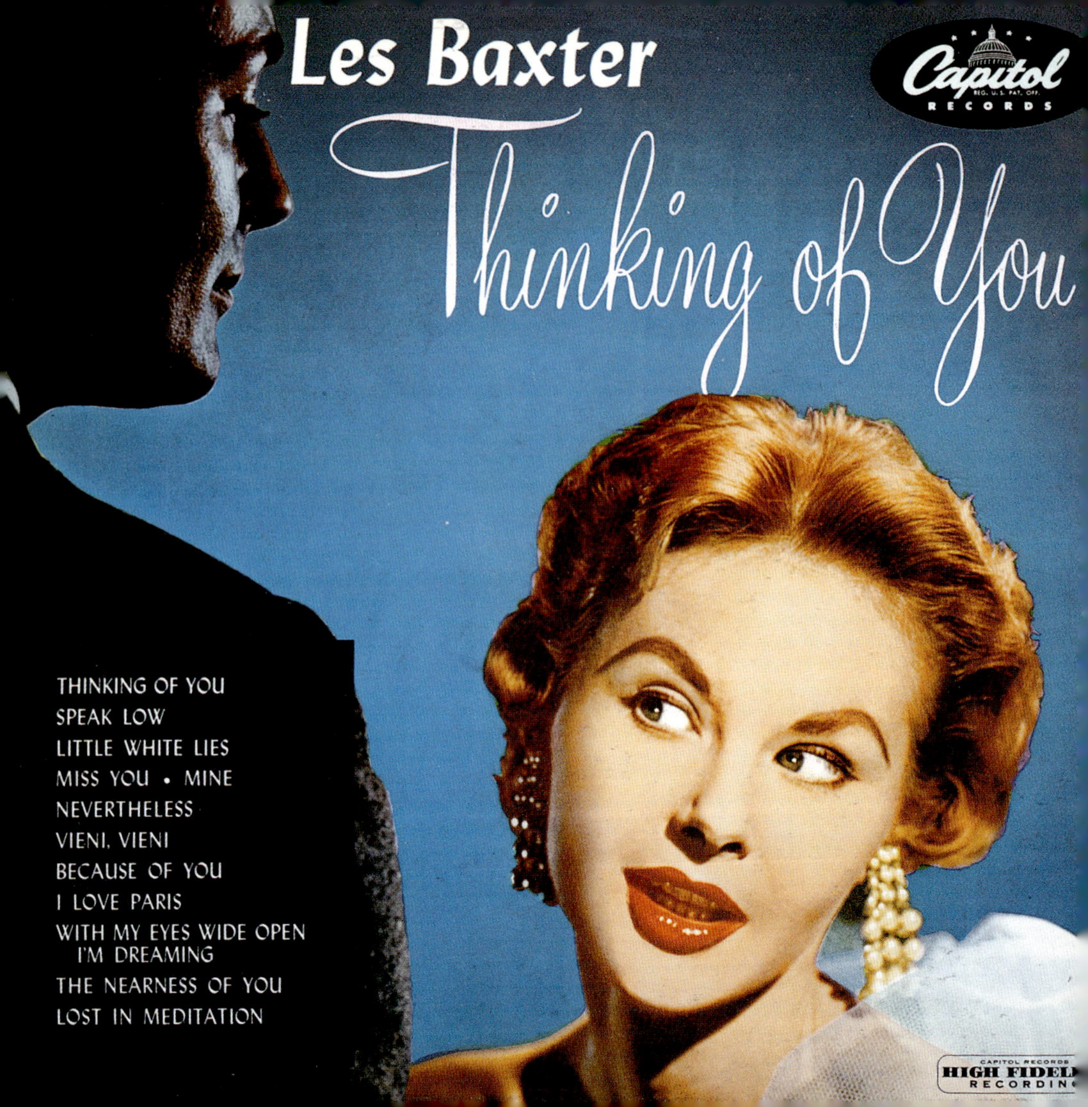
Les Baxter
Capitol
REG. U.S. PAT. OFF.
RECORDS
Thinking of You
THINKING OF YOU
SPEAK LOW
LITTLE WHITE LIES
MISS YOU • MINE
NEVERTHELESS
VIENI, VIENI
BECAUSE OF YOU
I LOVE PARIS
WITH MY EYES WIDE OPEN
I'M DREAMING
THE NEARNESS OF YOU
LOST IN MEDITATION
CAPITOL RECORDS
HIGH FIDELI
RECORDIN

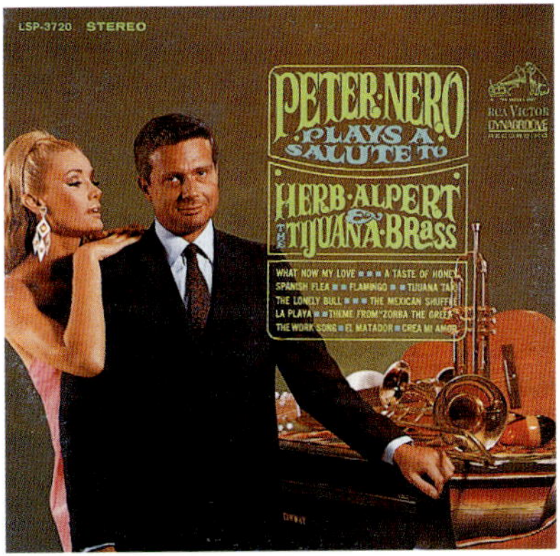
LSP-3720 STEREO
PETER·NERO
PLAYS A SALUTE TO
HERB·ALPERT
& THE TIJUANA·BRASS
RCA VICTOR
DYNAGROOVE
WHAT NOW MY LOVE
SPANISH FLEA
FLAMINGO
THE LONELY BULL
LA PLAYA
THE WORK SONG
EL MATADOR
CREA MI AMOR

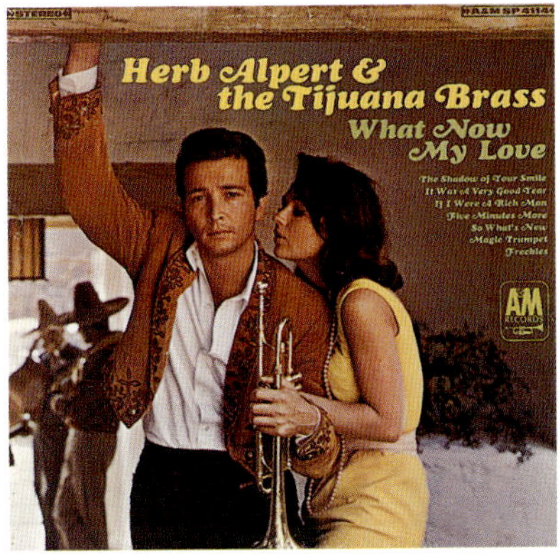
STEREO
A&M SP 4114
Herb Alpert &
the Tijuana Brass
What Now
My Love
The Shadow of Your Smile
It Was A Very Good Year
If I Were A Rich Man
Five Minutes More
So What's New
Magic Trumpet
Freckles
A&M RECORDS

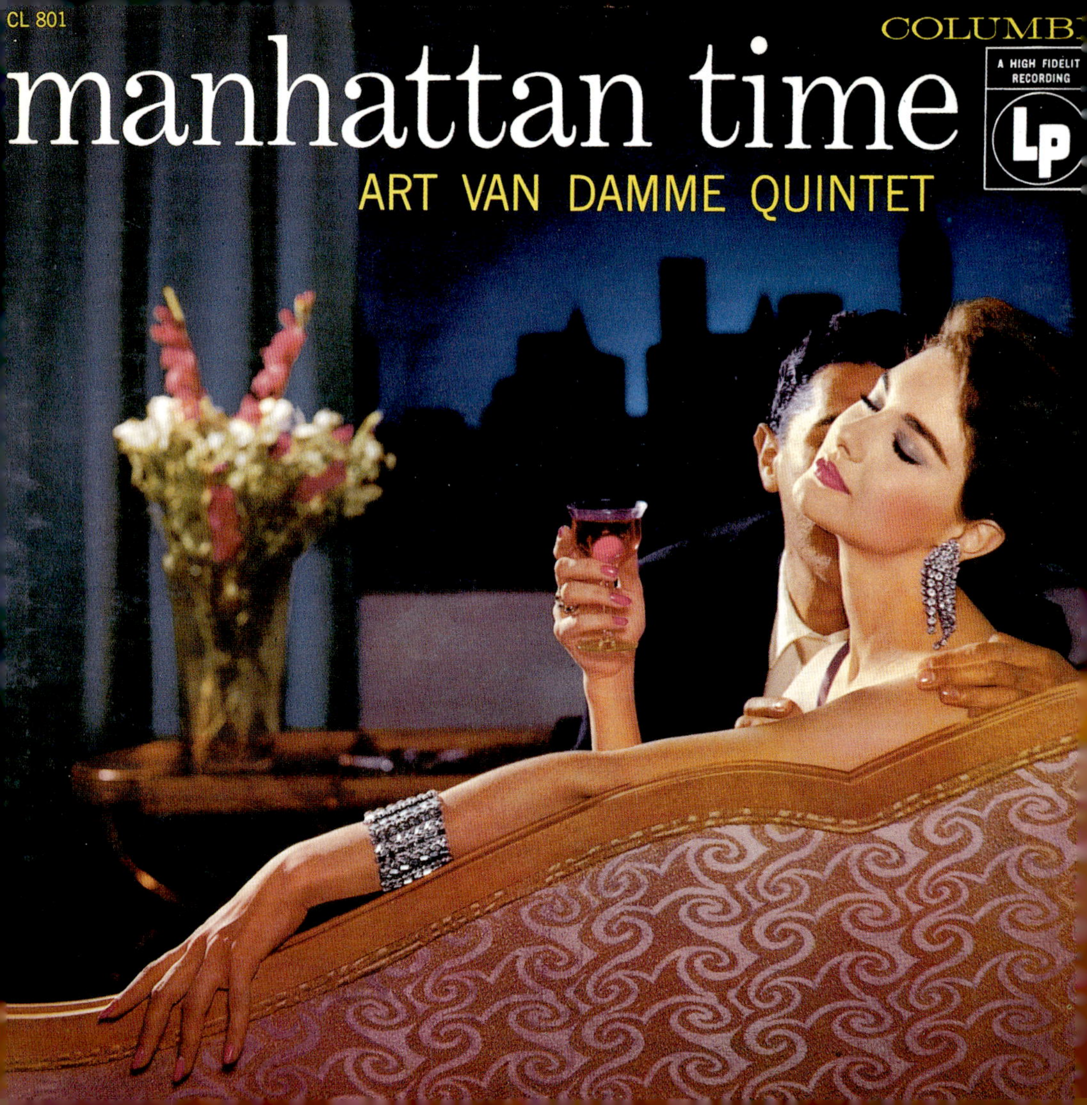
CL 801
COLUMBI
A HIGH FIDELIT
RECORDING
LP
manhattan time
ART VAN DAMME QUINTET

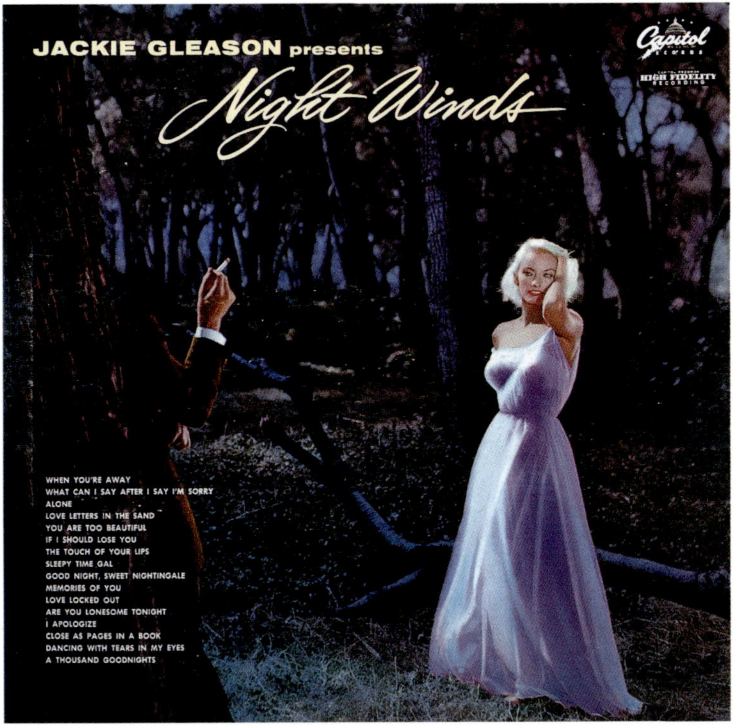

JACKIE GLEASON presents
Night Winds
Capitol
HIGH FIDELITY RECORDING
WHEN YOU'RE AWAY
WHAT CAN I SAY AFTER I SAY I'M SORRY
ALONE
LOVE LETTERS IN THE SAND
YOU ARE TOO BEAUTIFUL
IF I SHOULD LOSE YOU
THE TOUCH OF YOUR LIPS
SLEEPY TIME GAL
GOOD NIGHT, SWEET NIGHTINGALE
MEMORIES OF YOU
LOVE LOCKED OUT
ARE YOU LONESOME TONIGHT
I APOLOGIZE
CLOSE AS PAGES IN A BOOK
DANCING WITH TEARS IN MY EYES
A THOUSAND GOODNIGHTS

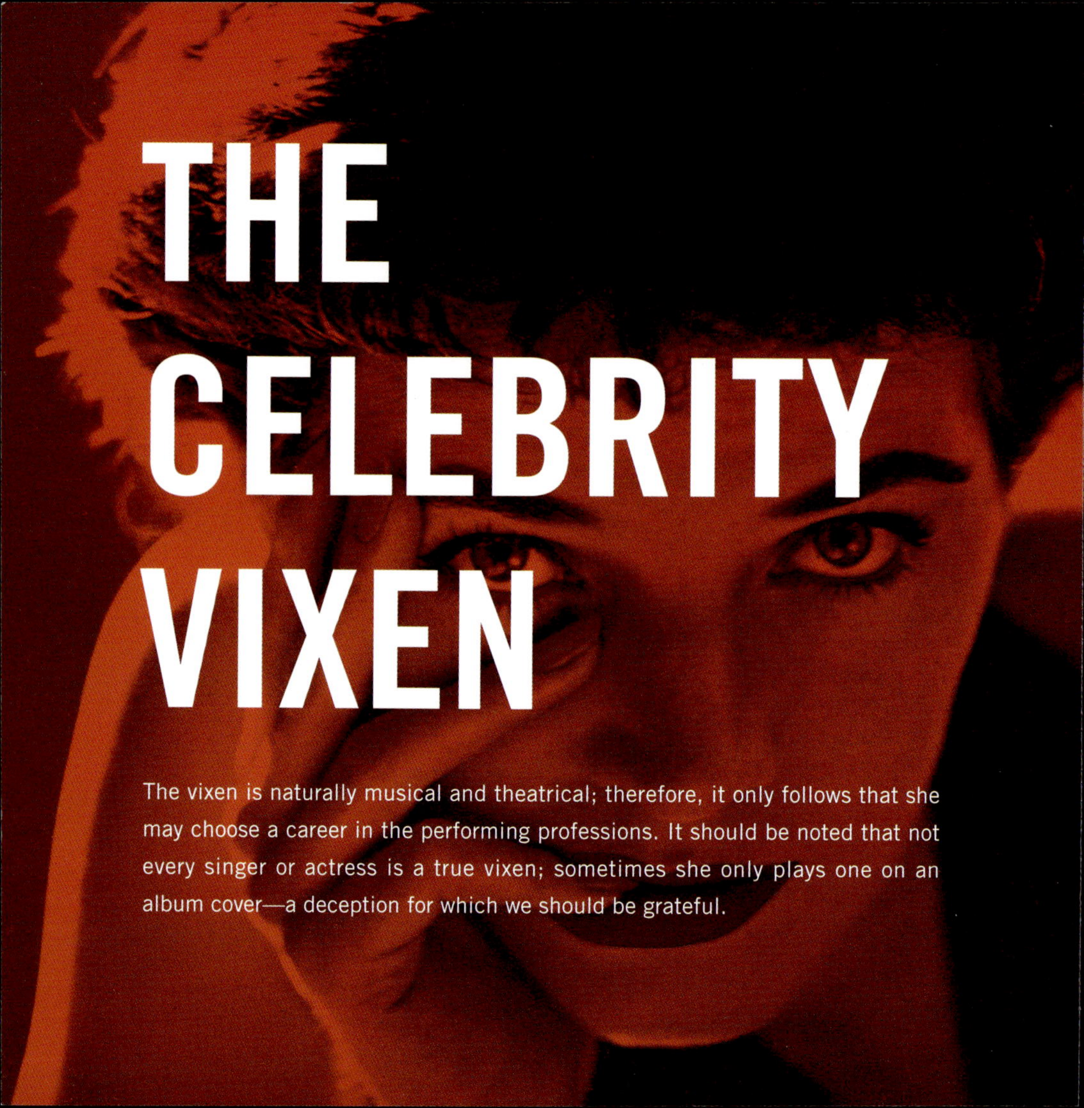

THE CELEBRITY VIXEN

The vixen is naturally musical and theatrical; therefore, it only follows that she may choose a career in the performing professions. It should be noted that not every singer or actress is a true vixen; sometimes she only plays one on an album cover—a deception for which we should be grateful.

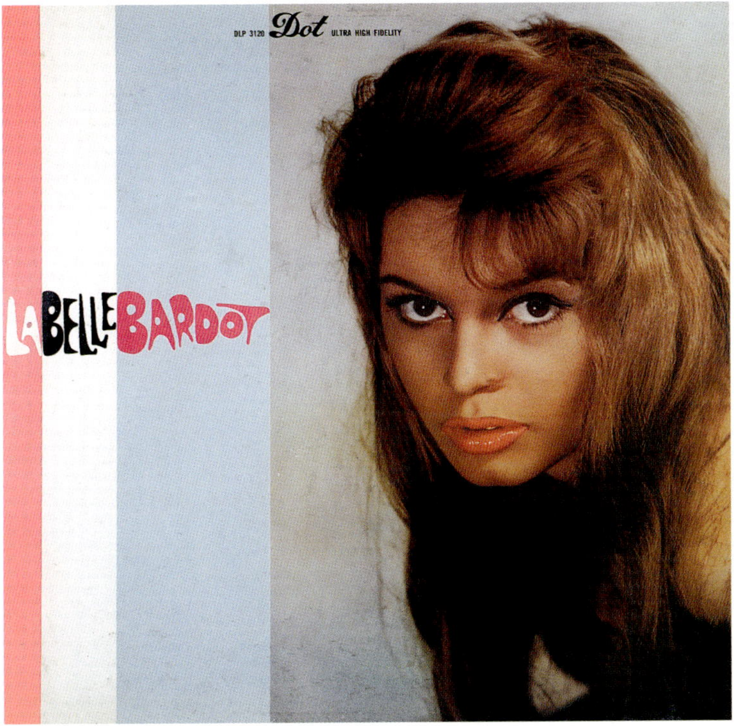

Liner Note: Isn't it wonderful how all of a sudden everyone is a connoisseur of foreign cinema! And just because of that scandalously adorable French wench, La Belle Bardot.

Liner Note: A staid member of the House of Lords shook his head and remarked in a dazed voice that she was "an arrangement designed to unhinge men's minds." Porfirio Rubirosa, renowned connoisseur of such matters, sighed and muttered that she was "fire in ice." Orson Welles . . . loudly proclaimed that she was "the most exciting woman in the world"! And the Maharajah of Cooch Behar summed up the Eartha-rized feelings of most men when he "bayed" . . . that he was "utterly destroyed" by this seething young enchantress!

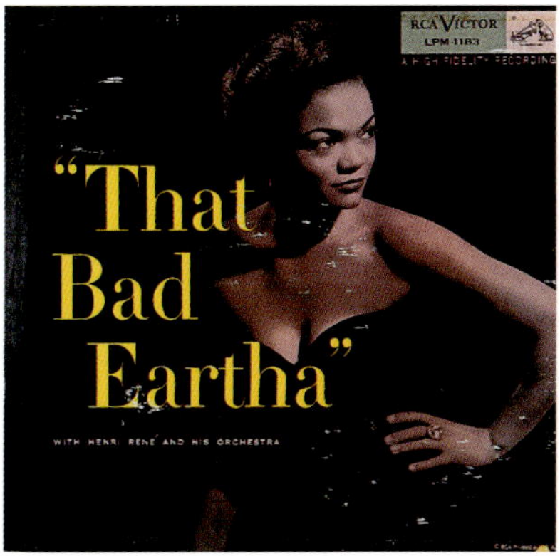
RCA Victor
LPM-1183
A HIGH FIDELITY RECORDING
"That Bad Eartha"
WITH HENRI RENÉ AND HIS ORCHESTRA

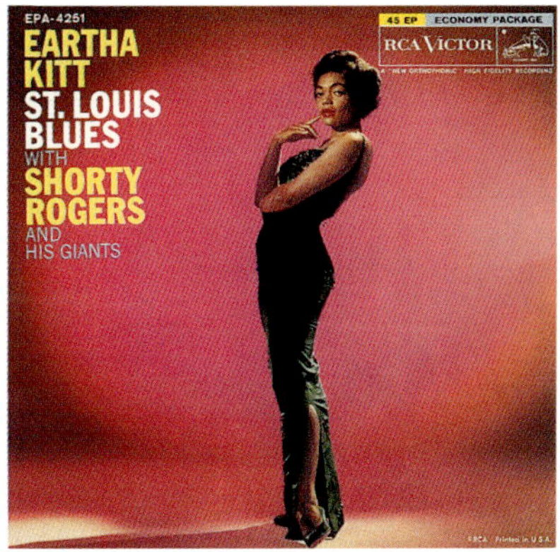
EPA-4251
45 EP
ECONOMY PACKAGE
RCA Victor
EARTHA KITT
ST. LOUIS BLUES
WITH
SHORTY ROGERS
AND HIS GIANTS

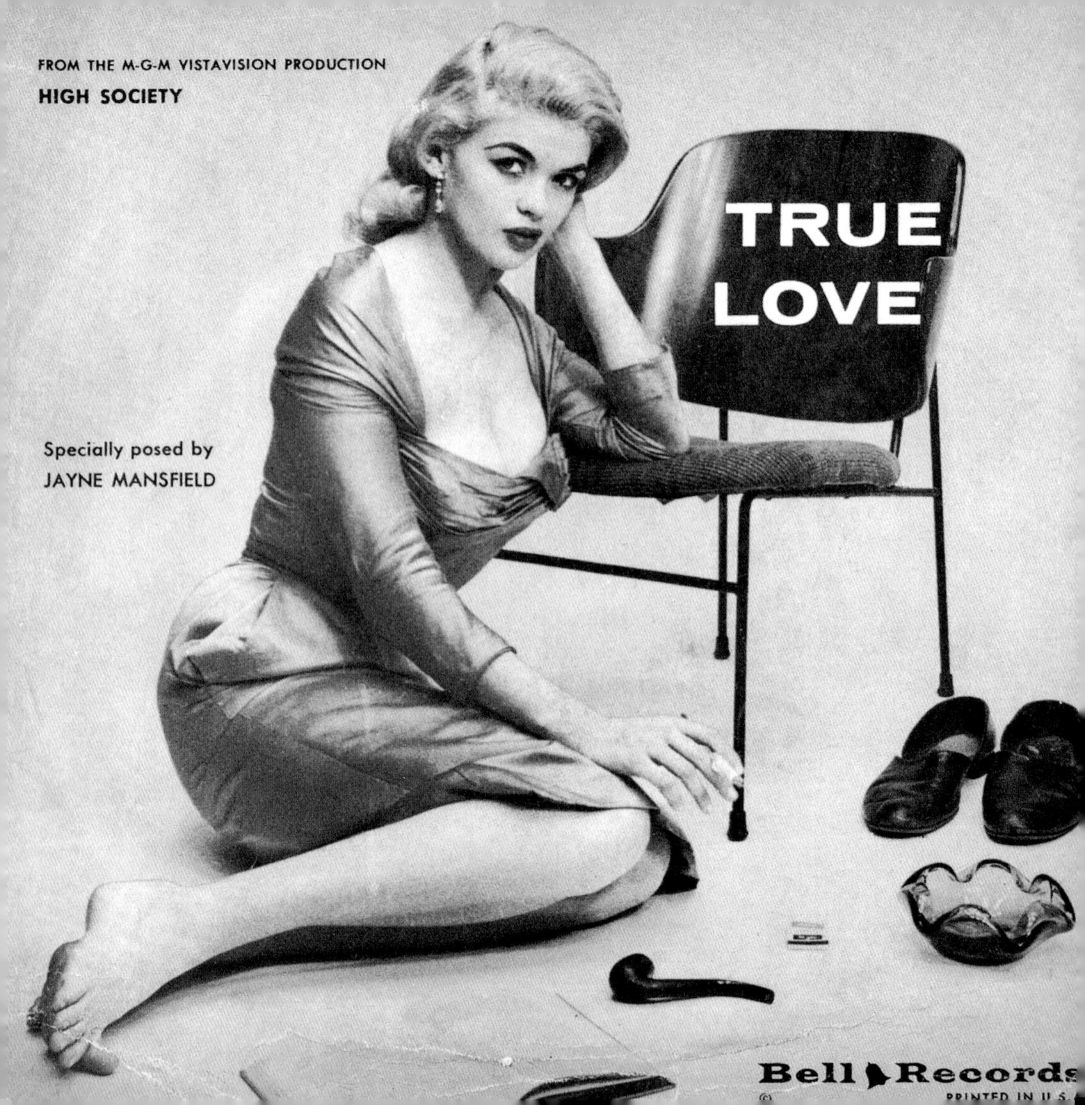
FROM THE M-G-M VISTAVISION PRODUCTION
HIGH SOCIETY
TRUE LOVE
Specially posed by
JAYNE MANSFIELD
Bell Records
PRINTED IN U.S.

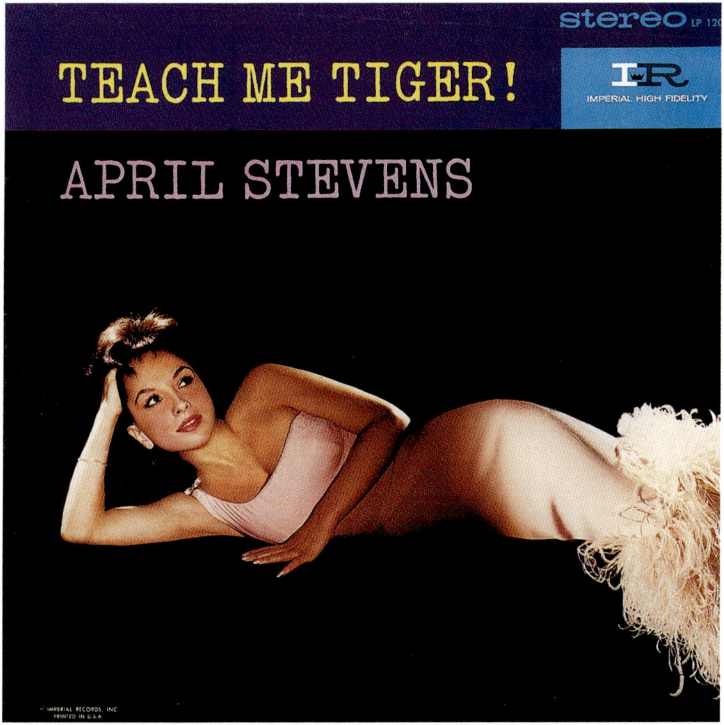

Liner Note: But a comment from one of her many fan letters explains her appeal best. "Your voice sounds as though you had a throat full of angora sweaters," the letter reads. "Other girl vocalists sing, but you actually talk to a guy, and boy, the things you say!"

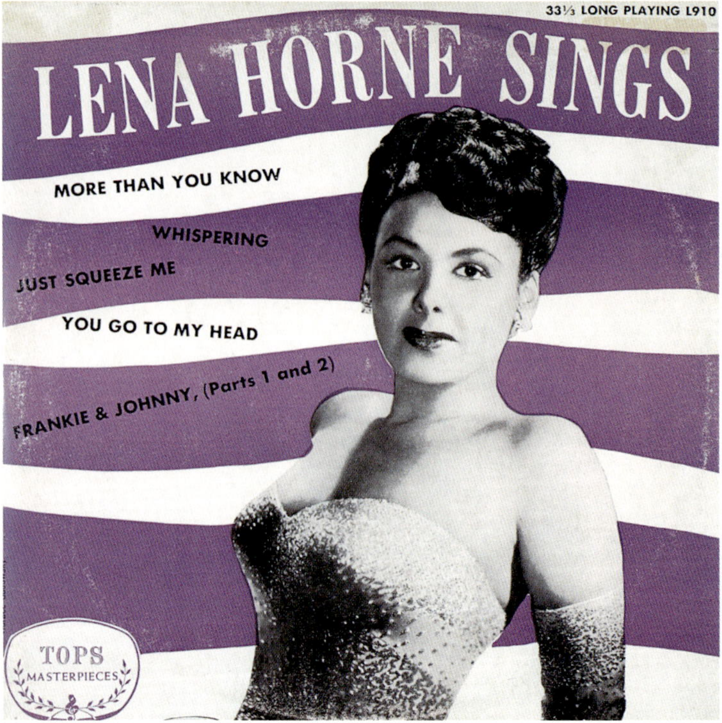
33⅓ LONG PLAYING L910
LENA HORNE SINGS
MORE THAN YOU KNOW
WHISPERING
JUST SQUEEZE ME
YOU GO TO MY HEAD
FRANKIE & JOHNNY, (Parts 1 and 2)
TOPS
MASTERPIECES

POLLY BERGEN'S

FOUR SEASONS OF LOVE

COLUMBIA
GUARANTEED HIGH FIDELITY

FRANK DeVOL AND HIS ORCHESTRA

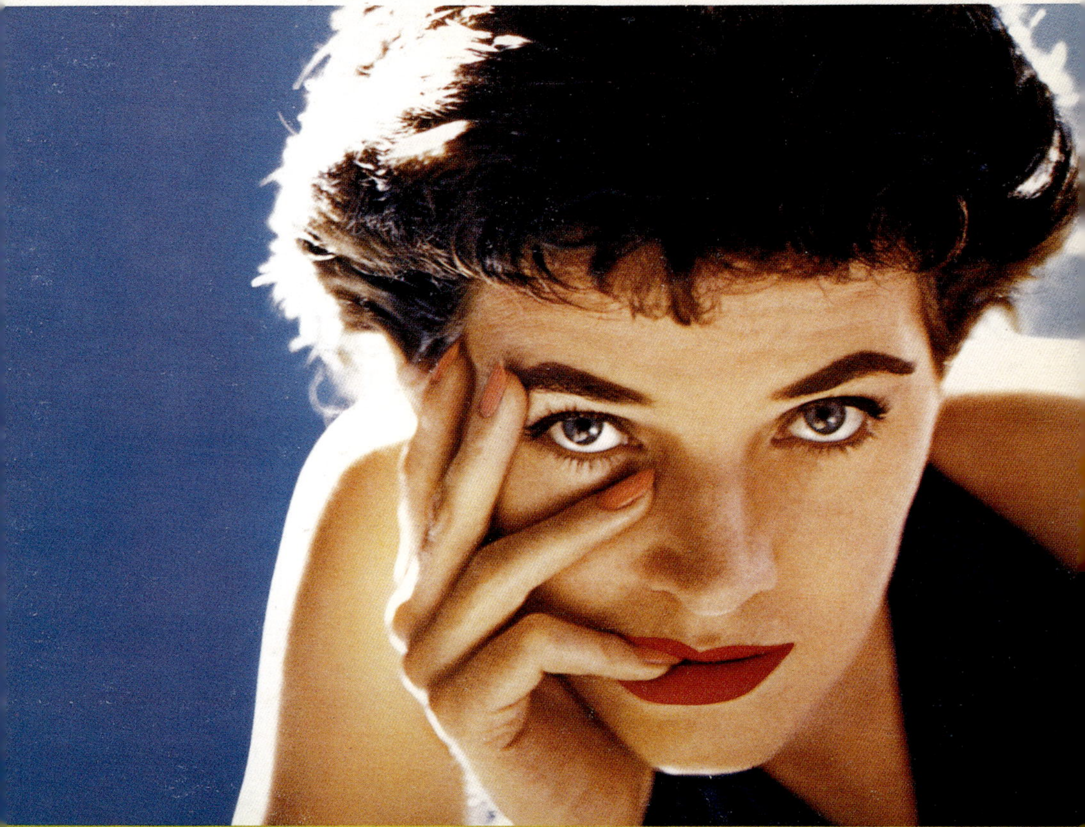

L 1451

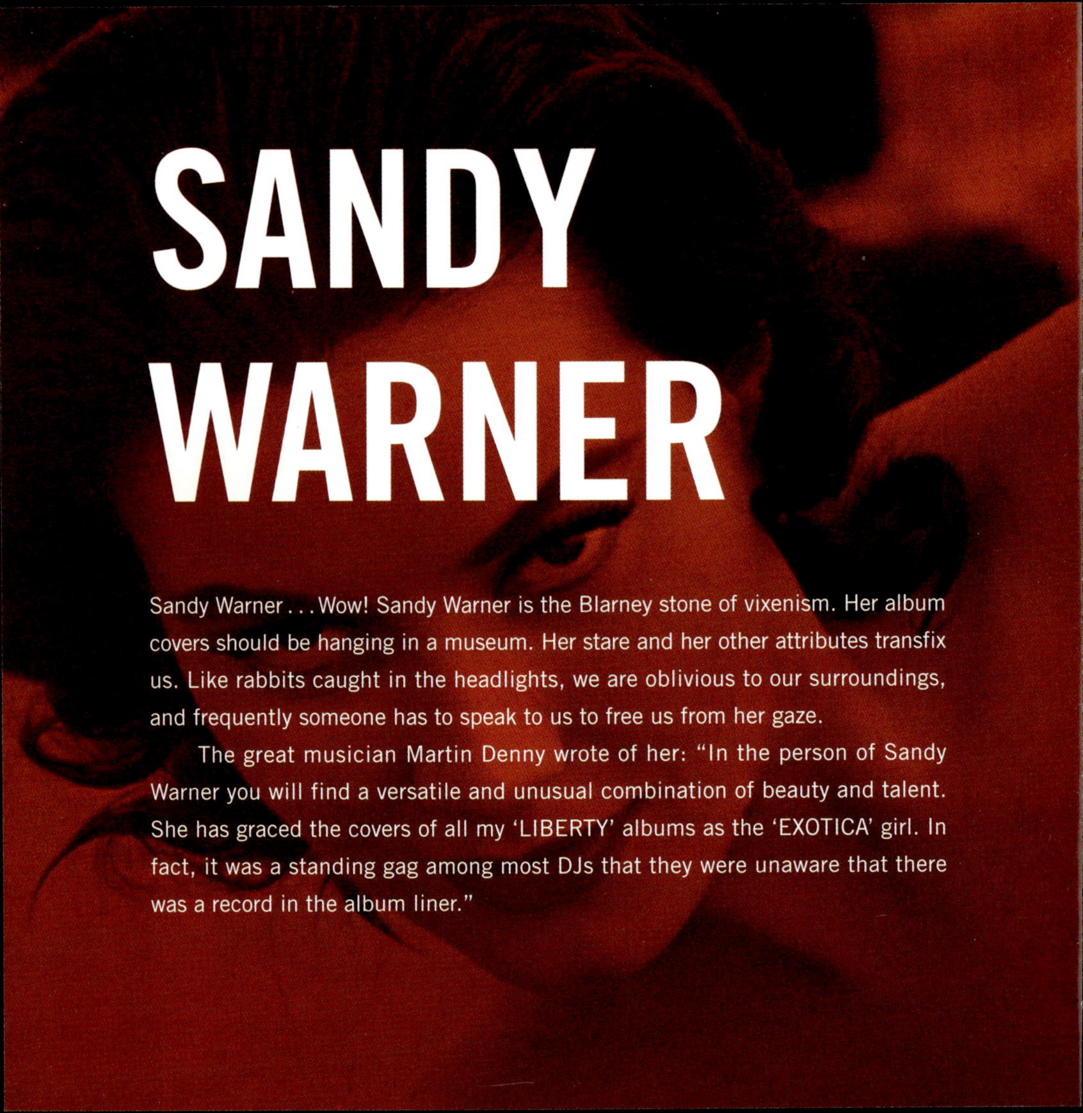

SANDY WARNER

Sandy Warner . . . Wow! Sandy Warner is the Blarney stone of vixenism. Her album covers should be hanging in a museum. Her stare and her other attributes transfix us. Like rabbits caught in the headlights, we are oblivious to our surroundings, and frequently someone has to speak to us to free us from her gaze.

The great musician Martin Denny wrote of her: "In the person of Sandy Warner you will find a versatile and unusual combination of beauty and talent. She has graced the covers of all my 'LIBERTY' albums as the 'EXOTICA' girl. In fact, it was a standing gag among most DJs that they were unaware that there was a record in the album liner."

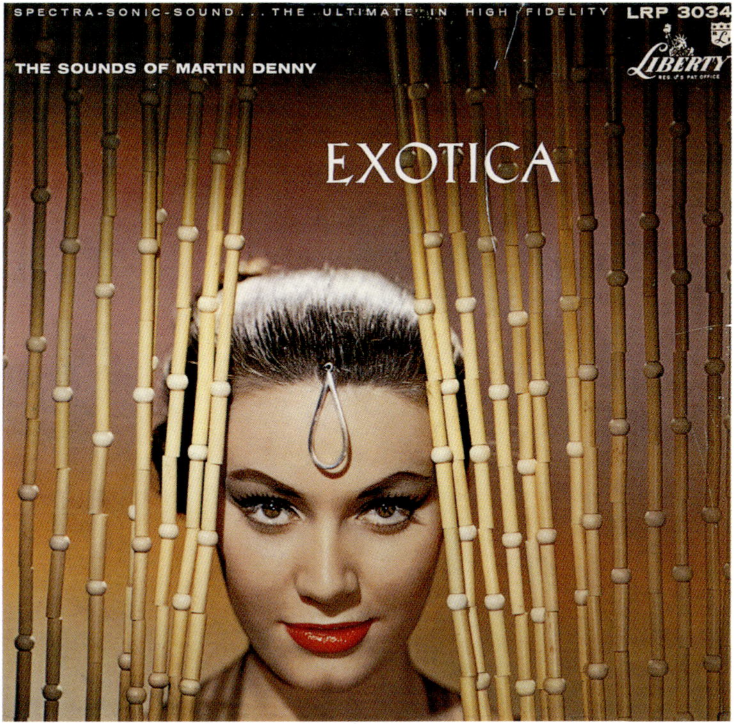
SPECTRA-SONIC-SOUND . . . THE ULTIMATE IN HIGH FIDELITY
LRP 3034
THE SOUNDS OF MARTIN DENNY
LIBERTY
EXOTICA

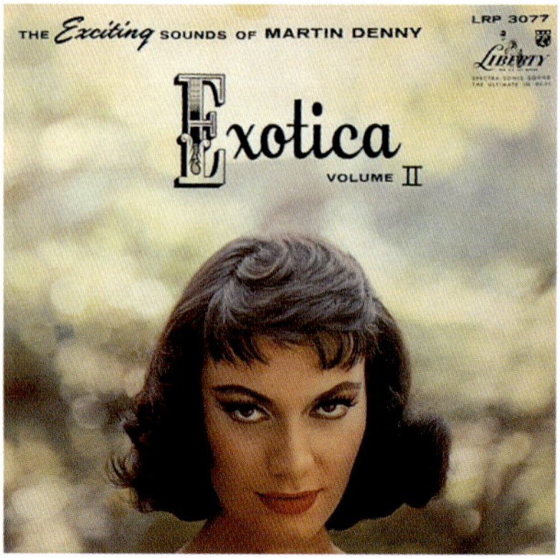
THE Exciting SOUNDS OF MARTIN DENNY
LRP 3077
Liberty
Exotica
VOLUME II

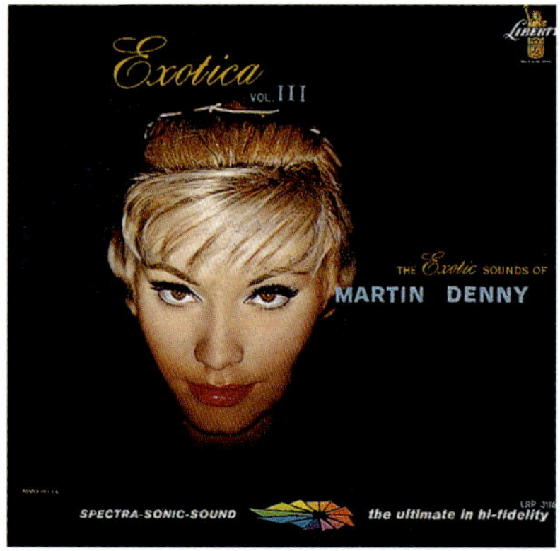
Exotica
VOL. III
Liberty
THE Exotic SOUNDS OF
MARTIN DENNY
SPECTRA-SONIC-SOUND
the ultimate in hi-fidelity

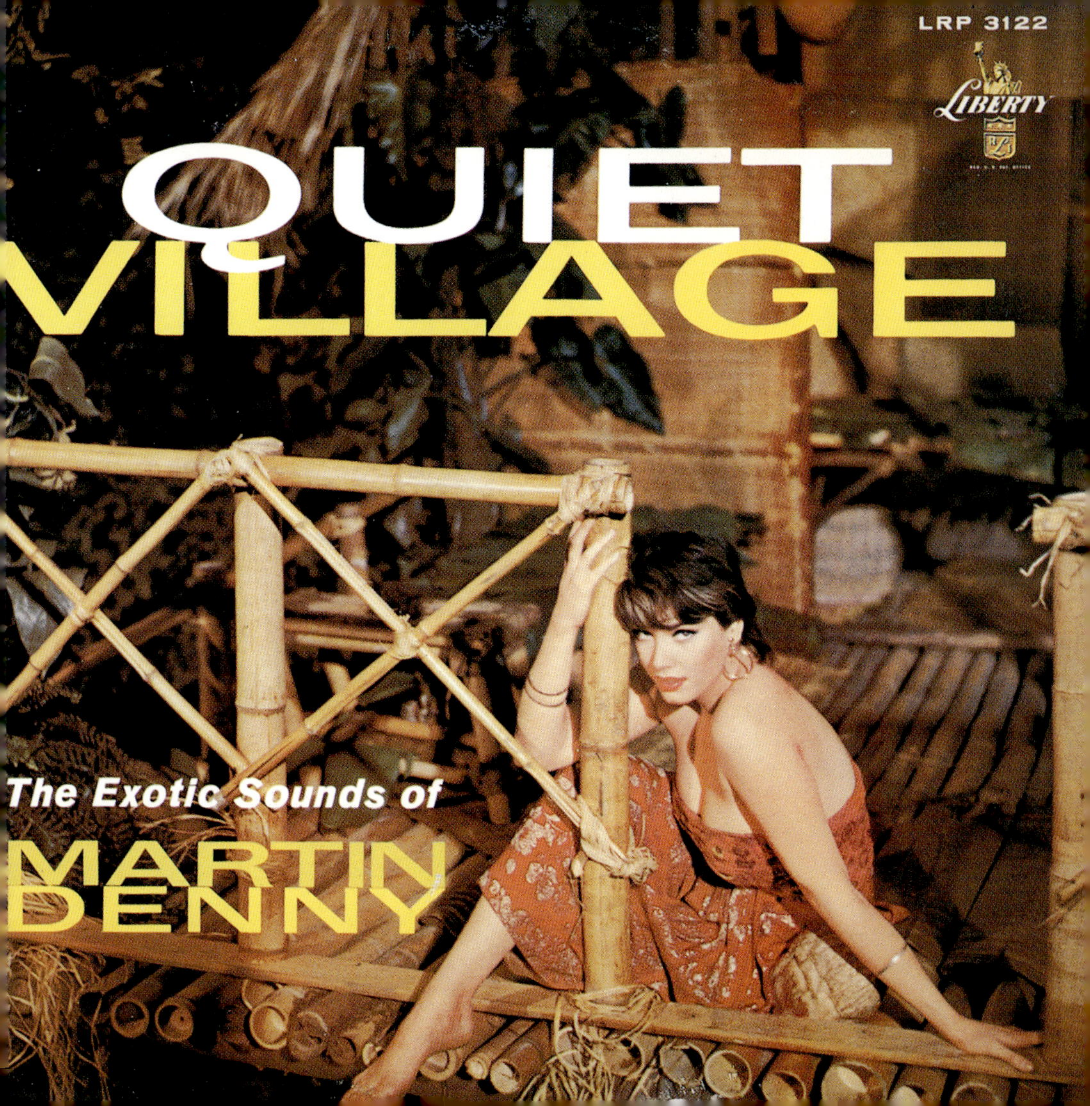
LRP 3122
LIBERTY
QUIET VILLAGE
The Exotic Sounds of
MARTIN DENNY

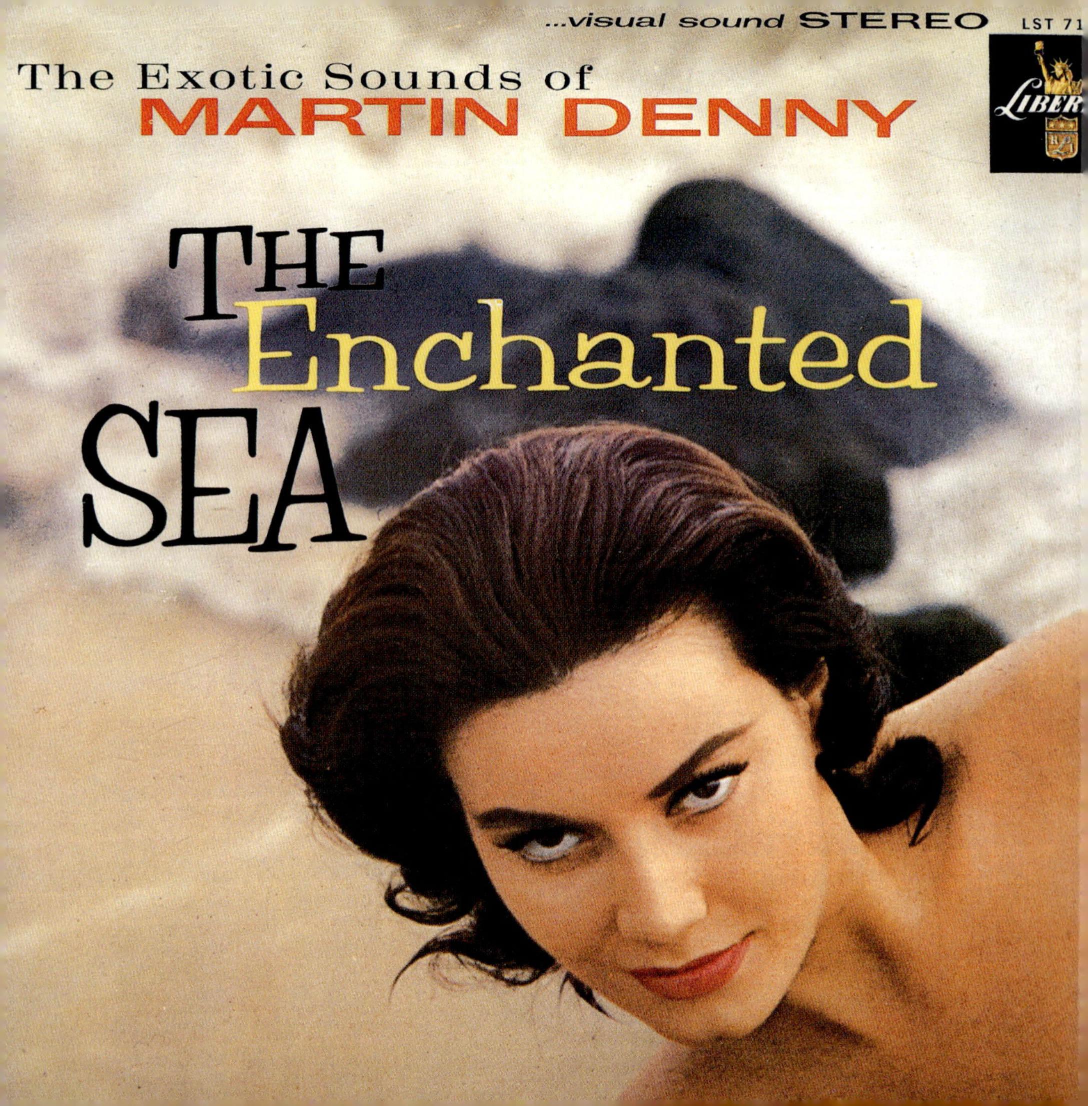
...visual sound STEREO
LST 71
The Exotic Sounds of
MARTIN DENNY
THE
Enchanted
SEA

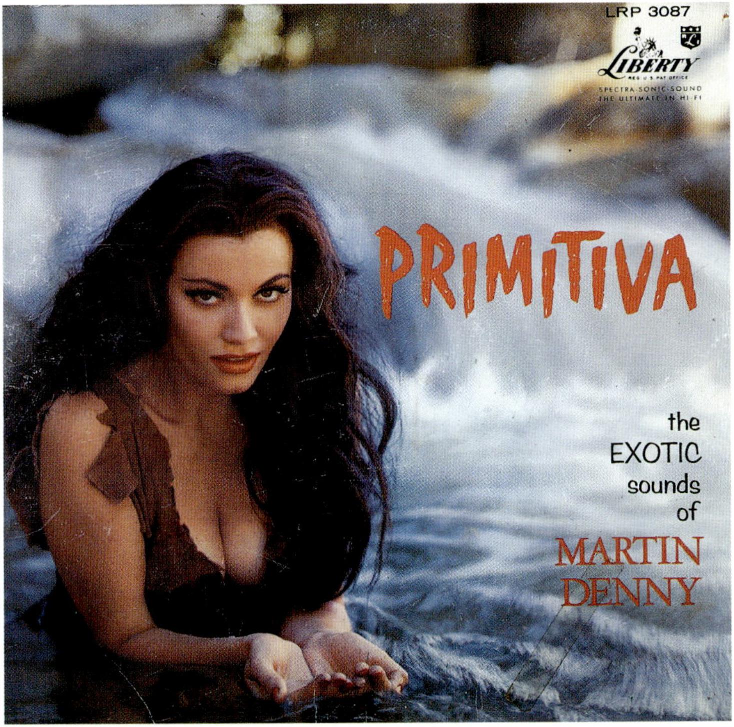
LRP 3087
LIBERTY
REG. U.S. PAT OFFICE
SPECTRA SONIC SOUND
THE ULTIMATE IN HI-FI
PRIMITIVA
the
EXOTIC
sounds
of
MARTIN
DENNY

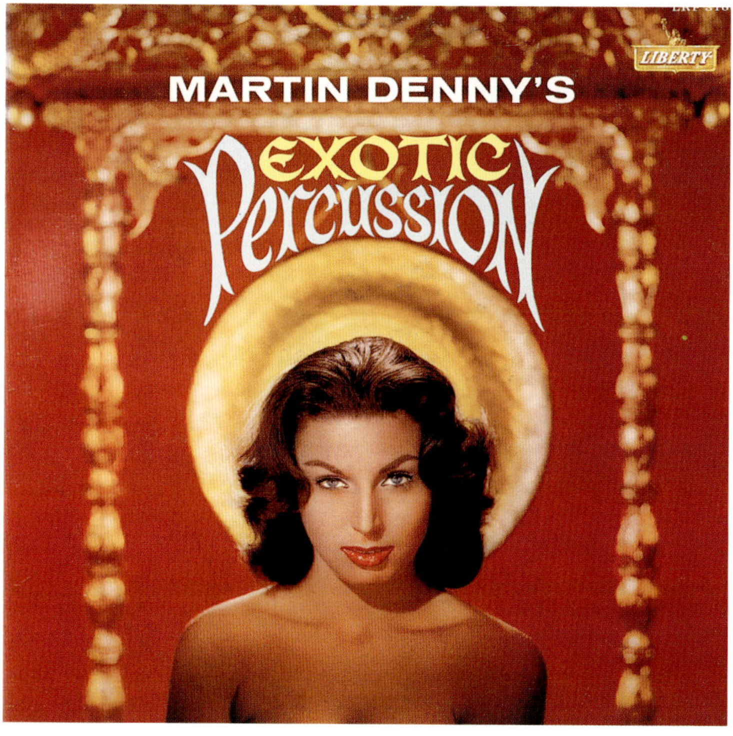
LIBERTY
MARTIN DENNY'S
EXOTIC
Percussion

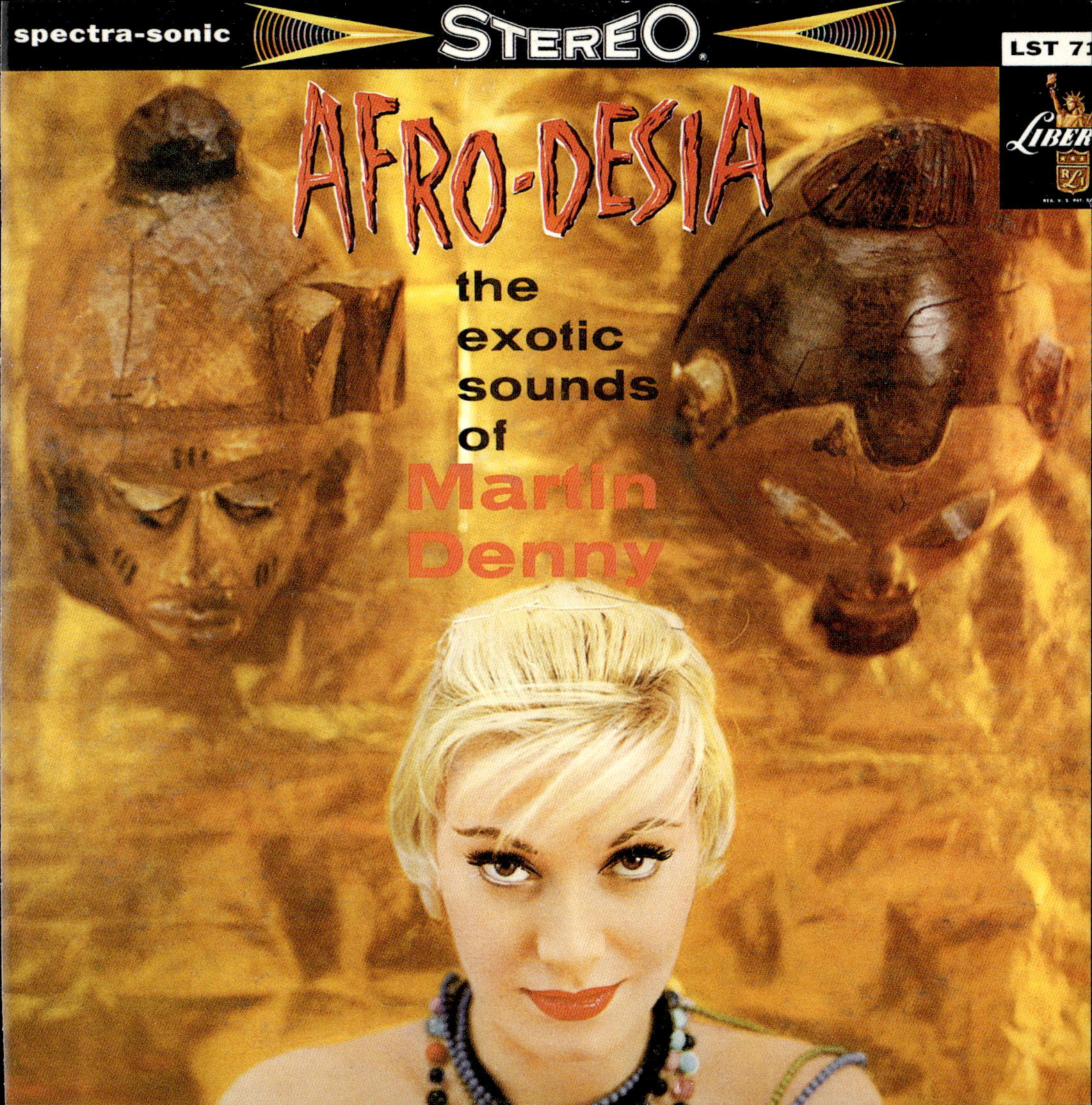
spectra-sonic
STEREO
LST 71
AFRO-DESIA
the exotic sounds of
Martin Denny

Vixens Are Not Perfect

Not all vixen album covers have that appeal. Some miss the mark—it's hard to do, but some manage. The mistake often seems to be that of taking the vixen out of her natural element and trying to make her "artistic" or avant-garde. Another grave mistake is asking a vixen to look wistful—she doesn't know how.

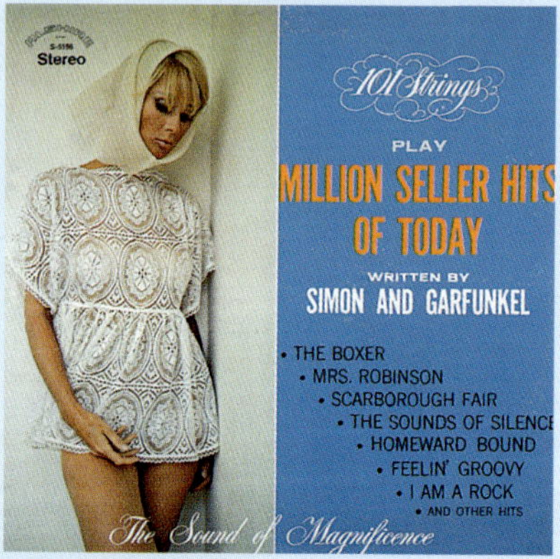

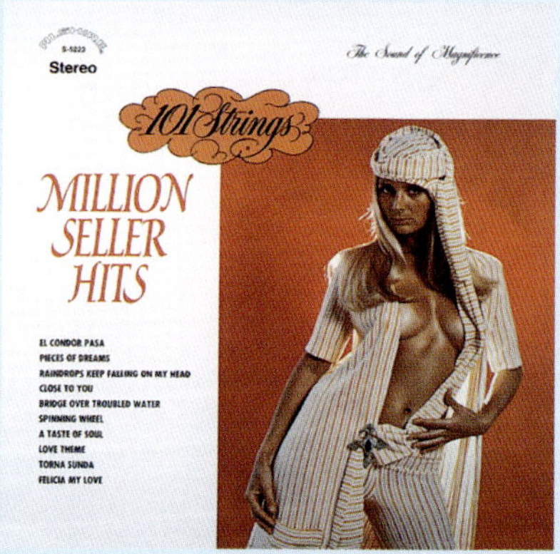

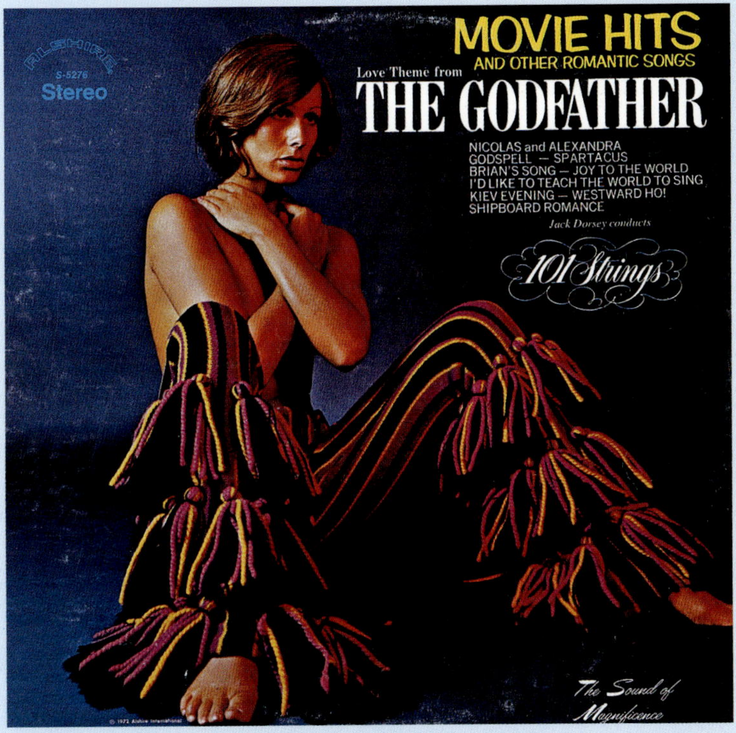
ALSHIRE
S-5276
Stereo
MOVIE HITS
AND OTHER ROMANTIC SONGS
Love Theme from
THE GODFATHER
NICOLAS and ALEXANDRA
GODSPELL — SPARTACUS
BRIAN'S SONG — JOY TO THE WORLD
I'D LIKE TO TEACH THE WORLD TO SING
KIEV EVENING — WESTWARD HO!
SHIPBOARD ROMANCE
Jack Dorsey conducts
101 Strings
The Sound of Magnificence

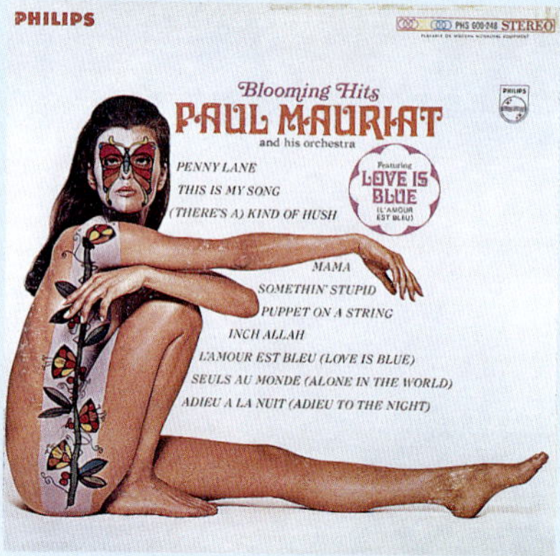
PHILIPS
PHS 600-248 STEREO
Blooming Hits
PAUL MAURIAT
and his orchestra
PENNY LANE
THIS IS MY SONG
(THERE'S A) KIND OF HUSH
Featuring
LOVE IS BLUE
(L'AMOUR EST BLEU)
MAMA
SOMETHIN' STUPID
PUPPET ON A STRING
INCH ALLAH
L'AMOUR EST BLEU (LOVE IS BLUE)
SEULS AU MONDE (ALONE IN THE WORLD)
ADIEU A LA NUIT (ADIEU TO THE NIGHT)

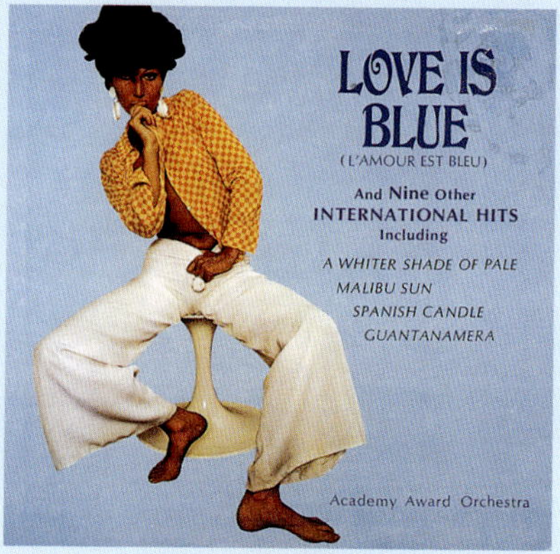
LOVE IS BLUE
(L'AMOUR EST BLEU)
And Nine Other
INTERNATIONAL HITS
Including
A WHITER SHADE OF PALE
MALIBU SUN
SPANISH CANDLE
GUANTANAMERA
Academy Award Orchestra

Epilogue

1:45 A.M. I poured Ed into a cab—he was mumbling something about having to work in the morning that I didn't quite follow—and climbed up onto my balcony for a nightcap. I stared out at Baghdad by the Bay and wondered about the fate of vixenism; I often get a little melancholy around closing time. More and more it seems the wholesome appeals of vixenism are being discarded for things with ever more shock value, like a boozer who always needs more to get high. Doesn't anybody appreciate innocent titillation anymore?

And where will the vixens go, and what will they do, once the market for their services has gone? You don't hear our esteemed politicians talking about that, do you? Well, I for one, I decided to myself, am going to give up my peripatetic and frivolous lifestyle and devote myself to the care and feeding of vixens, perhaps set up a foundation of some kind. I called out into the night, "Hey, vixens, don't worry —I care!"

Suddenly, I wondered if the guys had hit Chau's over in Chinatown for a late-night snack and a hand of rummy yet.

Credits

1. *For Adults Only* · Surprise Records. **6.** *101 Strings Play the Sugar and Spice* · Somerset Stereo Fidelity. **9.** *The Girl Friends* · Photography: Tony Guyther · Coral Records. **10.** *The Sweet and the Swingin'* · Capitol Records. **11.** *Music to Remember Her* · ca. 1962 · Capitol Records. **12 LEFT.** *Frat Hop* · Tops. **12 RIGHT.** *Boys! Boys! Boys!* · Tops. **13.** *Music for the Girl You Love* · Liberty Records · Photography: Garrett-Howard. **14.** *Italian Hits* · Somerset Stereo Fidelity. **15 LEFT.** *Music to Make You Misty* · 1953 · Capitol Records · Photography: Richard Nadel. **15 RIGHT.** *Music to Change Her Mind* · ca. 1962 · Capitol Records. **16 LEFT.** *Music for Relaxing* · Hollywood Records. **16 RIGHT.** *Relax with Victor Herbert* · 1954 · RCA Victor. **17.** *Music to Remember You By* · Hollywood Records. **18 LEFT.** *Music for Dining* · 1958 · RCA Victor. **18 RIGHT.** *Music to Make Housework Easier* · Request Records. **19.** *How to Strip for Your Husband* · ca. 1963 · Roulette · Illustration: Howard Nostrand · Design: Moskof-Morrison Inc. **20 LEFT.** *The World's Best Loved Waltzes.* **20 RIGHT.** *Honky Tonk Piano* · Halo. **21.** *Barbershop Ballads* · Tops. **25.** *Shangri-La* · Decca Records. **26.** *Irving Fields Plays Irving Berlin in Fabulous Hi-Fi* · Tops. **27.** *Warm and Willing* · ca. 1965 · Capitol Records · Photography: George Jerman. **28.** *I Only Have Eyes for You* · 1964 · RCA Victor. **29.** *Lush and Latin* · 1958 · Capitol Records. **30 LEFT.** *I Wish You Love* · Columbia Records · Photography: J. Frederick Smith. **30 RIGHT.** *Kostelanetz in Wonderland—Golden Encores* · Columbia Records · 1963 · Photography: Henry Parker. **31.** *Sexy Strings and Subtle Saxes* · ca. 1962 · Decca Records. **32.** *Levant's Favorites* · 1958 · Columbia Records. **33.** *I Love Paris* · Clarion. **34.** *I'm Looking Over a Four Leaf Clover* · Pickwick/33. **35.** *Moods of Mancini* · Wyncote Records. **36.** *The Immortal Ladies* · 1956 · RCA Victor. **37.** *Temptation* · 1960 · Kapp Records. **38.** *Latin Touch* · Coronet Records. **39.** *Come with Me to Far Away Places* · Mercury Records. **40.** *The Faraway Part of Town* · 1962 · Columbia Records · Photography: Horst. **41.** *A Taste of Honey* · Crown Records. **42.** *Battle of Bands* · Camay Records. **43.** *Our Golden Favorites* · 1967 · United Artists Records. **46.** *Black Satin* · 1958 · Capitol Records. **47.** *Satin Affair* · 1961 · Capitol Records. **48.** *Sax in Silk* · 1954 · RCA Victor. **49.** *Velvet Carpet* · 1956 · Capitol Records. **50.** *Frankie Carle Plays Cole Porter* · RCA Victor. **51.** *Strauss Waltzes* · 1955 · Columbia Records. **52.** *Shep Fields Plays for Cocktails, Dinner and Dancing* · Jubilee

Records · Photography: Stephen Haas. **53.** *Rhapsodies* · Columbia Records. **54.** *All I Do Is Dream of You* · 1962 · RCA Victor · Photography: Horst. **55.** *In a Sentimental Mood* · RCA Camden. **56.** *That Latin Feeling* · Decca Records · Photography: Hal Buksbaum. **57.** *The Best of Cugat* · Mercury Records · Photography: George Pickow · Model: Abbe Lane. **58.** *Mantovani/Hollywood* · London. **59.** *The Original Sounds of Ben McPeek* · RCA Victor. **61.** *Just a Little Lovin Will Go a Long Way* · Crown Records. **62.** *Honky Tonkin'* · Crown Records. **63.** *At the Golden Nugget* · Design Records · Photography: Philip Lustig. **64.** *Ellis in Wonderland* · ca. 1956 · Columbia Records · Photography: Hal Reiff. **65.** *Piano Witchcraft of Cy Coleman* · ca. 1963 · Capitol Records · Photography: Ken Veeder. **66.** *Other Worlds Other Sounds* · 1958 · RCA Victor. **67.** *Featuring the Magic Moods of Andre Previn* · Coronet Records. **69.** *Richard Hayman Conducts Pop Concert in Sound* · Mercury Records. **70.** *Canta Un Tiple* · Montilla Records · Photography: Gene R. Smith. **71.** *Slightly Latin* · MGM Records. **72.** *Forbidden Island* · ca. 1958 · Liberty Records · Design: Garrett-Howard. **73.** *Hawaii in Hi-Fi* · 1958 · Vik · Photography: Dave Hecht. **74.** *Aloha from Norman Luboff* · 1963 · RCA Victor. **75.** *Pianos in Paradise* · United Artists Records. **76.** *Port Said* · 1957 · Audio Fidelity Records · Photography: Bob Witt · Model: Nejla Ates. **77 LEFT.** *Skip Martin's Scheherajazz* · Somerset Stereo Fidelity. **77 RIGHT.** *Scheherazade* · Tops. **78.** *Mambo!* · Aamco Records · Photography: Otto Fenn · Design: Reid Miles. **79 LEFT.** *Pradomania!* · Omega Records. **79 RIGHT.** *The Dancing Beat of the Latin Bands* · RCA Victor. **80.** *Love Dances of Brazil* · Decca Records · Photography: Garrett-Howard. **81.** *Caribbean Rendezvous* · Crown Records · Photography: Todd Walker. **82.** *The Mills Brothers San Antonio Rose* · Dot Records. **83 LEFT.** *Rhapsody* · 1964 · RCA Victor. **83 RIGHT.** *Gypsy Passion* · ca. 1960 · Columbia Records · Photography: Peter Basch. **84 LEFT.** *Paris Swings* · 1959 · Capitol Records. **84 RIGHT.** *Rhapsody in Blue* · Columbia Records. **85.** *Made in France* · Surrey Records · Photography and design: George S. Whiteman. **86.** *It's Alaska* · Alaska Airlines. **87.** *Dutch Sax* · Capitol Records. **89.** *Whipped Cream and Other Delights* · 1965 · A & M Records · Model: Dolores Erickson. **90.** *Lady Godiva* · 1958 · Capitol Records. **91.** *A Little Spice* · 1957 · Davis Records. **92.** *For Men Only* · 1957 · Davis Records. **93 LEFT.** *Body and Soul* · 1960 · Pickwick/33. **93 RIGHT.** *Satin Brass* · Capitol Records. **94.** *Songs and Sounds of a Soft, Warm Mood* · Somerset Stereo Fidelity. **95.** *Young Man and a Maid* · Elektra Records. **96.** *Your Girl for the Night* · Ha-Ha Records. **97.** *Strip Along with Us* · Strand Records · Model: Libby Jones.

98. *David Rose and His Orchestra Play the Stripper* · MGM Records. **99.** *Music to Strip By* · Somerset Stereo Fidelity. **101.** *Ecstasy* · Columbia Records · Photography: Dirone. **102.** *An Evening at Goldie's New York* · Mercury Records · Photography: Dirone. **103.** *The Swinging Piano of Pete Jolly: Too* Much, *Baby!* · Columbia Records · Photography: Frank Bez. **104.** *Serenade for Love* · Mercury Wing. **105.** *Strictly for Lovers* · Tops. **106.** *Thinking of You* · ca. 1954 · Capitol Records · Photography: Sam Oppee. **107 LEFT.** *Peter Nero Plays a Salute to Herb Alpert and the Tijuana Brass* · 1967 · RCA Victor. **107 RIGHT.** *What Now My Love* · 1966 · A & M Records. **108.** *Manhattan Time* · 1955 · Columbia Records · Photography: Bottwin. **109.** *Jackie Gleason Presents Night Winds* · 1957 · Capitol Records · Photography: Ken Veeder. **111.** *La Belle Bardot* · Dot Records · Model: Brigitte Bardot. **113 LEFT.** *That Bad Eartha* · 1956 · RCA Victor · Model: Eartha Kitt. **113 RIGHT.** *St. Louis Blues* · RCA Victor · Model: Eartha Kitt. **114.** *True Love* · Bell Records · Model: Jayne Mansfield. **115.** *Teach Me Tiger!* · ca. 1960 · Imperial Records · Model: April Stevens. **116.** *Lena Horne Sings* · Tops · Model: Lena Horne. **117.** *Polly Bergen's Four Seasons of Love* · 1960 · Columbia Records · Model: Polly Bergen. **119.** *Exotica* · 1957 · Liberty Records · Photography: Garrett-Howard · Model: Sandy Warner. **120 LEFT.** *Exotica II* · ca. 1958 · Liberty Records · Photography: Garrett-Howard · Model: Sandy Warner. **120 RIGHT.** *Exotica III* · 1958 · Liberty Records · Photography: Garrett-Howard · Model: Sandy Warner. **121.** *Quiet Village* · ca. 1959 · Liberty Records · Photography: Ivan Nagy · Model: Sandy Warner. **122.** *The Enchanted Sea* · ca. 1960 · Liberty Records · Photography: Garrett-Howard · Design: Pate/Francis · Model: Sandy Warner. **123.** *Primitiva* · ca. 1958 · Liberty Records · Design: Garrett-Howard · Model: Sandy Warner. **124.** *Exotic Percussion* · 1960 · Liberty Records · Design: Pate/Francis and Associates · Model: Sandy Warner. **125.** *Afro-Desia* · Photography: Garrett-Howard · Design: Bill Pate · Model: Sandy Warner. **126 LEFT.** *Million Seller Hits of Today Written by Simon and Garfunkel* · Alshire. **126 RIGHT.** *Million Seller Hits.* **127.** *Alshire Movie Hits and Other Romantic Songs* · 1972 · Alshire. **128 LEFT.** *Blooming Hits* · 1967 · Philips Records. **128 RIGHT.** *Love Is Blue (L'Amour Est Bleu)* · Somerset Stereo Fidelity · Design: Chic Laganella.

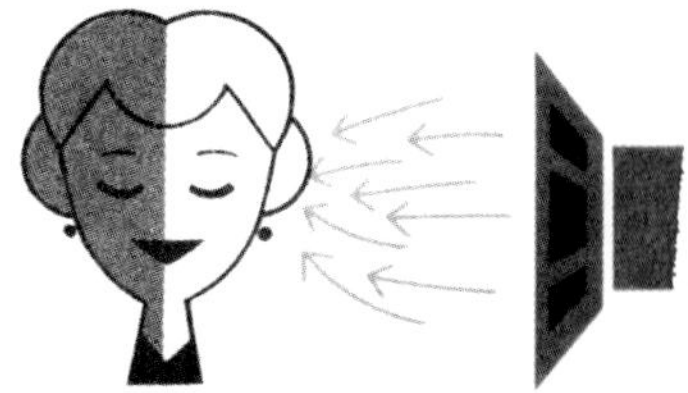

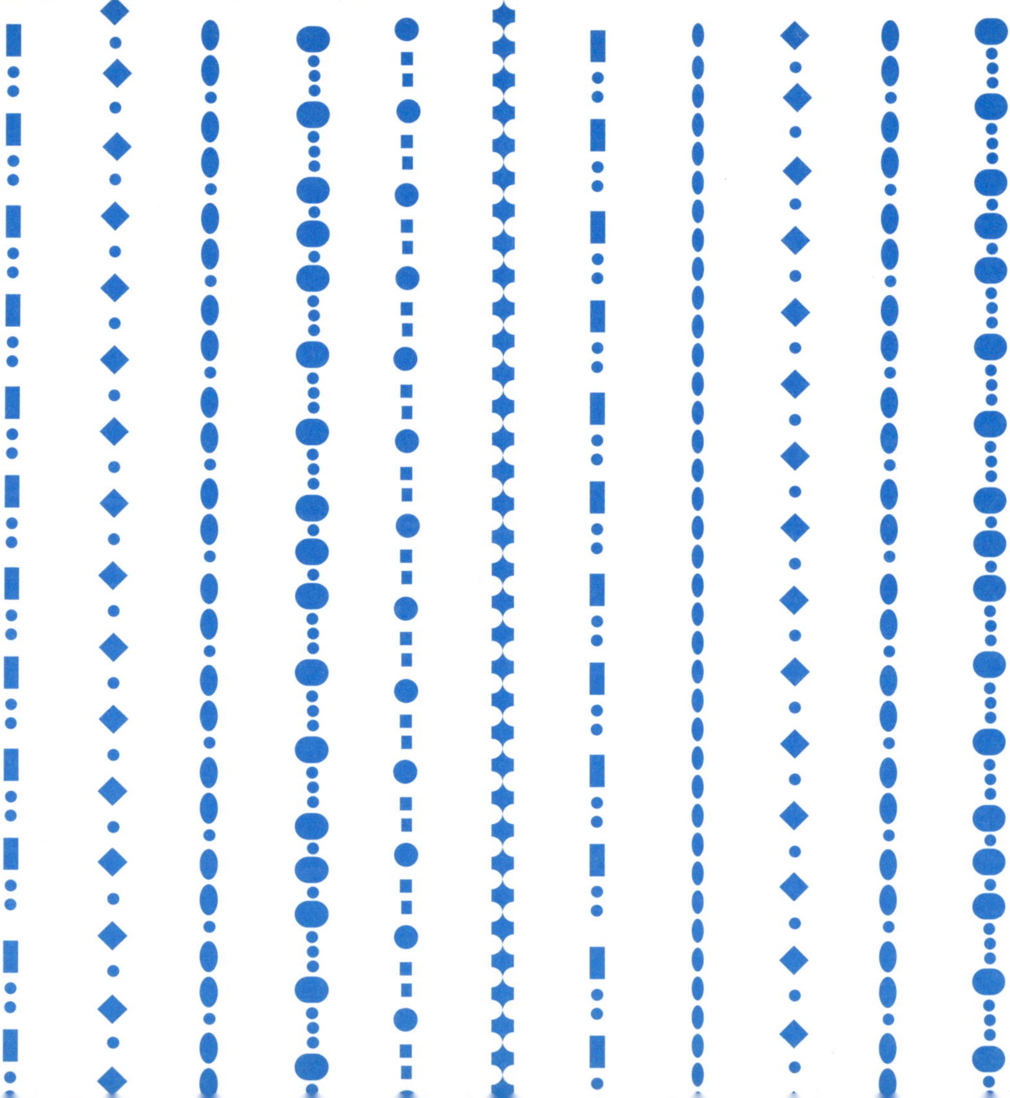

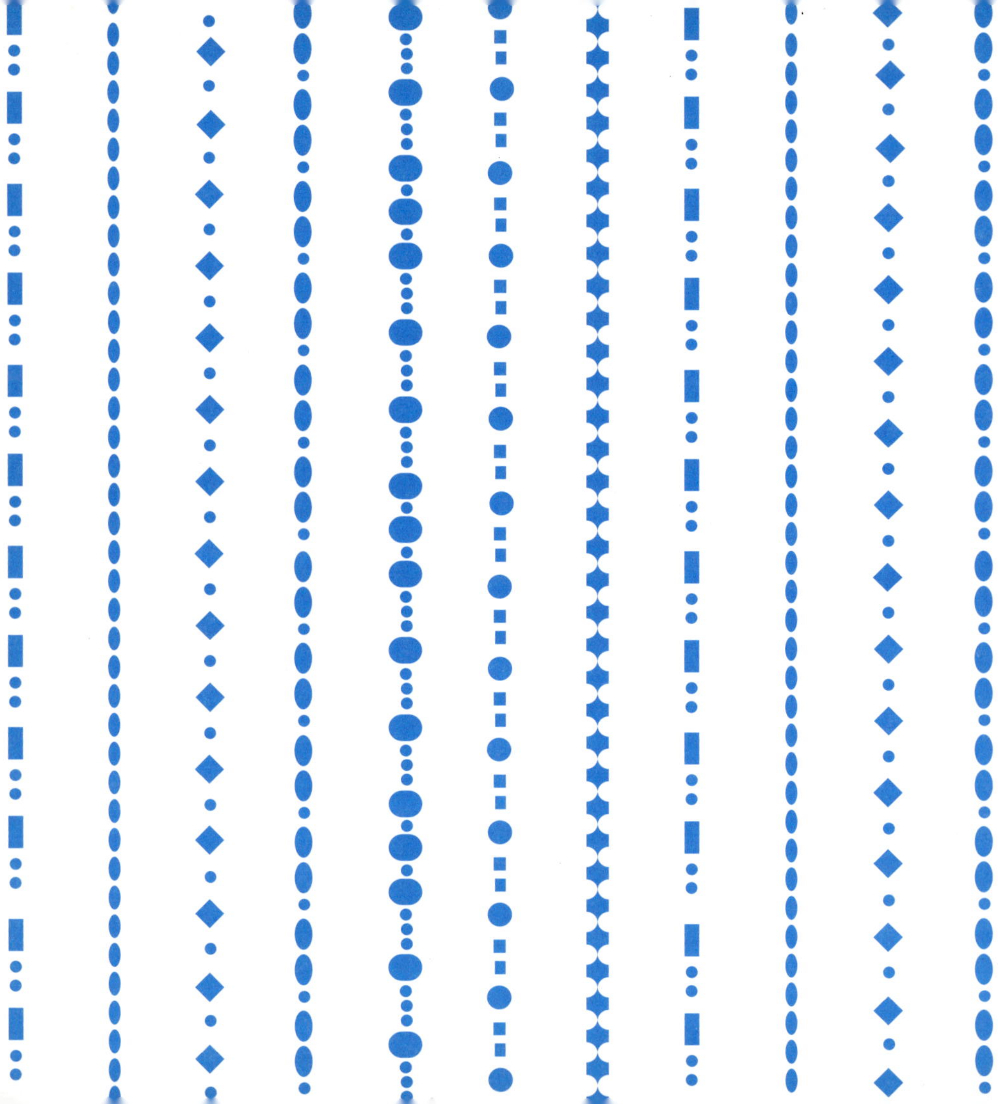